G000111675

Center for Basque Studies
Basque Classics Series, No. 3

Selected Writings of
José Miguel de Barandiarán:
Basque Prehistory and
Ethnography

Compiled and with an Introduction
by Jesús Altuna

Translated by
Frederick H. Fornoff, Linda White,
and Carys Evans-Corrales

Center for Basque Studies
University of Nevada, Reno
Reno, Nevada

This book was published with generous financial support obtained by the Association of Friends of the Center for Basque Studies from the Provincial Government of Bizkaia.

Basque Classics Series, No. 3
Series Editors: William A. Douglass, Gregorio Monreal, and Pello Salaburu

Center for Basque Studies
University of Nevada, Reno
Reno, Nevada 89557
http://basque.unr.edu

Cover and series design © 2007 by Jose Luis Agote.
Cover photograph: Josetxo Marin

Library of Congress Cataloging-in-Publication Data

Barandiarán, José Miguel de.
[Selections. English. 2008]
Selected writings of Jose Miguel de Barandiaran : Basque prehistory and ethnography / compiled and with an introduction by Jesus Altuna ; translation by Frederick H. Fornoff, Linda White, and Carys Evans-Corrales.
p. cm. -- (Basque classics series / Center for Basque Studies ; no. 3)
Summary: "Extracts from works by Basque ethnographer Barandiaran on Basque prehistory, mythology, magical beliefs, rural life, gender roles, and life events such as birth, marriage, and death, gleaned from interviews and excavations conducted in the rural Basque Country in the early to mid-twentieth century. Introduction includes biographical information on Barandiaran"--Provided by publisher.
Includes bibliographical references and index.
ISBN 978-1-877802-69-0 (pbk.) -- ISBN 978-1-877802-70-6 (hardcover) 1. Basques--Folklore. 2. Mythology, Basque. 3. Basques--Social life and customs. I. Altuna, Jesús. II. University of Nevada, Reno. Center for Basque Studies. III. Title. IV. Series.

GR137.7.B36313 2008
398.089'992--dc22

2008014798

The Center for Basque Studies wishes to gratefully acknowledge the generous financial support of the Bizkaiko Foru Aldundia / Provincial Government of Bizkaia for the publication of this book.

Selected Writings of José Miguel de Barandiarán: Basque Prehistory and Ethnography

Table of Contents

Acknowledgments

To my wife, Koro Mariezkurrena, with whom I visited several times at the home of D. José Miguel de Barandiarán. For this work, as with many other projects, she assisted with careful research of the bibliographical citations included in the introduction.

Introduction

by Jesús Altuna

N.B. It was only during the late twentieth century that the Basque Academy developed a standard orthography for the language designed to substitute Euskara Batua (Unified Basque) for its several dialects. Prior to then it was common practice for Basque writers to employ Spanish for place and personal names (including their own). Such was the case with José Miguel de Barandiarán (Barandiarango Jose Migel).

In this work, we have utilized modern Basque orthography for the names of Basque provinces: Araba (Alava), Bizkaia (Vizcaya), and Gipuzkoa (Guipúzcoa), while employing the commonly used English variants of Navarre (Navarra) and Lower Navarre (Basse Navarre). For cities and towns, we retained Barandiarán's usage, which was in many cases the Spanish form, but have added modern Basque orthography in parentheses after the names.

The Beginnings: Birth of a Vocation

José Miguel de Barandiarán is an exceptional witness to an entire century of the history of the Basque Country. He was born on December 31, 1889, and remained active until one year before his death, for in 1990 he was still writing a prologue to a book on ethnography. He died on December 21, 1991, ten days before his 102nd birthday.

Barandiarán was the youngest of nine children born to Francisco Antonio de Barandiarán and María Antonia de Ayerbe. They were farmers and lived on the farmstead called Perunezarra located in the neighborhood of Murkondoa in the town of Ataun, a rural village in Gipuzkoa. Murkondoa consisted of a dozen houses, and together with three other analogous neighborhoods formed the parish of San Gregorio, one of three in the town of Ataun. There were scarcely a thousand inhabitants in the parish of San Gregorio when José Miguel was born (photo 1).

Photo 1. San Gregorio de Ataun.

Photo 2. Perunezarra. Birthplace of José Miguel de Barandiarán.

The birth took place in the house called Perunezarra (photo 2). In and around it, during his childhood and adolescence, Barandiarán acquired intimate knowledge of lifestyles, traditions, customs, and myths that have since completely disappeared. His maternal language was Basque, or Euskara, and he began to learn Spanish (Castilian) only after attending the local school. Despite the students' complete ignorance of Spanish, the courses were taught in it as official policy. However, Barandiarán recalled that the teacher, who was an *Euskaldun* (that is, a fluent speaker of the Basque language), would frequently help them understand certain subjects with explanations in Euskara. He himself wrote that during those years in Ataun only the priests and a few rich people knew Spanish, and for that reason "it was considered by everyone to be a language for the rich and learned."[1] Basque, in contrast, was considered a language of the villagers.

The writer of these lines experienced this phenomenon, though under even worse circumstances. I refer to the years of the military uprising by General Franco when, as we will see later, Barandiarán had to flee into exile in Iparralde, or the Northern Basque Country in the French state. My first schooling took place in Berastegi, a town situated thirty-five kilometers from Ataun. The teacher who ran our school was sent away and another, completely ignorant of Euskara, was brought in from outside. As was the custom, we learned the four functions of arithmetic by singing, but the difficulties began when we attempted to solve mathematical problems.

In the text, which we did not understand, we would see two numbers. First we would add them together. We would then approach the teacher's desk, and he would pronounce our answer "good" or "bad." If the former, we would return to our places happy, as if we had accomplished something greater than a mere correct answer. If he said "bad" we retreated, saying, "*Erresta in beharko yu*" (We will have to subtract). We would subtract the smaller number from the larger and try the problem again. A second "bad," if that were his judgment, was more emphatic: "*Mul-ti-pli-car izango dek*" (It must be multiplication) and I remember that we would say the word "multiply" slowly, since it was new to us and we had to pronounce it carefully. If that was not the solution, we would return unhappily, saying "*Maixu onekin etzeok asmatzeik. Dibidir dek*" (With this teacher there's no getting it right. It's division). At times we were right the first time, sometimes on the second try, but maybe not until the fourth.

José Miguel, who lived in gentler times in this regard, had the good fortune that his teacher, though obliged by law to only use Spanish in his classroom, helped the students in Euskara, as needed.

In 1904 Barandiarán moved to Baliarrain, a small town of 216 inhabitants, near Ataun, where there was a preceptory or preseminary for students to begin their preparation for the priesthood. A priest, who was also the parish priest of the small town, would help them to learn Castilian Spanish, Latin, and other subjects related to their future studies. The exams were held in the greater Seminary of Vitoria, the diocesan see. When the Latin exams were given at the end of the first year, the chief examiner, who was scoring Barandiarán's test, said to him: "You know more Latin than Castilian. But you have to learn Castilian as well." Hearing this, the young lad, who was fifteen at the time, thought that they would fail him. He was greatly surprised on learning that, to the contrary, he had passed both courses in the same year. "It was one of the happiest days of my life," he would frequently say.

His joy was so great that he bought two rockets on his way home and fired them off on the road near his house. His mother saw him do this and thought he had become arrogant over his success. She took him to the orchard near his house, where there was an apple tree with branches sagging from the weight of the fruit. She showed him the tree and told him, "Son, you should be like that apple tree. The more apples its branches produce, the more humbly they hang down."[2]

The following term he moved into the Seminary of Vitoria. On returning home to spend Christmas vacation, just three days before Christmas, his mother died of pulmonary tuberculosis at fifty-six years of age. Her death caused the boy, who was not yet sixteen, one of the saddest days of his life. I heard him state this on numerous occasions during the long talks we had while conducting archeological excavations, often alone. I realized that that event was frequently on his mind, even though it had happened more than sixty years earlier. His biographer and nephew Luis Barandiarán recalls in his biography the tremendous effect that his mother's death caused José Miguel, quoting his uncle's exact words: "Many years passed without my mentioning my deceased mother. I did not want to acknowledge that she had died. Her memory was so vivid that I couldn't accept the idea of her absence. To say she had died seemed to me the same as killing her."[3]

For three years Barandiarán continued taking courses in philosophy and theology, but shortly before concluding his study for the priesthood, he suffered a crisis of faith and decided he must resolve his doubts before proceeding. He took an interest in other religions and came up with the idea of studying their history. At this point he read the book *Problémes et conclusions de l'histoire des religions* by Paul de Broglie (Paris: Putois-Cretté, 1904), which helped him greatly in resolving his doubts, as he was accustomed to say. Barandiarán found the topic pleasing and decided to explore it more deeply. It so interested him that in 1913, a year and a half before professing his vows, he took a course in Leipzig offered by Professor Wilhelm Max Wundt, one of the founders of scientific psychology, a specialist in ethnography and author of the massive work *Völkerpsychologie* (Leipzig: W. Engelmann, 1900–1920). Prof. Wundt greatly influenced Barandiarán, mainly regarding methodology and in particular the importance of belonging to the people one wanted to study. Whatever the case, Barandiarán later writes that although his stay in Leipzig was helpful, his poor knowledge of German prevented him from making the most of it. And he decided to study this language further since it was fundamental for his education in ethnological investigation.[4]

Barandiarán was ordained a priest at the end of 1914 in Vitoria, performing his first mass in the parish of San Gregorio de Ataun on January 1, 1915. That same year he graduated with a degree in theology from the University of Burgos and in 1916 was appointed professor at the Seminary of Vitoria, where among other disciplines (mathematics, physics, and geology) he taught prehistory and the history of religions. By this time he had already decided to study this last subject. Rather than being merely a student of it, he decided that he could make his own modest contribution by investigating the vestiges, memories, and traces of the religion of his fellow Basques that pre-dated the arrival of Christianity. Wundt encouraged him in this. Moreover, the topic was of interest to him in general terms, and he worked to have it offered as a course in the seminary, believing that those who were preparing for the priesthood should have knowledge of the subject. Acceptance of this idea was a long time coming.

Regarding this, a 1923 entry in his diary is of interest:

> After my visits to the museums and my classes in Germany, I became very enthused about participating in the Seminary, feeling that I was more qualified than before. But in Vitoria they were in no hurry to make use of my services. What happened taught me that I should not trust too much in the success of my plans, although it's important to make them and to prepare to put them into practice; they may be of some use eventually. Here's what happened: in the Seminary they installed a washing machine in October of this year. Subsequently, I was assigned to wash the clothing of everyone in the Seminary for three weeks . . . and for another two weeks at a later date, until the servant in charge of this chore had learned to operate the machine. During that time they excused me from my teaching duties, and I would wear a peasant's shirt when I was working in the laundry, during the most important time of the term, i.e., from early October until December.[5]

Turning to Barandiarán's archeological activities, the name Jentilbaratza (Orchard of Gentiles), which they use to designate a steep rocky hill in Ataun, led him to inspect the place and to initiate an excavation of it, helped by a peasant from the area who served as his assistant. There are some ruins of an ancient castle there. This was Barandiarán's first archeological expedition.

His assistant told Barandiarán that he knew where the last Gentiles[6] were buried, giving him directions to the place in Aralar where the tomb was located. They agreed to meet and go there on the following morning, but the peasant did not show up. Barandiarán decided to proceed alone, and when he arrived at Aralar he sat down on a pile of stones to rest and eat his sandwich. He began to poke around with his staff in the dirt of a molehill, and observed a human tooth in it. Then he looked at the pile of stones he had been sitting on and realized that it was actually a tomb at the center of which there were some large gravestones forming a kind of chamber.

Barandiarán saw a young shepherd nearby and asked him if he knew what those structures were. The young man answered in the affirmative and told him that it was a grave in which were buried the last Gentiles. After Barandiarán did further investigation, the boy told him a precious legend, that of Kixmi, which explains how the Gentiles disappeared with the arrival of Christianity, a legend collected by Barandiarán later in many other places and with different variations throughout the Basque Country.

It is quite interesting, from our current perspective, including that of these last fifty years, that it was a young shepherd and not an old man who narrated this legend. In effect, only the elderly remembered such legends a few years ago. But in the early twentieth century the young people still remembered them, at least in isolated parts of our country.

Barandiarán made a more thorough examination of the monument, which turned out to be a dolmen (photo 3). He drew a diagram of it and published the results, along with those of his investigation of others found nearby.[7]

Photo 3. Dolmen of Jentillarri, one of the dolmens discovered in Aralar in 1916. The cover was restored in 1960.

In response to this discovery he received a letter from Telesforo de Aranzadi,[8] who was excavating dolmens in the Navarre region of the mountains of Aralar, inviting him to join him in excavating the dolmens he had discovered. Enrique de Eguren would join them.[9]

Maturity and Lines of Investigation (1916–1938)

Following these discoveries and contacts with Aranzadi and Eguren, Barandiarán's investigative activity developed in two areas. In collaboration with the above-mentioned professors, he initiated a series of archeological excavations in caves and megaliths in the Basque Country, publishing the results of the investigations punctually. In addition, he began to collect a series of legends and popular beliefs, whose publication, starting in 1918, attracted the attention of important investigators in this field, as we will see below.

In the first instance, the three investigators came together primarily to undertake summer archeological excavations. In these projects, Aranzadi focused on the study of the human remains, Barandiarán on the artifacts, and Eguren on the fossils of mollusks, which were abundant in some of the prehistoric cave sites near the coast. The one dimension they lacked was a paleontologist to study the animal bones, which were so numerous in prehistoric sites.

In 1917, Barandiarán gave the inaugural address on Basque prehistory for the new academic course at the Vitoria Seminary.[10] The publication of this address is well-known and highly regarded by the Abbé H. Breuil, the famous French prehistorian, who wrote a letter to Barandiarán letting him know that he had read the address with genuine interest and telling him about some explorations he had made on a visit to the Basque Country.[11] Breuil advised him to contact the German prehistorian Hugo Obermaier (1877–1946), who was a professor of prehistory at the University of Madrid. Their relationship developed quickly.

That same year the Aranzadi-Barandiarán-Eguren team initiated excavations of several Gipuzkoan dolmens, activity that would lead them to broaden their investigations to all the dolmen sites of the Basque Country. The following year, in 1918, they also began another series of excavations in various caves, especially in Gipuzkoa and Bizkaia, among which the most significant are that of Santimamiñe and those of Urtiaga and Ermittia in Gipuzkoa. These caves hold important strata from the Upper Paleolithic, in addition to some later prehistoric

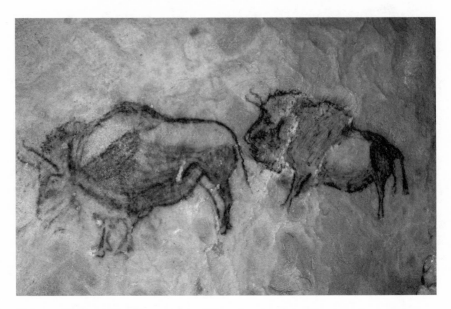

Photo 4. Santimamiñe. Bisons of the *Camarín,* or sanctuary.

strata with ceramics. In the cave of Santimamiñe there is also a sanctuary with cave art, which they also studied (photo 4).

The cave of Urtiaga also produced a collection of human remains, the most significant being several complete prehistoric crania, used by Aranzadi as the basis for important studies. We will comment on these remains later.

The excavation of some caves in Carranza in the westernmost part of Bizkaia dates from this same period, including the sites of Bortal and Venta Laperra. Participating in these excavations was the young Julio Caro Baroja, who recalls this experience as follows:

> While Don Telesforo was absorbed in his own thoughts, Don José Miguel [Barandiarán] spoke about Basque folklore, archeology, or general ethnography to me and a nephew of his from the Seminary who was working as his assistant. Whereas at the University I had to put up with the nuisance and boring analysis of Fernando de Herrera and other similar abominations, Barandiarán gave us very clear and precise ideas about the historical-cultural method, the latest investigations of Malinowski, the idea of God among the primitives, the thinking of Durkheim and Wundt . . . In short, I got a more thorough university education from a Paleolithic cave

in Bizkaia and the mouth of a Basque Catholic priest than from the halls of academe in Madrid.[12]

At the same time, they continued with the excavation of numerous dolmens, funerary monuments that span the period from the Neolithic to the Bronze Age. First, Barandiarán surveyed the high sierra and smaller mountain ranges where such monuments are found. He discovered numerous dolmens in the Gipuzkoan mountains of Aralar, Ataun-Burunda, Elosua-Placencia, Urbia and its environs, Pelabieta, Igoin-Akola, as well as other ranges in Bizkaia, Araba, and Navarre. The team participated in the excavation of some of these dolmens during the summer (photo 5). They published all of these studies in journals subsidized principally by the provincial councils overseeing the excavations.

Photo 5. Dolmen of Sasgastietako Lepua in the Megalithic site of Igoin-Akola.

We have indicated above that such projects continued until 1936. That was the year when the military uprising of General Franco interrupted Aranzadi and Barandiarán's excavation in the Gipuzkoan cave of Urtiaga. The military rebellion took place on July 18, but they kept working until the 24th, the date when they began to fear the consequences of the uprising. Aranzadi left for Barcelona, where his family lived, and Barandiarán fled to the northern Basque Country, in French territory, in September of that year as Franco's army advanced from

Navarre and Gipuzkoa toward Bizkaia. Eguren did not participate in
the Urtiaga project. The members of the team never saw each other
again. Eguren died in Vitoria in 1944, Aranzadi in Barcelona in 1945.
Barandiarán describes his flight as follows:

> Many people who were waiting to embark were crowded into the
> port.[13] The place is swarming with people, and is a good example
> of disorganization. A small boat labors to carry as many as it holds
> to the small steamships which, because of the low tide, await us
> beyond the wharf. Finally some forty-five of us fugitives embark on
> the steamship *El Angel de la Guarda* (Guardian Angel). Four or five
> Mendigoizales[14] armed with rifles board with us, in case it becomes
> necessary to defend us against those who wish to keep us from
> crossing. The stars maintain their silent course . . . We go for a long
> distance into the high sea, then turn right, toward St. Jean de Luz.
> We go without lights, to keep from being seen. Irigoyen scratches
> a flintstone to light his cigarette: he is showered with protests from
> all sides of the ship. On the way we do not meet any other ship.
> We arrive in Socoa at five in the morning. A sad voyage: with us
> go many young men from Motrico [Mutriku in Basque] who are
> fleeing the war and have no idea what they will do, where they will
> find shelter, nor where they should go once they arrive in St. Jean
> de Luz. Beside me is a lady who cries bitterly from time to time.
> Everyone is lamenting their own misfortune.[15]

Below, we will discuss Barandiarán's prehistory projects in the
northern Basque Country (1936–1953) and subsequent ones in the south,
once he returned there in 1953.

Barandiarán's second area of study during this period, his ethnographic projects, were more personal. In 1918, the Society of Basque
Studies (Eusko Ikaskuntza) was founded, and Barandiarán appeared
as a founding member, playing an extensive role within it. Among the
important milestones in this field, in addition to his active presence
at international conferences, are (in chronological order) the publication of an essay, "Contribución al estudio paletnográfico del Pueblo
Vasco. El magismo"[16] (1920), that aroused the interest of the famous
ethnologist, Wilhelm Schmidt, founder of the journal *Anthropos* and
distinguished member of the Historical-Cultural School in Vienna,
with whom Barandiarán subsequently maintained a long and extensive
relationship. As a result of this publication, in 1921 Schmidt invited him
to participate in the International Week of Religious Ethnology held in

Tilburg (Holland) in 1922. Barandiarán presented a paper on the religion of the ancient Basques.[17]

He was also instrumental to two further milestones in the development of Basque ethnology: the founding and publication of the monthly review *Eusko-folklore: Materiales y cuestionarios* (Eusko-Folklore: Materials and Questionnaires), which we will discuss below, and the founding and publication of *Anuario de Eusko-folklore* (photo 6), which after a number of interruptions is still being published today. Both publications were inaugurated in 1921. The first ceased publication in 1975.

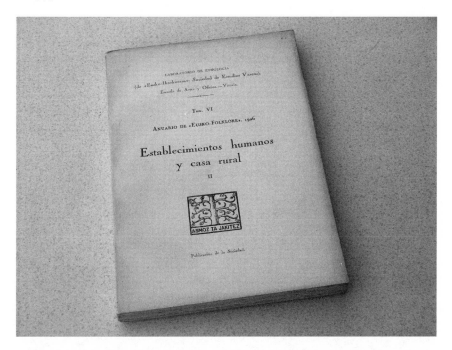

Photo 6. *Anuario de Eusko-folklore* (Basque Folklore Annual), Vol. 6, 1926.

Investigations Conducted during Exile

It is understandable that the pace of Barandiarán's investigations tapered off because of the military coup by General Franco and the world war that followed, leading to the German occupation of France. This diminished pace was particularly evident in the field of prehistory.

However, he soon renewed his investigations in ethnography in various places in Iparralde such as Doniztiri (called Saint-Esteben in

French), Heleta, Iholdi, and Liginaga, among others, under the patronage of Manuel de Ynchausti.[18] In addition, Barandiarán's international connections expanded through his participation in conferences and collaborations in journals. This was the case, for example, with Professors Bronislaw Malinowski, Raffaele Pettazzoni, Karl Bouda, Adolph Friedrich, and others. This last relationship led to his nomination in 1941 as a member of the Forschungsinstitut für Kulturmorphologie of the University of Frankfurt. Shortly before that, in 1938, he had been nominated as a member of the Commission Internationale des Arts et Traditions Populaires of Geneva.

In 1938, after two years of exile, he received an offer of a scholarship to study comparative ethnology in Great Britain, but he did not accept it, arguing that for the moment he preferred to continue studying the ethnology of the Basques, a topic that seemed urgent to him since their traditional culture, especially in its spiritual aspects of beliefs and myths, was rapidly disappearing, lending a sense of urgency to its documentation. Moreover, his stay in Iparralde allowed him to extend his investigations there, since until then Barandiarán had only conducted investigations in the peninsular parts of the Basque Country.

Photo 7. In the foreground, Bidartea House, in Sara, where Barandiarán lived between 1940 and 1953.

It is interesting to note that, once Barandiarán had established himself in Sara[19] in 1940 (photo 7), the year in which the Germans entered the northern Basque Country, the German military authority of the occupied zone gave him a safe-conduct pass so he could move freely in order to carry out archeological and ethnographic investigations. Barandiarán sent an emissary to Vitoria to bring back the archives that he had there in the seminary, since he needed them to carry out his present project. However, when this emissary crossed the French-Spanish border, the police confiscated these materials. Barandiarán informed the German military authority (*Feldkommandant* of Biarritz) of what had happened, and the next day he was in possession of the archives.

His search for prehistoric items led to his discovery of numerous megaliths (dolmens, tombs, and cromlechs) in Iparralde, which he reported in a publication.[20]

In 1946 he founded the Institut Basque de Recherche and the journal *Ikuska* and became the editor of another journal, *Gernika Euskojakintza: Revue des études basques* (Basque Studies Journal; *Gernika* was later dropped from the title) in which distinguished Bascologists from different countries collaborated. He also renewed publication of the *Eusko-folklore. Materiales y cuestionarios* mentioned above, which he humbly called "Hojas de Eusko-folklore" (Basque Folklore Leaflets). *Ikuska* continued to be published until 1951 and *Eusko-jakintza* continued until 1957. With all of this activity, he vigorously stimulated the cultural life of Iparralde.

During these years, especially the earliest ones of exile, he was intensely preoccupied with the political situation of the southern Basque Country, and with the Basque church in particular. He wrote important letters and commentaries such as those of 1937 with respect to the actions of the primate of Spain, Cardinal Gomá, who called Franco's military uprising a "Crusade," or the one concerning his own ecclesiastical hierarchy; or another, written in 1945, to Bishop D. Mateo Múgica, who was also removed from his diocese of Vitoria, which led the bishop to write his famous letter, "Imperatives of my conscience: an open letter to D. José Miguel de Barandiarán," concerning the consequences of the military uprising.

In connection with this, one of Barandiarán's first activities during the years in exile, at the request of Manuel de Ynchausti, cited above, was to gather personal accounts from many of the fugitives who fled from the southern Basque Country to Iparralde. From them he collected extensive information about the atrocities they had witnessed before fleeing. With these testimonies, presented with the rigor and method typical of Barandiarán in his ethnographic research, he produced a series of reports that have been preserved in Intxausti Baita, the house of Ynchausti and his descendants in Ustaritze. When the Germans entered Iparralde during the Second World War, to keep these testimonies from falling into their hands they were carefully buried in the chicken coop of a nearby house. They remained there until 1944, when they were recovered by Barandiarán himself once the Germans had withdrawn following the landing of the Allies in Normandy. Subsequently, they have been jealously preserved in the house of Intxausti Baita by Miren Ynchausti, daughter of Manuel Ynchausti. One hundred and thirty-six of these were recently published in *La Guerra Civil en Euzkadi* (2005).

Return from Exile

Barandiarán returned from exile in 1953, and inaugurated the Larramendi Chair at the University of Salamanca with the presentation of a short course on "The Current State of Basque Studies." He was offered the position and invited to present the course by the rector of that university, Antonio Tovar, who was interested in (among other things) researching Euskara.

In the neighborhood of his birth, Barandiarán built a new house, constructed according to the plans of the house Bidartea in Sara, where he had lived during most of the period of exile. He called this new house Sara (photo 8).

Photo 8. Sara House, constructed by Barandiarán in Ataun-San Gregorio on his return from exile.

In 1955, he renewed his archeological excavations in the cave of Urtiaga at the very point where he had abandoned them in 1936, but this time accompanied by different persons given that his co-investigator Telesforo de Aranzadi had died in 1945.

This is the period of important excavations carried out in numerous archeological sites such as the caves of Lezetxiki, Aitzbitarte IV, Marizulo, Ekain, Solacueva, Montico de Txarratu, Atxeta, and Axtor, among others, as well as studies of the Paleolithic sanctuaries of cave art in Altxerri and Ekain.

Photo 9. At the entrance to the Paleolithic site of Lezetxiki, with Jesús Altuna (1965).

These excavations, especially those of Lezetxiki (photo 9) and Aitzbitarte IV, were transformed immediately into field schools, where young students of prehistory who were finishing their university careers (Juan M. Apellániz, Ignacio Barandiarán,[21] and the author of these lines, among others) were learning field techniques under the direction of Don José Miguel.

The field school experience had a multiplying effect. These young men shortly thereafter initiated archeological excavations on their own account and, upon assuming teaching positions, began to develop their own students, assuring and greatly expanding prehistoric research in the Basque Country into the future.

Barandiarán gave up archeological fieldwork in 1974 after turning eighty-four, devoting himself thereafter to ethnographic activities. These had taken on a new luster after 1964, due to his appointment to the Chair of "Ethnology of the Basque People" at the University of Navarre, a position he held until 1980. This position carried with it the creation, in 1968, of the Etniker research groups (Etniker Euskalerria), primarily in Navarre and then in Gipuzkoa (1972) and Bizkaia (1973). The groups of Araba and Iparralde would be formed later. These groups continue working and publishing research connected to different aspects of traditional life throughout the Basque Country, using questionnaires originally elaborated by Barandiarán. From these groups, extensive studies of domestic diet (1990), games and children's songs (1993), funeral rites (1995), rites of birth and marriage (1998), cattle and sheep raising (2001), and popular medicine (2004) have been written and published. In this way, an ethnographic atlas of the Basque Country (Atlas Etnográfico de Vasconia, a series published in Bilbao by Eusko Jaurlaritza) is gradually being composed, one of Barandiarán's greatest dreams.

In 1972, the publishing house La Gran Enciclopedia Vasca began publishing the complete works of Barandiarán, with the issuing of the first volume. This project was completed in 1984, when volume 22, the last of the series, was published. The first volume includes an unpublished work titled *Diccionario ilustrado de mitología vasca* (Illustrated Dictionary of Basque Mythology), in addition to other works on mythology published between 1922 and 1960. The term "illustrated," introduced by the editor and with the illustrations also provided by him, did not please Barandiarán at all because of their popular (in the worst sense of the term) overtone. This first volume concludes with the legend of the disappearance of the last Gentiles, under the title "Kixmi, or the Sunset of the Gods," and is the same one he was told by the young shepherd of Aralar in 1916, at the beginning of his investigations.

The final years of Barandiarán's life were ones of homages, awards, medals, and honorary doctoral degrees from several universities. He remained lucid until his death, which came a few days before he turned 102 years of age (photo 10).

Plan of the Present Work

To select a handful of writings representative of Barandiarán's work from a total production of twenty-two volumes is no easy task. Inevitably, many interesting texts will have to be omitted. In any case, we offer here our selection, based on clear criteria.

Photo 10. Barandiarán at one hundred years of age, dedicating his last published work, *Euskal herriko mitoak* (Myths of the Basque People), to the Altuna family.

At the outset we should say that these are works written fifty or sixty years ago, and should be judged by the values prevailing in their time. I say this because many contemporaries are prone to be overly critical of past scholarship, alternatively treating it as either anachronistic or dismissing its value for not having been evaluated with today's methods and criteria. With this caveat, I have selected the following as particularly representative of Barandiarán's interests and thought:

1. *Mitología vasca* (Basque Mythology). Madrid: Editorial Minotauro, 1960. 162 pages. This work was published as the fifth volume of a series titled Biblioteca Vasca (Basque Library).

2. Several chapters of *El hombre prehistórico en el País Vasco* (Prehistoric Man in the Basque Country). Buenos Aires: Editorial Vasca Ekin, 1953. 257 pages. The chapters selected are 5 to 9, from the Mesolithic to the Iron Age.

3. Fragments of *Bosquejo etnográfico de Sara* (Ethnographic Sketch of Sara). *Anuario de Eusko-folklore*, published in seven parts (Volumes 17 to 24) between 1957 and 1972.

Basque Mythology

We chose *Basque Mythology* because it constitutes Barandiarán's own summary of his extensive investigations in that field over a period of forty-five years. Although it is a work published in 1960, and thus thirty years before the death of its author, it should be noted that it is a synthesis written when Barandiarán was already seventy years old, and hence a work of genuine maturity.

The book is dedicated to Telesforo de Aranzadi. The dedication ends with the words "Happy New Year." The editor added on his own account, "and until I hear from you," unaware of the meaning of the dedication. The phrase had, in effect, an eschatological sense, as Barandiarán pointed out to me when it was published, "because Aranzadi, who wasn't very pious, was, however, profoundly spiritual and we spoke on more than one occasion of life after death."

In a few words which the author himself addresses to the reader at the beginning of his work, Barandiarán humbly says that he is presenting "only a sampling" of the material collected. However, the book is far more than that. It is a systematic summary, which he divides into an extensive introduction, a thematic categorization which he includes under the epigraphs "Magic" and "Myths."

In order to achieve this synthesis of mythology in the work we are discussing, an indispensable step was the inauguration, in 1921, of the periodical *Eusko-folklore. Materiales y cuestionarios*, cited above, a work much beloved by the author. There were several interruptions in its publication due mainly to the Spanish Civil War and the subsequent exile which Barandiarán had to endure. Even so, despite the interruptions, it continued to be published until 1975.

It started out as a modest monthly publication, which Barandiarán edited from his Chair at the seminary in Vitoria. He called it "Hojas de Eusko-folklore" (Basque Folklore Leaflets) because of their brevity.

Here is the "Preliminary Note" introducing these "leaflets" in the first issue:

> Spontaneous products of the Basque spirit, in particular those that refer to early cultural conditions, evanescent remains of a past whose memory has come down to us in the form of legends, traditions, beliefs, customs and religious and magical practices; the mutual relations of these elements and their systematic categorization constitute the primary and immediate object of *Eusko-folklore*— this in regard to the descriptive part of the science, which must precede any scientific generalizations and the comparative study of

the materials. To investigate and collect such data is the first task to be undertaken. Such is the purpose of these leaflets, God willing and with the collaboration of all lovers of Basque folklore.[22]

These "Hojas" are published in three series. The first includes numbers 1–179, except for 146, which was lost while in press because of the war. This series is the one that was published in the aforementioned seminary between 1921 and 1936, with the interruption of the years 1931 to 1935, and it continued to appear with greater irregularity during Barandiarán's exile in Iparralde. There were even some numbers that could not be published for lack of funds, and which remained unpublished until 1966, when they were released in volume 4 of the Colección Auñamendi of Donostia-San Sebastián under the title *El mundo en la mente popular vasca: creencias, cuentos y leyendas* (The World in the Mind of the Basque People: Beliefs, Tales and Legends).

The second series consists of seven numbers and was published between 1947 and 1949 (during the exile in France) under the title *Euskofolklore. Documents et questionnaires* (Basque Folklore: Documents and Questionnaires). The first four appear in the journal *Herria* (1947) and the following three in the journal *Ikuska* (1948–49).

Finally, the third series, numbered 1–25, was published between 1954 and 1975 in the journal *Munibe* of the Sociedad de Ciencias Aranzadi in Donostia-San Sebastián. These "Hojas" provide the fundamental material for the work we are discussing here. In addition, they subsequently provided the material for the *Diccionario ilustrado de mitología vasca* (Illustrated Dictionary of Basque Mythology) mentioned above (Barandiarán, 1972).

Caro Baroja commented on these "Hojas": "If their scientific value is incalculable, their poetic value is no less so. In those monthly leaflets of *Eusko-folklore* so modestly titled Materials and Questionnaires, there is more genuine poetry than in many books of poetry, which are poetic more for form and intent than for depth and consequence. The poetic life of the Basque is expressed in them. Through it we see how he has lived poetically in this or that corner of this land during generations that have been at times hard and difficult."[23]

Barandiarán, on the other hand, in his collection of myths, legends, and tales in different parts of the Basque Country, beginning with those from near his family home and those of his region and town, was immediately aware of the multiple versions of a single legend. He collected these variants in the different places he visited throughout the length and breadth of the Basque Country during his archeological excavations, initially in the territories of Gipuzkoa, Bizkaia, Araba, and Navarre. Subsequently, exile allowed him to extend his investigations into the northern part of the Basque Country: Lapurdi (Labourde), Lower Navarre, and Zuberoa (Soule).

Nevertheless, Barandiarán was perfectly aware that he alone could not collect all of the different versions of each myth extant throughout the entire Basque Country, nor assess its distribution and importance within the different regions. He felt it was critical to create an atlas of such legends and myths in order to be able to assess their extent, relative chronology, etc. On the other hand, it was urgent to collect them quickly, since the transformation of the ways of life in Basque society, to which he was an exceptional witness, was erasing these traces of the past from the minds of his compatriots. They were no longer being passed from generation to generation, as previously, during long winter nights by the warmth of the hearth. The industrialization of many rural areas, the migration from country to city, and the diffusion of communications media were interrupting this process. Children nowadays, unlike those of yesteryear, prefer to turn on the television rather than listen to grandfather's "stories."

For this reason, the Basque Folklore Leaflets were subtitled "Materials and Questionnaires." Barandiarán's goal was for his students and collaborators, scattered throughout the Basque Country, to collect variants of the "materials" that he had gathered in a determined number of places. He provided a common methodology for such work to his collaborators, so that the data would be collected correctly and comparably. Furthermore, in each of the first issues he included a brief questionnaire by means of which he sought to persuade the readers of these leaflets to provide data from their own parts of the country. In any event, his collaborators were limited in number, and it was Barandiarán who collected the vast majority of myths.

In this regard it is worthwhile to say a few words about the ease or difficulty of collecting such information in a land that is a labyrinth of mountains and valleys, and in which the people are more reserved and circumspect than in the lowlands. It is easy to contact people on the Castilian plains, even without knowing Castilian well, as in the case of some American ethnologists, who have had no difficulty in doing so. But these same investigators encountered difficulty in the Valley of Pas (Cantabria), where the inhabitants are reluctant to tell their stories even to those who speak their language. In this respect it is useful to remember what we indicated earlier about Wilhelm Wundt, who spoke to Barandiarán about the importance of belonging to the people one wanted to study.

I myself have frequently tried the following experiment: on ascending some mountain in the Basque-speaking part of our country, at the most remote house on the mountainside I ask in Castilian how to get to a particular place in the area. The woman or man of the house comes to the upstairs window and without silencing the barking dog gives a curt direction with a slight motion and a couple of words. But if I ask in Euskara, she or he comes down to the front door, orders the dog to be quiet, and points the way with a panoply of gestures. It is easy after that to strike up a conversation.

Caro Baroja says in his portrayal of Aranzadi and Barandiarán that the latter enjoyed certain advantages over him in collecting ethnographic data: he spoke Euskara well and wore a clerical tunic. Caro's own command of Euskara was inadequate and, besides, he wore a suit and tie.

I would say to my dear friend Caro Baroja that he is correct in what he says about Euskara. That is in fact precisely what I have been saying, but with regard to clothing I disagree with him. In the first place the tunic might have been an advantage in the past, in some circumstances, but in others it was an obstacle. As for the suit and tie, nothing could be easier than dispensing with them and wearing good cotton trousers instead.

I often would go with Barandiarán to houses in the area where we were conducting excavations during the sixties, a period in which, at least among us, the use of tape recorders had not become common. We would do this on Sundays, our day of rest from work in the caves. Barandiarán would chat at length, aimlessly and in a friendly manner, with the elders of the household on topics that concerned them, such as the weather, crops, and hard domestic chores, establishing a climate of complete trust. Little by little he would lead the conversation to topics that were of interest to him, asking about their customs or beliefs about lightning, caves, or many other aspects of their world of representation. I would observe how easily information about beliefs and myths would begin to come out, along with ancient knowledge and sayings.

After this lengthy conversation, Barandiarán would take out his field journal and begin to take notes, in order not to rely on memory for so much material. You would then see an expression of unease in the informant, as Barandiarán urged them to repeat a particular legend. You could tell that they wanted to amend it, to dress it up in some manner, since it was now being written down. But as Barandiarán had already heard it, he would frequently say, "You told me earlier . . .," by way of getting them back on track.

The book *Mitología vasca* (Basque Mythology) is a brief, systematic summary put together by Barandiarán from the wealth of material about spiritual culture salvaged by him from an entire world of representations. It was one that he knew vividly from his childhood, but which he saw dying and disappearing forever from the imagination of his people.

The reader will note that among the many images of different spirits collected by Barandiarán, that of Mari stands out, a feminine spirit, known also by other names and appearing in different forms, with her family, her symbols, her dwellings and the way those who go to her for advice should behave when visiting her there, her attributes, her functions, the cult she professes, her rules, and the punishments she can inflict. Barandiarán considers that "this spirit constitutes a thematic nucleus or point of convergence of numerous mythic themes of different origins: some Indo-European, others of ancestral background. But if we consider some of its attributes (the control of terrestrial forces and of subterranean spirits, its identification with various telluric phenomena, etc.) we are inclined to consider it as a symbol—perhaps a personification—of the Earth."[24]

Another fundamental element of this work is the house (*etxe*), not only as a dwelling but as material support, as temple and cemetery, as a common focus for the living and dead members of the family, which implies a cult, with its functionaries, the main one being the *etxekoandre* or lady of the house.

Thus, the reader will gradually become familiar with the mythology of an ancient people that has jealously preserved its personality until recent times. The very latest period, with the entire complex of mental changes it entails, has had a significant effect on that personality.

At this point, we must mention an element that has not followed this path to extinction: the Basque language. It has come down to us intact. Let us consider it.

Of our European prehistory, except for a single element, a single witness, we are left with nothing but ruins. Some of these are quite beautiful and have come down to us well preserved—for instance, the sanctuary of Ekain. But even in this case the context is missing. Why, in effect, did the Paleolithic painters go so far into the cavern to make their paintings? What were they seeking? What was their image of the universe? What were their sorrows, fears, and joys? The bones of those people, their instruments, and even their paintings were fossilized and remain accessible to us, but not their thoughts and beliefs. We are left only with those beautiful ruins.

But I mentioned that there is one exception. We are left, in effect, with a unique and still vibrant witness of European prehistory. It is still alive in this corner of the Gulf of Bizkaia. I am referring to Euskara; call it proto-Basque or whatever you like. When, at the beginning of the first millennium before Christ, the Indo-European languages spread westward, all of the prehistoric languages of this continent disappeared, with this one exception.

One of the potent branches derived from Indo-European, Latin, with all the weight of the Roman Empire behind it, surrounded Euskara's territory. Spanish and French, Latin's progeny, made deep incursions into it, but, surprisingly, the Basque language lived on. We have abundant reasons to continue preserving it, but for those who do not acknowledge them, the following might suffice: Euskara, as I have said, is the only cultural legacy of European prehistory. If we are making efforts to maintain the broken remains of a dolmen, a cromlech, or a menhir, and we should indeed do so, how can we not work to preserve this unique patrimonial linguistic legacy? Europe as a whole should preserve Basque as the only living treasure of its millenary past.

At the present time, despite all of the language's many deaths and rebirths, the *ikastolak* or Basque schools and the vital sentiments of the people have led to the recovery of the language in certain areas and its intensification in others. Euskara's entry into the university has eliminated the perception throughout the Basque Country that it is considered the language of villagers, as we said at the beginning of this presentation.

Concerning the appeal by UNESCO (United Nations Educational, Scientific, and Cultural Organization) during the 1960s to save the treasures of Nubia, a rescue operation in which I had the honor to participate, André Malraux said, "There is only one act over which neither the indifference of the constellations nor the eternal murmur of the rivers prevails. This is the act whereby man rescues something from death."[25] Barandiarán is a man who has rescued many things from death. His collection of *Basque Mythology* is the best testimony to that.

Some had commented, during his old age and then after his death, that Barandiarán did little more than collect data without elaborating on it—that he did not interpret his materials. He heard this criticism during his final years and said, "If we don't collect this data today it will slip through our hands, it will never be collected and much less interpreted, for you cannot interpret what doesn't exist. There will be time later for interpretations."[26] We have before us the grand patrimony of materials he rescued. Here is the quarry in which contemporary anthropologists can act, analyze, investigate, organize, interpret, and compare Basque culture with that of other peoples. Oddly enough, those critics demanding such interpretations from the man who collected the materials are nowhere to be found working in that quarry.

It is indeed true that Barandiarán is often too laconic, that we would have welcomed more extensive commentary from him concerning such materials, but there is a large gap between this and the antiquarian that he has been accused of being.

Mitología vasca brings to a close an analytical index undertaken by Julio Caro Baroja and published in a series of editions by Txertoa of Donostia-San Sebastián, along with a prologue by Caro Baroja himself. To complete the presentation of this work I want to quote a few paragraphs from this prologue:

> We have before us the complete *Mitología vasca* [Basque Mythology]. Our guide is the most qualified man who exists, who ever did exist and who will probably ever exist (given the decline of the Basque people) to speak to us on this topic, which he presents in a systematic, organized fashion that the dictionaries of the language fail to reflect . . .
>
> This book is an admirable model for approaching what is or, more accurately, what was the Basque world of myth up until the epoch in which its author, still a child, first encountered it in the land of his family: late nineteenth- and early twentieth-century Ataun. Later the vision broadened as Barandiarán, after delving into the study of the history of comparative religions and cultural anthropology, went about traversing his country, step by step . . .
>
> Barandiarán, like no one else, has taught us about the cardinal ideas that dominate the minds which accept such myths as something real. Chief among these, in my judgment, is the idea that "all things that have names exist." That is, that the mythical beings are not symbols or allegories, as the ancient and more or less symbolist mythologists and philosophers believed, nor are they the products of verbal confusions that lend themselves to equivocal concepts, which then take on a profile conforming to what others believe. No. They are products of the known and physically knowable world. Not only the sun, or the moon, or the stars, as animated entities, but also others that do not have that same corporality but which are described with particular forms: *Tartalo*, the *basojaun*, the *lamiak*, the "Lady," whether she be from some other mountain or from a familiar place, and countless others.[27]

Prehistoric Man in the Basque Country

Barandiarán's other activity, as a prehistorian, also occupied a large part of his life. After 1917, when he embarked on his first archeological excavations with Telesforo de Aranzadi and Enrique de Eguren in the Gipuzkoan dolmens of Aralar, which he discovered, he devoted every summer until 1936 to working on excavations, preferably on dolmens and caves in which Paleolithic strata were most pronounced. During his seventeen-year exile, this activity tapered off significantly and, although the prospecting expeditions in the northern part of the Basque Country were numerous, leading to the discovery of many sites, he worked only occasionally in that region.

But after his return from exile, every year until 1974 he initiated new excavations, especially in Paleolithic caves. His excavations in the Mousterian strata of Lezetxiki, Aitzbitarte IV, and Ekain date from this epoch. Barandiarán also worked on Mesolithic sites and the Neolithic ones with ceramics such as Marizulo and Solacueva, as well as some dolmens. These summer projects entailed for Barandiarán long hours of work at other times of the year documenting and publishing the results of his investigations.

Barandiarán would write several overviews of Basque prehistory. The first of these, *El hombre primitivo en el País Vasco* (Primitive Man in the Basque Country), was published in the Colección Zabalkundea by Ediciones Vascas of Donostia-San Sebastián in 1934. It appeared in two editions, one in Castilian and the other in Euskara. It has 112 pages followed by eleven photographs.

The work begins by explaining what little is known about the Lower Paleolithic in the Basque Country. Rather than isolating the Mousterian period as a separate stage of the Middle Paleolithic, he includes it with the Lower Paleolithic. He then deals extensively with the Upper Paleolithic, for which more evidence is available, proceeding on to the Neolithic, the Calcolithic, and the Bronze and Iron Ages. He concludes the work with a chapter dedicated to the period of Romanization of the area.

In this work, he frequently correlates his ethnographic data with specific archeological discoveries. He often said that certain contemporary prehistorians resort to the culture of so-called "primitive peoples" of Africa to explain specific prehistoric findings, establishing ethnographic parallels between peoples far removed in space and time, while failing to probe deeply into their own people, that is, those living very close to the site of the discoveries, where they might also find such parallels and without having to invoke remote cultures.

Later on, in 1953, he published another synthesis entitled *El hombre prehistórico en el País Vasco* (Prehistoric Man in the Basque Country) with Editorial Ekin, the Basque publishing house in Buenos Aires. This work is much more extensive (267 pages), but in a format similar to the earlier collection. This major expansion is the result of the passage of almost twenty years between the two editions, during the course of which, naturally enough, much more information became available. Thus, for example, it includes more information about geography, orography, and climate changes during the Quaternary, the glaciations and the alluvial deposits, as well as the Isturitz site and the introduction of the parietal art of the Lower Paleolithic, discovered in the interim between the two editions.

In this work he clearly defines the Lower Paleolithic, about which little was known at the time, but which extends into the Middle Paleolithic, including the Mousterian period of the cave of Isturitz (Isturitze) and the shelter found in Olha.

Of course, it includes no information about the great cave art sanctuaries, such as Altxerri and Ekain in Gipuzkoa and other minor finds in Iparralde, since they had yet to be discovered. He continues introducing ethnographic data that he had collected by relating it to the prehistoric discoveries. Finally, this work includes an extensive appendix with a catalog of the prehistoric sites known in the Basque Country at the time. He organizes the living sites by province and the Megalithic monuments by mountain chain.

Later, in 1972, he published one further synthesis, this time only in Euskara, titled *Lehen euskal gizona* (Early Basque Man) with Editorial Lur in Donostia-San Sebastián. This is a smaller work, with only 120 pages. Although it contains far more information, with the inclusion of the excavations made from 1955 to 1970 and the important discoveries of the sanctuaries of Altxerri and Ekain with Paleolithic cave art, it is much more parsimonious with respect to both reflection and interpretation. It is as if, over the long course of the years, Barandiarán had seen how ideas, theories, and interpretations had come and gone and consequently decided that such treatment was less important than the presentation of the raw data.

He does not, in fact, reproduce the series of reflections and interpretations of his earlier works. At forty-four years of age he had had the audacity to make claims that he no longer ventured to defend at sixty-three. Thus, in the two earlier works, among other things, he draws specific conclusions about matters such as hunting methods employing instruments still used by Basques in his day, such as ropes (*bizto* or *lakio*), the sling, and the *malota*, a kind of catapult, and naturally the *usategieta* netting system for hunting doves in Etxalar or Sara. In this later work such ethnographic parallels disappear. On the other hand, he is even more reluctant to posit general interpretations. He is more cautious in relating the prehistoric past to the ethnographic material he collects in the present.

This procedure of simply presenting the data without attempting to interpret it (which we mentioned earlier) contrasts with his highly interpretive treatment of the traditional spiritual culture that was on the verge of disappearing even as he was collecting and rescuing it from extinction. Nevertheless, it remains true that his most recent treatment and summary of Basque prehistory lacks a clear interpretive dimension.

Whatever the case, the facile relationship he established in the 1934 and 1953 works between the mythical world underlying present reality and what was revealed in the prehistoric discoveries was gradually becoming blurred and open to skepticism. Not only was Barandiarán growing skeptical of his own previous acumen, he began questioning many of the affirmations made by his famous contemporary prehistorians. Thus, when he saw them distinguish between cultural levels, blithely labeling them as Magdalenian V, Magdalenian VIa and VIb, connecting the results of the Cantabrian to the stratification or schemata of the sites in the French Dordogne, he would frequently say that if future investigations were conducted that way in the Basque Country, serious errors would result. In effect, if in their zeal to classify and stratify by geological epoch one kind of instrument is used in Urbia, Urbasa, and Aralar; another in Berastegi, Segura, and Abadiano (Abadiño), and a third in Getaria, Bermeo, and Elantxobe, prehistorians would reach conclusions about the existence of three cultures which they have sought to categorize according to different geological periods, but without realizing that they are three different activities (the first pastoral, the second agricultural, and the third piscatorial) of a single people.

For the reasons explained in the previous paragraphs, we have chosen to present here certain sections from the 1953 work *El hombre prehistórico en el País Vasco*, rather than that of 1972, because it is in the earlier edition that one can see more clearly how Barandiarán makes frequent reference to data that have survived, according to him, until his own time. Those sections are chapters 5 through 9 of the text that refer to the Mesolithic, the Neolithic, and the Age of Metals.

We wish to remind the reader again, and especially here in this work on prehistory, of what we said at the beginning of our presentation of the selected works: that they should be judged according to the precepts of their own time. Since 1953 many advances have been made in the field of prehistoric investigation, not only in our general knowledge (it should suffice to recall that the great sanctuaries of cave art like Ekain and Altxerri were discovered subsequently) but also in methods and general perspectives concerning the prehistoric peoples of southwestern Europe.

In the chapter referring to the Mesolithic, Barandiarán also considers the human being that could have inhabited the Basque Country then, mentioning the craniums discovered in the cave of Urtiaga in the Azilian strata. Already at the beginning of the long chapter preceding it, which we omitted from this selection, he speaks at greater length about this detail and presents the hypothesis offered by Aranzadi and later accepted initially by others, including the author of these lines.

Aranzadi and Barandiarán had found a series of craniums in the cave of Urtiaga, all well preserved, one of which they attributed (with some uncertainty) to the Magdalenian, two others to the Azilian, and one (of a child) to the Eneolithic. These craniums have been the object of numerous anthropological studies, the first of which was done by Aranzadi (1948). According to him, the oldest cranium (B_I), probably Magdalenian, had Cro-Magnonoid features. The Azilian craniums (A_I and A_2) were intermediary between Cro-Magnon and the present-day Basque type. Finally, the cranium from the Eneolithic is of the Basque type. Thus, the present-day Basque type probably derived from Cro-Magnon man in this area of the western Pyrenees, just as in other regions it produced the Alpine type and the Mediterranean type.

This stratigraphic and consequently chronological categorization, combined with Aranzadi's anthropological classification concerning the origin of the Basque population, has been reiterated in many books and published articles. However, the craniums appeared in a zone in which the roof of the cave had collapsed onto the floor, causing, on the one hand, problematic stratigraphy and, on the other, certain difficulties in the course of the excavation, especially given the methods of the epoch in which this took place (1935–36). Regarding this, Barandiarán later said that, "Both the study of the site of Urtiaga as well as that of the human remains found in it should be completed by means of new investigations and methods, which can confirm or perhaps rectify our current conjectures."[28]

The suspicion that the craniums could have been buried subsequently was reasonable, given that during the Calcolithic the cave had a sepulchral function. This being so, it was possible that they might have been commingled with artifacts of the Magdalenian and Azilian epochs, depending on the depth of the burial. It was also possible that the strata could have been altered subsequently, given that in that area of the cave we identified the remains of a badger, a burrowing animal that makes dens, frequently inside caves, displacing strata. There were also remains of a cat and domestic goat, clearly from a later period.

Our earlier speculation predated development of radiocarbon dating techniques. Then, for many years, the analysis of C14 required a large quantity of bones, meaning the destruction of the craniums in question, which was inadmissible. But when radiocarbon analysis with the mass accelerator was invented, they could be dated with only a few tenths of a gram of bone matter. This allowed us to send three samples taken from the temporal bone of the ear. Two of them belonged to cranium B_I and the third from A_I. The result was 3,475 years plus or minus 120 for one of the samples of B_I, 3,445 plus or minus 110 for the second sample of this cranium, and 3,430 plus or minus 100 for cranium A_I. Therefore, the three craniums belonged to the Bronze Age. The morphological differences between them could very well have been due to the individual variability occurring within a population.

There are numerous examples regarding the relationship Barandiarán establishes between current observations and prehistoric data, backdating them in some cases to prehistoric times. For instance, in the chapter on the Neolithic he relates the domestication of bovines with hunting techniques of semi-wild cows that he was familiar with in his youth in mountainous zones of the Basque Pyrenees. Or when taking into account the climactic conditions of the Pyrenees, Barandiarán extrapolates from the present to then posit transhumance in prehistoric times. In this way, he explains the presence of certain new cultural elements in both lowland Aquitania and the valley of the Ebro as caused by contacts with mountain dwellers in the course of lengthy transhumant journeys, rather than by immigrations from without. He regards the latter to be improbable, given the homogeneity in the physical anthropology of populations in the zones near the Pyrenees.

He also links the distribution of recent shepherd dwellings in the Pyrenees, as well as in many other mountain ranges in the Basque Country (such as Aralar, Urbia, Urbasa, Abodi, and Gorbea (Gorbeia)) with the presence of dolmenic sites. He even notes such details as the absence of dolmens in places with poor pasturage and, to the contrary, the frequent construction of the shepherd's hut right upon a dolmen or a tomb.

Barandiarán dedicates an important chapter to language, in which it is interesting to note the importance he gives to the names of specific instruments used today—*aizkora* (axe), *aiztzur* (hoe), *azkon* (arrow), *aizto* (knife), and *zulakaitz* (chisel), all of which contain in their root the word *(h)aitz* (stone). This suggests to him that their names date from a time when these instruments were made of stone. He repeats this observation in the 1972 book.

This is a truly suggestive idea to which linguists have returned time and time again. Most recently, Joaquín Gorrochategui (2001) has taken up the topic. He believes that it proves that the ancestors of the Basques knew the Neolithic culture in which these instruments were made of stone. However, it is not exclusive to them as such terminology can also be found in other languages. He offers the example of the German word *Messer* (knife), which means etymologically "knife for meat," as in the Old English *mete-seax*. Now this *seax* is related to the Latin *saxum*, stone. What can be affirmed is that in Euskara the proportion of such compounds is greater than in the surrounding languages.

Barandiarán also posits as evidence of the antiquity of the language the names *urraida* (from *urre*, "oro" (gold) and *aide* (similar)), and *zirraida* (silver and *aide*), corresponding to copper and tin, indicating that their formation correctly follows the order of the historical appearance of use of these metals. The source words *urre* and *zillar* would have preceded the diffusion of copper (Eneolithic or Calcolithic) and of tin (Bronze Age). In support of this he also offers the Basque names for lightning (*ozme*) and thunder (*ozminarri* or *ozkarri*) with the names for sky (*ortz*) and stone (*arri*).

Barandiarán dedicates important sections to religion both in the chapter on the Eneolithic and the one on the Bronze Age. He draws attention to the orientation of the dolmens, whose chambers are oriented east to west, as is the placement of the cadavers deposited in them, laid out in the direction of the sun star. He notes that "they are visible signs of a world of beliefs, ideas and intentions,"[29] which he relates to a probable veneration of the sun. Additional evidence of this are the words *Ekhaina* (month of the sun, June) and *Eguberri* (new sun, Christmas).

Today we may think that the Eneolithic and the Bronze Age are too many thousands of years removed for us to try to relate traditional Basque culture with some of those beliefs using only the data collected by Barandiarán in the Basque countryside. However, some of the parallels beg explanation.

With respect to his activity in the field of prehistory, two aspects stand out. First, Barandiarán's collection of materials was significantly better and more systematic than that of many of his colleagues who were working at the same time in the Cantabrian region. We ourselves have seen materials from caves in Asturias and Cantabria, scattered among different museums, without stratigraphic references. We can learn nothing from them. In contrast, during the late 1960s and early 70s, three doctoral dissertations, and subsequently parts of others, have been written using the materials excavated by Barandiarán (in combination with others). This was possible because his materials are preserved in perfect chronological order by century and with stratigraphic references. Those from Bizkaia are in the museums of Bilbao, those from Gipuzkoa in museums of Donostia-San Sebastián. The three doctoral dissertations are those of his disciples Ignacio Barandiarán (1967), Juan María Apellániz (1973 and 1974), and the author of this presentation (Altuna, 1972), who approached Barandiarán after his return from exile.

On the other hand, the publications of Aranzadi and Barandiarán do not possess the rigor and quality of those of today's prehistorians. When Barandiarán was writing the memoirs of his excavations in solitude, he kept track of each and every artifact appearing in the site, including making drawings of them. However, his stratigraphic references and attributions of particular strata to one of several cultures were excessively spare. He failed to publish the analyses that his descriptive reports should have generated.

In any event, within the historiography of prehistoric investigations in the Basque Country, in contrast to the pioneer or initial period, the Aranzadi-Barandiarán-Eguren team initiated a second stage, that of consolidation, which started with the excavations of dolmens in Aralar in 1917 and lasted until 1937, that is, until the Spanish Civil War and Barandiarán's subsequent exile. This work is of indisputably greater maturity. In short, they elevated prehistoric investigation in the Basque Country from the level of aficionados to a scientific one. It is the latter to which contemporary investigations are heir.

In any case, to my mind, in light of future developments in the two fields, Barandiarán's contribution to ethnography is of greater importance than his work in prehistory. In effect, had he not excavated the numerous sites that he did, they would have remained intact and could have been examined later. On the other hand, had he not collected the legends and myths when he did, they would have been lost forever since they have subsequently died out.

An Ethnographic Sketch of Sara

Barandiarán produced an ethnography worthy of note. It is entitled *Bosquejo etnográfico de Sara* (An Ethnographic Sketch of Sara). In 1937, after residing off and on for an entire year in different towns of Iparralde (Doniztiri (Saint-Esteben in French), Iholdi, Uharte-Hiri, Liginaga, etc.) where he was conducting ethnographic projects, Barandiarán settled in Biarritz. He resided with his niece Pilar, who had moved there from Ataun. (With exquisite diligence she subsequently tended to the three homes that her uncle would live in until his death.) Three years later, toward the end of 1940 and five months after the Germans invaded this part of Labourde, Barandiarán moved to Sara, where he established his residence definitively for the next thirteen years.

In Sara, as he says at the beginning of his study, he conducted "different investigations designed to learn the traditional ways of life of the inhabitants of Xareta, especially the town of Sara."[30] Xareta (a wooded region) is a name that is given to the region around Sara in a legend. Today, the region is made up of the towns of Ainhoa, Sara, Urdax, and Zugarramurdi, the first two administered by the French state and the other two by the Spanish, but it has no name.

The configuration of this region or valley, two of its towns belonging to the Spanish state despite its location at the western end of the Pyrenees range, is curious. This reality of a small valley of four towns, two belonging to France and the other two to Spain, has been very convenient for the inhabitants, who for many years dedicated themselves to smuggling. The anecdotes that Barandiarán told about it are innumerable.

One of them refers to a homeowner from Sara who night after night took calves from Sara to Zugarramurdi. He would gather together the calves from other herders in Iparralde on a meadow in Sara at midnight before driving them across the border. One night, a man bringing him the calves arrived late, or just as dawn was beginning to break, and they were surprised by French gendarmes. The smuggler from Sara began to lament and cry out that those calves had wandered over from Spain and were eating his grass, and he tried to shoo them toward the Spanish side of the border. The gendarmes pitched in. So that morning the contraband crossed with the help of the police.

One day, many years later, when I was driving through that region in my car, a man signaled for me to stop. He asked me if I would take him to Zugarramurdi. He got in and I steered the conversation to the topic of smuggling. He himself had been a smuggler years ago. When I asked him how he did the smuggling, he answered, "*Gauez eta eskuaraz*"—"At night and in Basque."

Returning to the work we are discussing, this excellent and exemplary monograph, which Barandiarán modestly entitled *Bosquejo etnográfico de Sara*, was published in installments in the *Anuario de Eusko-folklore* between the years 1957 and 1972 (volumes 17–24). Previously, in 1947, Barandiarán had published "Le calendrier traditionnel de

Sare" in that journal and later, in 1981, the songs of love "Amodiozko kantak," also in the *Anuario de Eusko-folklore*, vol. 30.

His ethnography of Sara starts out with a description of the natural landscape: the soil, the hills, the caverns (with sketches), the climate, the vegetation, and the fauna. It continues with an exhaustive toponymy, including the names of houses, huts, orchards, properties, meadows, pastures, woodlands, chestnut groves, streams, etc. He then discusses the human landscape and economy, subdivided into agriculture, forestry, cattle herding, communication, and transportation.

Barandiarán also dedicates a long chapter to the different professions and industries, such as the production of lime to fertilize the planted fields, the coal mines, shops for washing and weaving wool. He dedicates a very important section to hunting and relates it to the prehistoric world. This chapter ends with the trades of blacksmith, carpenter, quarry worker, mason, mechanic, tinsmith, painter, cobbler, ox-driver, and others less common.

The following chapter he dedicates to human establishments and the *etxe*, or rural household. This is followed by a chapter on work, dealing with farm equipment, tools for cutting wood, for making beverages, for the textile industry, for dairy farming, for measuring, instruments for transportation and for hunting.

It is impossible to include the entire "sketch" in the present work. I have opted for three chapters that are particularly representative of Barandiarán's ethnographic work:)

1. "Human Establishments and the Rural House." *Anuario de Eusko-folklore* 20 (1963–64): 85–109.

2. "The Household." *Anuario de Eusko-folklore* 23 (1969–70): 77–128.

3. "Hunting." *Anuario de Eusko-folklore* 18 (1961): 157–71.

1. *Human establishments.* The house or *etxe* has been a favorite topic of Barandiarán in his investigations, as we have indicated in our discussion of *Basque Mythology* in which he dedicates a whole chapter to it. In his ethnography of Sara, he begins by speaking of the structure of the *etxe*, both exterior and interior, with its outbuildings, house types, and floor plans. He gives the names of all the houses in Sara (which we omit in this selection to save space and because they are not that relevant in a work such as this), and the spiritual safeguards against threats, both natural—inclement weather or snakes and toads—and preternatural, especially against evil spirits. At times he speaks of natural forces such as wind or lightning, but these are considered to be preternatural.

Once Barandiarán has described the main house in all of its aspects, along with the outbuildings (granaries, fertilizer sheds, pigsties, folds, chicken coops, lime bins, sheds, benches, and the family tomb in the church or cemetery), he then speaks of the temporary shelters which the household may have in the mountains, totally or partially dedicated to the herding of sheep (both for the shepherd himself, who sleeps there at night, and for the flock). Finally, he describes in detail the furnishings and equipment in a rural house (also excluded from this selection).

2. *The Household.* In this chapter he covers blood relationships, clothing, food, and rites of passage—birth and baptism, first communion, youth, courtship, marriage, and death. He concludes with the neighborhood, describing the relationships among households within it.

3. *Hunting.* The hunt constitutes an activity of great interest in Sara, as well as in the nearby Navarrese municipality of Etxalar. It is a professional activity handed down from some remote period and practiced with the same methods they might have used in the very distant past. Barandiarán collected its artifacts with great care. He says of it that, "It is one of the testimonials of the solidarity between past and present."[31]

He begins by listing the quarry, animals to be eaten (different species of birds, hare, rabbit, and wild boar) as well as those to be defended against (badger, fox, marmot, wildcat, and weasel), and then discusses the professional hunting that we mentioned above: dove hunting.

This form of dove hunting involves controlling the flight of the birds toward a net by stationing people along the flanks of their passage through the mountains during their annual fall migration from the more northern zones of Europe to lands further south in the Iberian Peninsula. The doves are captured alive and sometimes entire flocks are netted. Later, they are sold. Twelve houses in Sara form a society with the right, since time immemorial, to conduct this hunt. The society pays the municipality for the exclusive monopoly.

The dove hunt is famous throughout the Basque Country, notoriety that justifies selection for this book of the detailed description of it which Barandiarán provides in his study of Sara.

Epilogue

To conclude the presentation of these works by Barandiarán, I want to emphasize another of his contributions. He was a teacher who knew how to form teams around him, both in the field of prehistory and in that of ethnography. In the former, in Barandiarán's very first year, the Aranzadi-Barandiarán-Eguren team (who were referred to as *"los tres tristes trogloditas*" (the three sad troglodytes)) was constituted. Barandiarán agreed that they were indeed "troglodytes," since they went from cave to cave, but that there was nothing "sad" about them. This team worked together for twenty years, until broken up by the war that brought so many ills to the Basque Country.

After the end of his exile, Barandiarán did not lock himself up in Ataun. He spent long periods of time in Donostia-San Sebastián and Bilbao organizing and categorizing the materials from the excavations done in Gipuzkoa and Bizkaia during the years before the war. As I said earlier, I was among the several young men finishing university studies during those years who came under his influence. Under his guidance and encouragement we began to work in the caves, since the excavations had suddenly started up again, especially in the three provinces of Gipuzkoa, Bizkaia, and Araba.

We have already indicated that this beginning had an exponential influence, since those young students of his went on to occupy university professorships and to educate the next generation. If, at that time, three or four excavations were begun each year in the Basque Country, without any possibility of working on them simultaneously given that Barandiarán was the only principal investigator, today far more are being conducted, and simultaneously. There is greater specialization among the investigators, consequently current investigations are conducted in interdisciplinary fashion and are producing results that are more sophisticated and precise than those of that earlier period.

The same must be said in the field of ethnography. The previously mentioned Etniker groups that developed under Barandiarán's direction are now efficiently developing an ethnographic atlas of the Basque Country, which was one of the dreams of the master. On the other hand, a wealth of research material awaits the attention of today's anthropologists in the Hojas de Eusko-folklore, as we noted in our discussion of them.

On balance, then, Barandiarán was not only a founding figure within Basque anthropology; writ large his legacy lives on in both manifest and latent forms.

Notes

1. J. M. de Barandiarán, "Nacimiento y expansión de los fenómenos sociales," *Anuario de Eusko-folklore* 4 (1924): 194.

2. José Miguel de Barandiarán, personal conversation with author.

3. L. Barandiarán, *Barandiarán, patriarca de la cultura vasca*, 34–35.

4. J. M. de Barandiarán, *Diario personal (1917–1936)*. Vol. 2, 513.

5. Ibid., 531.

6. Name used to designate some extraordinary creatures from Basque mythology from before the introduction of Christianity.

7. J. M. de Barandiarán, "Prehistoria vasca. Monumentos del Aralar guipuzcoano," in *Euskalerriaren alde* 6 (1916): 561–65.

8. Telesforo de Aranzadi (1860–1945) was a native of Bergara, a small town located in the same province of Gipuzkoa. When he met Barandiarán, he was a professor of anthropology at the University of Barcelona. Barandiarán always considered him his mentor. L. Barandiarán, *Cartas a José Miguel de Barandiarán (primera etapa, 1915–1936)*, 7.

9. Enrique de Eguren (1888–1944) was a native of Vitoria and professor of geology at the University of Oviedo.

10. J. M. de Barandiarán, "Discurso leído en la solemne apertura del curso de 1917 a 1918 en el Seminario Conciliar de Vitoria."

11. L. Barandiarán, *Cartas a José Miguel de Barandiarán*, 101.

12. J. Caro Baroja, *Los Baroja*, 236–37.

13. The Port of Mutriku, a small town on the eastern coast of Gipuzkoa.

14. Mountain people, of whom there have always been many in the Basque Country.

15. J. M. de Barandiarán, *Diario personal (1917–1936)*, Vol. 2, 731–32.

16. In *Extractos de la Asociación Española*, 39–73.

17. J. M. de Barandiarán, "La religion des anciens Basques," 156–68.

18. Manuel de Ynchausti was a Basque lawyer and entrepreneur who patronized many Basque cultural activities. He was born in the Philippines and held U.S. citizenship. He purchased a house called Intxausti Baita in Ustaritze (Lapurdi/Labourd).

19. A town on the French-Spanish border (known as Sare in French).

20. "Catalogue des Stations préhistoriques des Pyrénées basques," *Ikuska* 1 (1946): 24–40.

21. Juan María Apellániz was a professor at the University of Deusto; Ignacio Barandiarán is still a professor at the University of the Basque Country.

22. *Eusko-folklore. Materiales y cuestionarios* (Vitoria), nos. 1–12 (1921): 1.

23. J. Caro Baroja, "D. José Miguel de Barandiarán. Antropólogo," in *José Miguel Barandiarán-eri omenaldia*, 22.

24. J. M. de Barandiarán, *Mitología vasca*, 106–7.

25. André Malraux, *Culture*, May 1960.

26. Personal conversation with author.

27. J. Caro Baroja, "Prologo," *Mitología vasca*, by J. M. de Barandiarán, 6, 9–10.

28. J. M. de Barandiarán, "Antropología de la población vasca," *Ikuska* 1 (1947): 210.

29. J. M. de Barandiarán, *El hombre prehistórico en el País Vasco*, 158.

30. J. M. de Barandiarán. *Bosquejo etnográfico de Sara*, in *Anuario de Eusko-folklore*, 17 (1957–1960): 148.

31. J. M. de Barandiarán, *El hombre prehistórico en el País Vasco*, 55.

Bibliography

Altuna, Jesús. *Fauna de mamíferos de los yacimientos prehistóricos de Guipúzcoa. Con catálogo de los mamíferos cuaternarios del Cantábrico y del Pirineo Occidental.* (Doctoral Thesis). *Munibe* (San Sebastián) 24, nos. 1–4 (1972).

Apellániz, Juan María. *Corpus de materiales de las culturas prehistóricas con cerámica de la población de cavernas del País Vasco meridional. Munibe,* 1973, suppl. 1.

———. *El grupo de Los Husos durante la prehistoria con cerámica en el País Vasco.* Estudios de Arqueología Alavesa 7. Vitoria: Diputación Foral de Alava, Consejo de Cultura, 1974.

Aranzadi, Telesforo de and José Miguel de Barandiarán. "Exploración de la cueva de Urtiaga (Itziar, Gipúzkoa) [part 2]. Con un estudio de los cráneos prehistóricos de Vasconia." *Eusko-jakintza* (Bayonne) 2 (1948): 307–30.

Barandiarán, José Miguel de. "Antropología de la población vasca." *Ikuska* 1 (1947): 193–210.

———. *Bosquejo etnográfico de Sara.* In *Anuario de Eusko-folklore* 17–24 (1957–1972).

———. "Catalogue des stations préhistoriques des Pyrénées Basques." *Ikuska* 1 (1946): 24–40.

———. "Contribución al estudio paletnográfico del Pueblo Vasco. El magismo." *Extractos de la Asociación Española para el Progreso de las Ciencias. Congreso de Bilbao,* 1919. 6 (1ª parte), 39–73. Bilbao, 1920.

———. *Diario personal (1917–1936). Desde los primeros trabajos científicos hasta el exilio.* 2 vols. Colección Sara 6. Astigarraga (Gipuzkoa): Fundación Barandiarán, 2005.

———. *Diccionario de mitología vasca.* Donostia-San Sebastián: Editorial Txertoa, [1984].

———. *Diccionario ilustrado de mitología vasca.* In *Obras completas de José Miguel de Barandiarán,* Volume 1, 9–258. Bilbao: La Gran Enciclopedia Vasca, 1972.

————. "Discurso leído en la solemne apertura del curso de 1917 a 1918 en el Seminario Conciliar de Vitoria." Vitoria: Editorial Montepío Diocesano, 1917.

————. *Euskal herriko mitoak / Mitos del pueblo vasco.* [San Sebastián]: Caja de Gipúzcoa, 1988.

————. *Eusko-folklore. Materiales y cuestionarios.* Nos. 1–12, Vitoria: Seminario Conciliar de Vitoria, 1921.

————. "Exploración de la cueva de Urtiaga," *Gernika, Eusko-jakintza* (Bayonne) 1 (1947): 13–28, 265–71, 437–56, 659–96.

————. *La Guerra Civil en Euzkadi. 136 testimonios inéditos recogidos por José Miguel de Barandiarán.* Presentation by José María Gamboa and Jean-Claude Larronde. Milafranga: Editorial Bidasoa, 2005.

————. *El hombre prehistórico en el País Vasco.* Buenos Aires: Ekin, 1953.

————. *El hombre primitivo en el País Vasco.* Colección Zabalkundea 3. Donostia-San Sebastián: Beñat Idaztiak, 1934.

————. *Lehen euskal gizona.* San Sebastián: Editorial Lur, 1972.

————. "Leyendas de Goierri. Cómo se propagó en nuestro país el cultivo del trigo." *Euskalerriaren alde* 8, no. 169 (1918): 10–11.

————. *Mitología vasca.* Colección Biblioteca Vasca 5. Madrid: Editorial Minotauro, 1960.

————. "Nacimiento y expansión de los fenómenos sociales." *Anuario de Eusko-folklore* 4 (1924): 153–229.

————. "Prehistoria vasca. Monumentos del Aralar guipuzcoano." *Euskalerriaren alde* 6 (1916): 561–65.

————. "La religion des anciens Basques." In *Compte-rendu analytique de la IIIe session de la Semaine d'Ethnologie Religieuse* [held in Tilburg (Netherlands)], 156–68. Enghien, 1923.

Barandiarán, Luis. *Cartas a José Miguel de Barandiarán (primera etapa, 1915–1936).* Donostia-San Sebastián: Caja de Ahorros Municipal de San Sebastián, 1989.

————. *Barandiarán, patriarca de la cultura vasca.* Madrid: Editorial Sociedad de Educación Atenas, 1992.

Barandiarán Maeztu, Ignacio. *El Paleomesolítico del Pirineo Occidental. Bases para una sistematización tipológica del instrumental óseo paleolítico.* Monografías Arqueológicas 3. Zaragoza: Seminario de Prehistoria y Protohistoria, Facultad de Filosofía y Letras, Universidad de Zaragoza, 1967.

Barbier, Jean. *Légendes du Pays Basque.* Paris, 1931.

Caro Baroja, Julio. *Los Baroja*. Madrid: Taurus, 1972.

———. "D. José Miguel de Barandiarán. Antropólogo." In *José Miguel Barandiarán-eri omenaldia*, 19–25. Oñati: Sociedad de Estudios Vascos, 1979.

———. "Prologo." In *Mitología vasca*, by José Miguel de Barandiarán, 5–11. San Sebastián: Txertoa, 1979.

Gorrochategui, Joaquín. "Planteamientos de la lingüística histórica en la datación del euskara." *XV Congreso de Estudios Vascos* 1, 103–14. San Sebastián: Sociedad de Estudios Vascos, 2001.

Basque Mythology

by José Miguel de Barandiarán

To Don Telesforo de Aranzadi, my former professor
and companion during twenty years of
investigations in the Basque Country.
Happy New Year and until I hear from you.

TO THE READER

In this little book we have collected some beliefs which, conforming to magical and animistic concepts, manifest themselves in the lives of the Basque people. We cannot be sure if in previous times they had the same theoretical basis that they have today, since we frequently observe that words, expressions, rituals, and objects lose their original meaning and take on new significance in the service of other ideas and other designs.

We have taken them just as they came to us and have arranged them in groups according to the objects and their thematic affinities, and we have described them succinctly with the greatest fidelity possible.

We offer, then, a handful of current phenomena that may give the reader an image, albeit partial, of one of the least known aspects of the Basque tradition.

It will be easy to discover in this sketch of our mythology certain gaps due to the author's limitations and the lack of adequate research. Unfortunately, such research will come too late for many elements of our traditional life which have already been lost or distorted.

In effect, no matter how strong our attachment to tradition, it is not sufficiently powerful to prevent the propagation of many ideas, beliefs, and customs, some of which are accepted without any resistance at all and others are partially accepted or result in compromise and distortion.

We have been witness to the reactions provoked in rural areas by recent attempts to reach the moon through man-made machines. The news of the successes of would-be moon travelers has spread to every small town. Alongside those who accept the achievement as something they always believed possible, there are others who believe that man will not be able to remain on the lunar surface without the help of some appropriate supporting structure; otherwise, he will inevitably fall to earth from sheer weight. Only insects—a man from Albistur told me—will be able to walk up there the way they do on the ceiling of a room. Others, finally, doubt than man can ever reach our satellite, because they believe the moon is a divine being that will not permit any mortal to approach it.

Change, then, is fast and widespread. New ways of living, new ideas and new ideals are replacing tradition. A civilization based on the preponderance of technology and machinery, with its own elements and its own problems and solutions, is developing here as elsewhere in the world. For this reason it is urgent that we research all aspects of traditional life and record the data that manifest and describe them. This task will provide data that will be directly useful to science. This will lead to the determination of regional variances of the phenomena, the demarcation of their respective areas and, finally, the indication of the strata or phases of their historical development.

Reserving for later publications what science may eventually say, given the current state of our research we focus here only on the first task, that is, the presentation of a portion of the material we have collected. If in doing this we succeed in awakening new interest and intensifying the study into our ethnography, we will have satisfied one of our goals.

Sara (Lower Pyrenees), December 12, 1959

INTRODUCTION

Every myth seeks to explain one or several realities. It involves, naturally, a representation or mental equivalent of phenomena and objects in the same way—though not to the same degree—that the concepts and definitions of contemporary science do.

The majority of myths represent objects and aspects of nature, such as *eguzkiamandre* (sun), *odei* (thunder, storm cloud) and *sugaar* (lightning). There are others that refer to human endeavors (cultural mythology), such as the growing of wheat, the origin of certain tools, and the operations of forges (ironworks). Finally, some myths respond to purely subjective creations, such as *inguma*, *gerixeti* (ghosts of ancestors, soul), etc. . . . In all of them, the coefficient or element that imbues them with life and significance is tradition, or interpretations consecrated by tradition.

In our case, this coefficient is characterized by an undercurrent of animism in which phenomena and objects are explained through the intervention of spirits and divinities. This varies from one community to another and from one social class to another. For this reason it may be useful for us to situate the myth within the context of our culture, indicating the zones it occupies or the regions where it prevails.

Cultural Gradation

We should point out, first of all, that two categories of elements make up this complex network of ideas and knowledge constituting "our world of representations": elements from the external world proceeding from the natural landscape and from human groups foreign to ours, and internal elements which are our own mental traditions. The former provide material and possibilities for action; the latter orient and condition our activity. In a house, on a funeral stele, or in a rural hollow it is easy to identify traces of our forests and cliffs, but also traces of our ancient traditions.

It is natural, therefore, for the same phenomenon to be seen or felt and represented in a different way by different human groups and even by different individuals from the same group. The world of representations of an individual is always something personal, which does not completely coincide with that of others. So it is not only within the totality of human groups that different ethnicities can be identified, but cultural gradations exist within a single group, so that individuals occupy different levels of an environment. Narrowing our focus to our Basque people, we can say that in some, mechanistic ideas predominate, in others providential ideas, while many others are under the sway of magical and animistic concepts that lend themselves to the perpetuation of numerous forms of ancient cultures and mythologies.

Even within a single individual, alongside a system or world of representations that generally occupy his center of vision, there exist other worlds situated in peripheral zones, like spirits lurking and waiting for the chance to come into play and usurp a fellow spirit whenever that one seems inefficient and inadequate.

When the vicissitudes of life lead us into a situation that conflicts with our customary way of thinking, without fail there appears one of these marginalized systems into which that situation fits or within which it may be easily and coherently justified.

Such systems are not all of equal value, of course. Magic, myths, science, and the Christian complex are not equivalents, objectively speaking. But in all of them generally we see the pulse of inspiration and a tendency toward an ideal that surpasses us and whose definitive realization we situate in the future. Thus, the future—let us say in passing—serves us as a stimulus for human progress, that is, as a factor of our conduct and, therefore, of our present moment.

Christianity and Paganism

Like all ethnic groups, the Basque people forged a culture, a way of life that reflects the attitude of man when confronted with the fundamental problems of his existence.

One of the aspects that must be considered in that attitude is religion. Above all, the Christian ideal has played a predominant role for many centuries. But around it and sometimes filtered through it, or apparently developing on the margins of every religion, other concepts exist—magic, mythology, mechanistic notions—horizons of paganism ready to assume equal influence when circumstances favor their ascendance.

Myth, like all forms of religion, surfaces as the expression and vehicle of an ideal, born into a magical or animist environment despite the materialistic character of the entity that frequently serves as its object. The representation of the serpent *heren* (*herensuge* or *lerensuge*) consists of that of the spirit or divinity *heren* as an ideal of power.

Universally accepted as an explanation and expression of an idea, in earlier times myth has served as inspiration for the most educated men and the most respectable institutions.

Mythical beings act through enchantment and magic. Only through magical procedures can we approach them or defend ourselves from them. *Maindi* extracts from a hazelnut (*urr*) a garment made with golden thread (*urre*). We defend ourselves from *odei*, "storm spirit," through gestures and the presentation of *uztaibedar*, "a celestial or rainbow herb"; from the projectile of *urtzi* or *mari*, "thunderbolt," by holding up an axe or a sharp thorn.

Animism in particular is the propitious environment for myth. Animism posits a spirit or divinity in the face of every function, every phenomenon, and behind every mystery: everything is pervaded by divinity, things are divine, sacred, with no need for action by secondary causes.

But our idea of the gods is generally imprecise, lacking a clear profile. Each of us suffuses it with content appropriate to our culture and our level of education. Often in various representations of the same divinity there is scarcely any common element except the name, which is, however, sufficient for the formalism that satisfies the needs of the ingenuous man.

The animist concept of the world was common among the ancients: everything was sacred. Later, the profane enters the scene when natural phenomena begin to be given a new explanation, without direct recourse to the gods. In this way a duality of beings and things is established: some belong to the world of the spirits (*aideko*); others, to nature (*berezko*)—two worlds into which we can only enter and act by using their respective laws and techniques.

The influence of the profane, i.e., laicization, began to spread as man began to rationalize, dominate, and transform the world.

Once men succeed in explaining many of the phenomena of nature that were formerly regarded as mysteries or functions of the gods, they begin to consider the latter as non-existent or purely imaginary entities: mythical beings in the sense of being fictitious. So the sacred retreated as science advanced, and the science/religion dualism was established as a confrontation of incompatible opposites. In effect, the secular attitude seemed justified if the divinities were merely a complement of our former insufficiency, something unrealizable; the recognition of the divine proceeds fundamentally from another factor, to something implicit in the question, "What am I?" If the reference to God is not based on our failure, but on the incessant activity of the world and on the very action which, under its influence, we continue to perform, then we would have to conclude that the sacred had not actually retreated, but that we had left it out of our calculations, offering premature solutions to the problem before posing it in all its dimensions.

The change introduced by the appearance and progressive expansion of the profane in the animist world was not, however, as profound as might have been thought. The notions of science that kept evolving thanks to observation, intuition, and experimentation could only be represented in scientific language (not in everyday, common language) through the mediation of mathematical characters invented wholly by man. Lucretius' maxim, *utilitas expressit nomina rerum* (the names of things express their utility) could be applied to science as well as mythology, and the new spirits, projections of the human mind no less than the old ones, obeyed laws similar to the laws of the old spirits: man was present in both.

Levels of Knowledge

In seeking to describe the religion and mythology of a people, it is important to ascertain, to the extent possible, the degree of adhesion to those beliefs and myths in the consciousness of the members of the group. In this respect, considering the mental attitude of the Basque toward myths, it is important to recognize the popular mode of expressing them and the level of knowledge manifested in that mode.

According to a popular saying, the real is comprised of not only everything perceived by the senses and concluded and affirmed by reason, but also everything that has a name. People say, *"Izena duen guztia omen da,"* which means that if there is a name, there must be a thing. There is this difference, however: what you perceive yourself is certain, it is something personally known and, therefore, it can be expressed categorically, as in these phrases: *au ala da,* "this is so," and *au esan dute,* "this is what they say"; what is known through someone else's testimony, or through references, is not affirmed categorically and without reservation, and the sentences expressing it are prefaced by *omen* or *ei* (depending on the region), which refers them to their sources, as in the following examples: *au ala omen de,* "they say that this is so," and *au esan omen dute,* "we are told that they say this," and so on . . . It is important to keep in mind this difference in category of meaning so we can better appreciate the value of the affirmations of Basque narratives, mythical or not. Myths, of course, belong to the second category today, even in the appreciation of the most innocent.

Sources of Our Investigation

From what has been said, we can conclude that in order to completely understand Basque mythology we will need to be familiar with the magical and animistic concepts that constitute its base, its preamble and its context.

There are very few documents or references from ancient authors to take us back to the times when paganism was still a living religion among Pyrenean populations. There are hardly any reliable documents dealing with animism and the practice of magic prior to Christianity. Allusions to the religion of the Basques by Strabo, Lampridius, and the poet Prudentius contribute little to our investigation. More helpful are inscriptions from the Roman period and even prehistoric monuments and ruins. Many of the archeological materials are connected with religious beliefs and cults. Arranged chronologically, they can give us an idea of some of the more salient features of the religious practices or the religions practiced in the Basque Country before the introduction of Christianity. That is the path I followed in an article entitled "Huellas de artes y religiones antiguas del Pirineo vasco" (Traces of Ancient Arts and Religions of the Basque Pyrenees) (in *Homenaje al M. I. Sr. Dr. D. Eduardo de Escárzaga*. Vitoria, 1935). In the present work, we will give preference to ethnographic data, focusing especially on the popular traditions of the Basque people that can provide us with materials for the study of magic and the attempt to reconstruct present-day mythology which, if used wisely, can clarify many problems related to the religion of the ancient people of the Pyrenees.

This is not the first time this subject has engaged my interest. In 1919, I presented to the Congress of the Asociación Española para el Progreso de las Ciencias (Spanish Association for Scientific Advancement) held in Bilbao, a work entitled "Contribución al estudio paletnográfico del pueblo vasco. El magismo" (Contribution to the Paleoethnographic Study of the Basque People. Magic), which was later published in the Proceedings of that association. Two years later the same work, somewhat expanded, was published in the journal *Euskalerriaren alde* (San Sebastián, 1921).

I investigated mythological topics even more thoroughly in a work published in the book *Homenaje a Fritz Krüger* (Mendoza, 1952), the text of which has served me greatly in composing the present essay.

Here is a list of publications related to our topic:

Barandiarán, José Miguel de: "Contribución al estudio paletnográfico del pueblo vasco. El Magismo," in *Actos del Congreso de la Aso-*

ciación Española para el Progreso de las Ciencias. Congreso de Bilbao, 1919. Bilbao, 1920.

———. *Fragmentos folklóricos. Paletnografía vasca,* in *Euskalerriaren alde* (San Sebastián) 10 (1921): 182–90, 224–32, 396–402, 431–43, 452–70. (Also published as a booklet by San Sebastián: Imprenta de Martín, Mena y Ca., 1921.)

———. *Eusko-mitología* (Meetings of Euskaltzaindia during Basque Culture Week in Durango). Bilbao, 1922.

———. "La religion des anciens Basques." In *Compte-rendu analytique de la III session de la Semaine d'Ethnologie Religieuse,* 156–68. [Held in Tilburg (Netherlands), 1922]. Enghien, 1923.

———. "Mari, o el genio de las montañas." In *Homenaje a don Carmelo de Echegaray,* 245–68. San Sebastián: Diputación de Guipúzcoa, 1928.

———. "Huellas de artes y religiones antiguas del pueblo vasco." In *Homenage a D. Eduardo de Escárzaga,* 128–39. Vitoria, 1935.

———. "Sur les anciennes religions des Basques." In Congreso Internacional de Ciencias Antropológicas y Etnológicas, Copenhagen, 1938. *Compte-rendu de la deuxième session,* 368. Copenhagen, 1939.

———. "Die prähistorischen Höhlen in der baskischen Mythologie." In *Paideuma.* Leipzig, 1941. (Later published in Spanish as "Las cavernas prehistóricas en la mitología vasca," in *Cuadernos de historia primitiva* (Madrid), Year 1, no. 2 (1946): 71–89.

———. "Les recherches anthropologiques au Pays Basque," address presented at the Royal Anthropological Institute of London, April 11, 1946. (Later published in *Obras completas de José Miguel de Barandiarán,* Volume 6, 111–19. Bilbao: La Gran Enciclopedia Vasca, 1974.

———. "Croyances populaires basques," address presented at the Centre International de Synthèse, in Paris, July 13, 1947.

———. "Etat actuel des études ethnographiques basques." Address given at the session of the Commission Internationale des Arts et Traditions Populaires. Paris, October 2, 1947.

———. "Le Calendrier traditionnel de Sare." In *Ikuska,* 1947, nos. 2 and 3, pp. 47–57, 77–78.

———. "Matériaux pour une étude du peuple basque: à Uhart-Mixe." In *Ikuska* 1 (1947): 107–25, 167–75 and 2 (1948): 135–51.

———. "Les symboles magiques au Pays Basque." Address presented in the Congrès International d'Archéocivilisation. Paris, July 2, 1948.

————. "Ele-zaar." Various articles published under this heading in the journal *Eusko-jakintza* (Bayonne) in 1 (1947): 487–90; 2 (1948): 345–46, 385–88, 593–94; 3 (1949): 299–300, 393–98; and 4 (1950): 259–78.

————. "De la vida tradicional vasca. Valores de algunos símbolos." In *Homenaje a D. Luis de Hoyos Sainz,* Vol. 2, 36–44. Madrid, 1950.

————. "Materiales para un estudio del pueblo vasco: in Liginaga (Laguinge)." In *Ikuska* 1947, 1948, 1949, and 1950.

————. "Contribución à l'étude de la préhistoire et de l'histoire ancienne des populations pyrénéennes. Etat actuel de cette étude en ce qui concerne le peuple basque." Address read at the IXe Congrès International des Sciences Historiques. Paris, August 18, 1950.

————. "Contribución al estudio de la mitología vasca." In *Homenaje a Fritz Krüger,* Vol. 1, 101–36. Mendoza: Universidad Nacional de Cuyo, 1952.

————. "Cuevas y simas en las creencias y mitos del pueblo vasco." In *Homenaje a D. Joaquín Mendizábal,* 71–75. San Sebastián: Museo de Telmo, 1956.

————. *Eusko-folklore.* Articles on Basque mythology published 1921–1959. Vitoria, Bayonne, Sara, San Sebastián, 1921–1959.

————. "Persistances culturelles rurales." In *Visages de l'homme. Cahiers d'histoire et de folklore.* Dol-en-Bretagne, 1959.

Various Authors: *Anuario de Eusko-folklore* (16 volumes published since 1921).

Azkue, Resurrección María de. *Euskalerriaren yakintza.* Madrid: Espasa-Calpe, 1935–1945.

Webster, Wentworth. *Basque Legends.* London, 1879.

Cerquand, M. "Légendes et récíts populaires du Pays Basque." In *Bulletin de la Société des Sciences, Lettres et Arts de Pau,* 1874–1875.

Vinson, Julien. *Le Folklore du Pays Basque.* Paris: Maisonneuve, 1883.

Barbier, Jean. *Légendes du Pays Basque, d'après la tradition.* Paris: Delgrave, 1931.

Caro Baroja, Julio. *Algunos mitos españoles y otros ensayos.* Madrid: Editora Nacional, 1944.

————. "Sobre la religión antigua y el calendario del pueblo vasco." In *Trabajos del Instituto Bernardino de Sahagún,* Volume 6. Madrid, 1948.

Barriola, Ignacio María. *La medicina popular en el país vasco.* San Sebastián: Biblioteca Vascongada de los Amigos del País, 1952.

MAGIC

The world of the sorcerers, like any other, consists of things and their representations. But, according to them, the two are bound together by a force called *adur*, so that whatever action we take in connection with the latter, heeding certain conditions, must inevitably affect the former. It could be said, then, that there exists a unique sympathy between the object and its image or representation.

The following cases will give an idea of the different forms in which this singular concept is manifested among the Basques.

Light as Symbol or Representation

For the sorcerer, the wax candle represents the body; the light is an image of the spirit that gives it life.

Consulted by a resident of Ataun who wished to know who had stolen his cow, an *azti*, seer, from Tolosa advised him to light a wax candle, which would represent the thief. As the candle gradually burned down, the thief would waste away. In this way, he would be exposed.[1]

Some peasants from Aldaba twisted a candle and lighted it, hoping that this would twist the body and snuff out the life of an individual they wished to harm or upon whom they wished to avenge themselves for an insult.[2]

A farmer from Elduayen (Elduain), wishing to punish some young men who stole a hoe from him and hung it from a cherry tree on Ainbialde mountain, took a candle to the church intending to burn it. The village priest discouraged him from carrying out his plan.[3]

When a person suffers a long illness, in Berástegi (Berastegi) you will hear them say: "*Orri bate batek argizarie piztu zook*" (Someone lit a candle against him).[4]

In Leiza (Leitza) when it was time to pick apples, it was the custom for the owner of the apple orchard to ask his neighbors for help. This usually happened in the afternoon, and the workers were treated to a snack right there in the orchard. If the owner was rich, he would have wine served on a silver tray called a *barkillo*. One day, the family from the Maxurrenea or Marikurrenea house went with their neighbors to work in the orchard they owned in the place called Inguruarte. During the snack one of the neighbor women served wine to the workers on a *barkillo*. Afterwards, she placed the tray on the edge of a hollow spot high up on the trunk of an old apple tree. But when she gathered up the silverware and the tablecloths she forgot the *barkillo*. The Maxurrenea family noticed that it was missing and asked where it was, to no avail, because the neighbor who had gathered up the valuable tray couldn't remember where she had left it. The owners, suspecting that the woman had stolen their *barkillo*, twisted a candle and burned it before a saint, expecting that the supposed perpetrator of the theft would thereby be punished. But the neighbor lady suffered no mishap at all. Instead, in the Maxurrenea orchard an apple tree withered and died. It was cut down and, to everyone's surprise, the *barkillo* was found in the hollow in the trunk of the tree. The magical force, they said, had acted on the apple tree that concealed the *barkillo* and made it wither.[5]

In order to pay some debts he had incurred, a man from Leiza (Leitza) sold a pig without telling his wife. She believed that the animal had been stolen by one of her brothers-in-law, and to punish such an outrage, she twisted a candle and burned it. Shortly thereafter her husband died of a mysterious disease, which was attributed to the magical effect (*adur* in Basque) that detected the true culprit.[6]

In Pasajes de San Juan (Pasai Donibane), the person who seeks to discover who has done him harm kneels before a lighted candle in order to assure the success of his investigation.[7]

In Sara, a girl who was having an affair with a young man from her neighborhood threatened to light a candle (*xirio*) against him if he didn't keep his promise to marry her.

In Oyarzun (Oiartzun) this procedure is also known. The sorcerer offers a candle to a saint and then lights it. According to my informant,[8] an individual from Iturralde died when he was a victim of this magical operation carried out by his former girlfriend.

In Elduayen (Elduain) and in Ataun, it is believed that this magical spell turns against its author if that person commits the same act for which she is trying to punish someone else.[9]

The Coin as Image

The coin generally bears an effigy which, in popular belief, can represent any person. It can be used, therefore, as an object of magical spells.

On a certain occasion, a resident of Ataun named José Antonio, from the Semao farm, discovered that some items of his clothing were missing. Wishing to find out who the thief was so he could punish him, he bent a five-cent coin and threw it into the Calvario hermitage located in that town, hoping that the thief would become stooped the way the coin was bent.[10]

In Aya (Aia) this form of magic is also practiced.[11]

According to my informant from Villafranca, this practice is also known in that town and considered a serious curse.[12]

In Beasain this curse consists of throwing a bent coin into the fireplace and simultaneously lighting a candle to St. Anthony. On one farm a herd of pigs died. The deed was attributed to a woman from the same town who habitually practiced that form of magic.[13]

In 1921, in the church of Santo Cristo de Lezo, the discovery of several bent coins deposited in the alms dish was attributed to the same kind of magic.

In Abadiano (Abadiño), magical spells of this sort also occur at times, repeated on nine consecutive days.[14]

Grains of Salt, Wheat, and Ginger in the Practice of Magic

A remedy used in Tolosa, Urnieta, Andoain, and Oyarzun (Oiartzun) for curing certain swellings or lesions on the neck, called *gaingilla*, also belongs to the same circle of ideas as the preceding. It consists of the fasting patient holding a grain of salt in his hand and making the sign of the cross with it on the ailing body part while holding his breath and repeating this spell [the + signs indicate the sign of the cross]:

Gaingillak dira + Bederatzi; Bederatziak + Zortzi; Zortziak + Zazpi; Zazpiak + Sei; Seiak + Bost; Bostak + Lau; Lauak + Iru; Iruak + Bi; Biak + Bat; Gaingillak egin dezala zirt-zart (the lesions are + nine; the nine + eight; the eight + seven; the seven + six; the six + five; the five + four; the four + three; the three + two; the two + one: make the lesion *zirt-zart*, "destroy itself"). With these last words the grain of salt is thrown into the fire which immediately crackles, making the sound *zirt-zart*. The patient should take another grain and repeat the operation, always accompanied by the same formula, until nine grains of salt have been thrown into the fire. This must be done for nine consecutive days.[15]

In Bedia and in Cortézubi (Kortezubi), they use grains of salt to cure warts: you rub the latter with the former. The grains used in the rubbing will be thrown into the fire, the patient making every effort to stay far enough away to keep from hearing the inevitable crackling. In this way the warts will vanish in the same way their images, that is to say, the grains of salt, will have vanished.[16]

In Oyarzun (Oiartzun), the person who has warts and wants to heal them takes the same number of grains of salt. After the usual rubbing, he puts them in a handkerchief or a piece of clean cloth along with an *ardite* (today it would be a different coin) and lays them at a crossroads. The traveler who picks up that bundle and takes the coin that is inside it will acquire the warts whose images were in there with it.[17]

"If you have warts on your hands, as I did"—a farm worker from Cortézubi (Kortezubi) said to me once—"take as many grains of wheat as there are warts, one for each wart, and rub them with their corresponding grains. Afterwards you'll place the wheat you used beneath a stone, and as it gradually spoils, your warts will be healed without fail."[18]

In Garayo (Garaio, Araba) and in Garay (Garai, Bizkaia) they use the same procedure to cure warts.[19]

In Llodio (Laudio), the person with warts has to place underneath a stone the same number of juniper berries, making every effort not to look at them while putting them there. Then he should move away from the stone, saying: "I've got warts, I'm selling warts, I'm leaving them here and I'm running off." As the juniper berries gradually decompose, the warts are healed.[20]

In Cortézubi (Kortezubi), they also use raw apples to heal warts. They cut the apple in four sections and rub the warts with them. Then they place the sections at a crossroads. If a passerby picks them up and eats them, the warts will move to his hands.[21]

Herbs, Shrubs, and Trees in Magic

In Elduayen (Elduain), they use the sap from reeds to cure warts. Then, sprinkling a few grains of salt on the reeds, they place the mixture underneath a pile of garbage. When the reeds have rotted away and the salt has dissolved, the warts will disappear.[22]

In Bedia, they tie some reeds together in a bundle and place it underneath a rock on a well-traveled road. They believe that when the reeds rot, the warts will disappear.[23]

According to superstitions in Oyarzun (Oiartzun), a person who has warts and wishes to cure them should pull up several reeds from the ground with his hands crossed behind his back so he can't see the plants at the moment of uprooting them. Afterwards he must make the sign of the cross with the reeds over the warts, then place them in the chimney of the fireplace where they will dry quickly. As the herbs dry out, the warts will begin to shrink, then disappear.[24]

To cure the skin condition called herpes, the patient has to walk around a rose bush every day for nine consecutive days, while repeating this formula: *Arrosa arrosakin*—"*arrosa* with roses." This makes the herpes disappear, according to the inhabitants of Andoain.[25]

It used to be the custom to take children suffering from *arrosa* to visit the Virgin of the Rose who is worshipped in the parish church of Santa Eufemia de Bermeo. Many of the sick who attended that church would use a handkerchief to touch the part of the image that corresponded to the afflicted limb and then touch the limb itself with the same cloth. They would then place the cloth at the foot of the Virgin.[26]

In his work *Medicina popular en el país vasco*, Ignacio María Barriola writes: "In Goizueta we found this variation: at high noon, three persons will stand around a rose bush with the sick child and, beginning at the sound of the first bell marking twelve o'clock, they will pass the child from one to another while reciting: *Arrosa arrosakin, Arrosa arrosangana, Ama Santa Rosak eraman dezala beregana*, 'The rose with the roses, the rose to the roses, may the mother Santa Rosa take it away with her.' The event ends with the praying of the Creed, an indispensable act of faith in so many similar rituals in which, truly, faith is the principal ingredient."[27]

I have here a practice for curing hernias which can be observed in Amorebieta (Zornotza) on the night of the 23rd to the 24th of June in a grove situated beside the hermitage of San Juan. It must be performed by two brothers born one after the other from the same womb. They split the trunk of an oak tree with an ax and keep the two sides separated by means of a chock. The split serves as the image of the hernia. When the midnight bell begins to toll, one of the brothers takes the person with the hernia in his arms and passes him through the opening while saying "Eutsi, Anaiye" (Take him, brother), and so delivers him into the arms of the other. The latter receives him, saying, "Ekatzu, Anaiye" (Give him to me, brother), and immediately returns him to the first brother around the outside of the trunk to the right (not through the split) while saying "Eutsi, Anaiye." The first brother receives him, answering, "Ekatzu, Anaiye." This is performed three times as the bell tolls midnight. They leave the shirt of the sick man hanging on the oak tree and pull the two sides of the split trunk back together, tying them with ropes. If the oak tree survives, the sick man will be cured, but if it dies the hernia cannot be cured.[28]

In Sara, this ritual is performed by three individuals named Juan Bautista. Meeting at a bent oak tree, they transfer the hernia victim

from hand to hand around the tree three times during the first and second bells of the tolling of midnight on Saint John's Eve, saying: "To,
Batista (Take him, Baptist); Ekar, Batista (Give him to me, Baptist); To,
Batista; Ekar, Batista." This operation should be done without prior
notice so that the evil spirits who might interfere are not forewarned. A
son from the Arberua farmstead was the object of this operation in the
oak grove of Berrueta. My informant from Ibarsoro-Behere swore that
a nephew of his was cured using this same procedure.

In Larraun, according to Azkue, two men named Juan participate.
The first says: "Juanek uzten zaitu" (John leaves you). The other, receiving the herniated man, responds: "Juanek artzen zaitu" (John receives
you). In Ulzama three men named Juan say the words "To, Juan; Ar
Zak, Juan" and "Tori, Juan," meaning "Take him, Juan." In Ochandi-
ano (Otxandio), it is twin brothers named Juan and Pedro. This custom
is also known in Urbina (province of Araba), Aezcoa (Aezko), Roncal
(Erronkari), Donazaharre and in Barcus (Barkoxe). In this last region
the formula was "To, Yohane; ekarrak, Yohane" (Take him, Juan; give
him to me, Juan).[29]

These beliefs about the curative power attributed to the oak tree as
well as to Saint John's Eve and to individuals named Juan, belongs to
the Indo-European thematic tradition, which attained wide currency in
the ancient world.[30]

The following practice observed in Sara belongs to the same circle
of ideas. When a wound becomes infected, they say this about it: "ure ta
suak artua" (attacked by water and fire). In such a case, water is boiled
in a clay pot into which seven or nine pebbles have already been placed.
The pot is emptied by pouring its contents into a cauldron and placing
the pot upside down inside the cauldron so that it covers the pebbles.
Scissors open in the form of a cross are placed on top of the clay pot,
and two laurel branches also forming a cross are laid on the scissors;
a comb is placed on top of the laurel branches; the infected member is
placed on top of the comb. If the water retires, spontaneously entering
the pot, this means that the cause of the infection has been removed and
the infection will be cured.

In Oyarzun (Oiartzun), they use this procedure for infections and
for swellings that are caused, they say, by dizziness. They put five white
stones and five laurel leaves in the pot. The operation is repeated several
times, in uneven numbers.

In Lizarza (Lizartza) they practice the same procedure, but without
stones.

In a case from Donostia-San Sebastián cited by Don Ignacio María
Barriola, the remedy for the "dizziness" injury is carried out in an analo-

gous manner, but using three laurel leaves and twelve white stones and by placing scissors, a knife, and a comb crossed on top of the pot. The injured member is held over the pot covered with a rag for ten minutes. "If the wound was caused by dizziness, the pot swallows the water from the cauldron, and the steam attracts the inflammation."[31]

Animals in Magic

The male goat is considered a healthy animal that rarely becomes ill. Because of this, in Ataun and in Sara it is said that his presence in the stable guarantees the health of the livestock sheltered there.

In Ereño, there was an individual suffering from a heart condition. A healer and seer (in Basque, *astue*) from Mundaca was consulted, and she ordered that two hens be killed. She tore the heart out of one of them, and after sticking pins into it, she buried it, guaranteeing that the man's illness would fade away as the hen's heart putrified.[32]

Cranial Cavity and Teeth

In San Victor de Gauna, the skull of the saint has been preserved. The pilgrims who climb up to the hermitage use it as a cup for drinking the water they pour into it for the purpose of healing sicknesses of the head or to prevent headaches. The same practice is observed in San Gregorio de Sorlada.

The teething of children is encouraged, according to magical thinking, by wearing the teeth of a hedgehog (*llodio*) or wild cat (*larrabezua*) or the tooth of a horse (*bedia*) around the neck.[33]

Sprinklings

According to magical thinking, a beneficial effect is attributed to certain symbolic operations. To make it rain in a time of drought, in some towns they moisten the image of a saint by sprinkling it with water or submerging it in a well. We have observed practices such as this in Ataun, in Alsasua (Altsasu), in Astigarraga, etc.[34]

Magical Axe

To indicate where a lightning bolt (an imaginary *Ceraunia* or stone axe) should strike and to keep it from striking a house during a storm, they place an axe in the doorway with the blade pointing upward, according to reports from Mañaria, Llodio (Laudio), Urrialdo, Nafarrete (Nafarrate), Elduayen (Elduain), Ataun, etc. This custom, which won widespread acceptance among the Basque people in ancient times and spread to many countries in Europe, is still practiced in some villages, inspired by the spirit of magic.[35]

Simulated Sewing

The same spirit can easily be recognized in certain practices used in cases of muscular distension. A rag is placed over the injured or afflicted member. The rag represents that member. If it is a leg, a sock is placed on it so that the imagery will be more perfect. Using a needle and thread without a knot in the end, the person acting as magician perforates the cloth several times as if he were sewing it. As he does this he prays the "Our Father" in reverse order. In Maruri-Jatabe they recite this formula at the same time: *"Zain tiratu / Zain urratu / Zana bere tokian sartu"* (Damaged muscle, torn muscle, may the muscle be put back in place). Gernika, Ajanguiz (Ajangiz), Maruri-Jatabe, Guerricaiz (Gerrikaitz), and Bedia form one of the focal points of this practice in our country.[36]

Solstice Fires

On the night of June 23, Saint John's Eve, in addition to the practice noted above, a number of rituals also inspired by magical thinking can be observed, for instance, the custom of burning sheaves of straw in cultivated fields in the hope that such combustion will cause the burning of the enemies of the crops planted there. In Larrabezúa (Larrabetzu), they carry a burning sheaf over the property, singing *"Gure soloan lapurrik ez / Badago bere erre beitez / Pistiek, zapoak, sugeak erre, erre / Eta peste txarrak erre, erre"* (On our property no thieves / if there are any, let them be burned / let the wild beasts, the toads, the snakes be burned, burned / and the harmful pests be burned, burned). A similar custom exists in Amorebieta (Zornotza) and in Oyarzun (Oiartzun).[37]

Finally, here we have a custom, considered to be a pantomime of magical inspiration that I described in a work published in the year 1947 with the title of "Calendrier traditionnel de Sare" (*Ikuska*, no. 3). In Sara on St. John's Eve they make a bonfire in front of each house or at a crossroads. The inhabitants form a line and walk single file clockwise around the fire while praying the rosary. This custom, common throughout the Indo-European world, mobilizes the magical force that keeps the sun on its annual course.[38]

Names and Things

Names are signs, generally the first signs or representations of things, their audible images. According to Basque folklore, things are closely connected to their names; everything has a name, it is commonly thought. And vice versa—it is customary to say that every name is connected to a thing: "*Izena duen guztia omen da*," which means that there isn't any name that does not correspond to some reality, so that beyond the world of our concepts and objects, nothing exists. The popular phrase or saying regarding magical power and the attributes of witchcraft, "*Direnik, ez da sinistu bear; ez direla, ez da esan bear*" (One must not believe they exist; one must not say they do not), is a compromise between this belief and Christian faith.

It is natural that in an environment where the magical conception of the world prevails, it is thought that by manipulating their names, one can influence things themselves. Therefore, in our country it is commonly believed that a curse (in Basque, *birao, birau*) leveled against a name affects the object it represents. In Sara they use the words *birao* and *otoitzgaxto* to express this kind of anathema which, by virtue of magical power or *adur*, brings sicknesses or misfortunes to the person or animal named in the curse. Only the person who initiated the curse can undo it. This is why they say that the person affected by a curse will suffer for a long time and take a long time to die, because God cannot receive the person until the one uttering the curse withdraws it.

Not long ago, a young man who came from Andoain got in an argument with a laborer from Ataun. When he found out that the laborer was suffering from lumbago, he told him: "You're suffering this because of the curse I've leveled against you repeatedly over the past few days."

This form of magic is basically the same as that mentioned frequently in medieval documents and which was commonly practiced by the pagans before Christianity. Thus, Macrobius, in *Saturnalia*, Book III, says that the Romans tried to keep secret the names of the tutelary god of Rome and the Latin name of his city so that they could not be evoked magically by their enemies. The same writer reveals the formulae with which the Romans evoked the tutelary gods of the cities they sought to conquer. Numerous examples acknowledging the magical power of names are documented in the book *Die magischen Heil-*

und-Schutzmittel aus der unbelebten Natur by S. Seligmann (Stuttgart, 1927).[39]

* * *

In the examples of magic described above, it is easy to discern the various phases of a long cultural process. The ways of life in different prehistoric periods have left their stamp. Indo-European culture has also left its mark. Christianity and paganism are mixed together there, too.

Such examples permit us, on the other hand, to consider practices of this kind as cases of social formalism, or rather, a regime in which form prevails over substance. The person who simulates a cloudburst by sprinkling water on the statue of a saint and then waiting for the saint to bring the needed rain fulfills a formula, just as an initiate enacts a formula—the delivery of a speech—to gain membership in a society, or dons a uniform to demand a certain attitude from his fellow citizens.

One who preaches and recommends a behavior without practicing it is content with the form. One who prays without focusing on the words is merely satisfying the form. One who adjusts his conduct to what has been sanctified by custom, behaving as others behave, is heeding formulae in the clear expectation that they will produce their effect, exactly as one utters a curse in the belief that the letter of his formula will bring harm to his enemy. In social formalism we acknowledge the truth of *forma dat esse rei* (form gives being to things). But with this difference: in non-magical formalism, the quasi-mystical force that characterizes magic—*adur*—is lacking; it is a laicization of magical rituals. In both cases, however, there is an automatism comparable to that of a mechanism of precision. In both cases man is seen entrusting his fate to the form, to the formulae, fluctuating on the surface of social life. The Basque calls this *legea egin*, fulfilling the law, keeping up appearances.

THE MYTHS

Beyond the conception of the physical universe or phenomena as something that obeys the normal interaction of natural agents, beyond magical concepts or fate, whose manifestations we have analyzed, a different vision of the world is apparent in many beliefs and popular legends, a world in which spirits or natural humanized forces play an important part.

The World of Beliefs

The earth is known directly only in part, in the locale or region that one has inhabited. Concerning the rest, in popular stories there are only vague references, often legendary, which present it as something immensely large, whose limitless surface forms a perceptibly horizontal plane, with prominences of solid land formed by its mountains and with the waters of the ocean.[40]

The surface of the earth is not immobile, for some regions rise, others fall, and many mountains grow like living beings.[41]

Inside the earth there are vast spaces where rivers of milk run; but these are inaccessible to man as long as he lives on the surface. There are certain wells, pits, and caverns that connect with them, like the Urbión well, the sinkholes of Okina and Albi and the Caves of Amboto, Muru, and Txindoki. From subterranean regions such as these certain atmospheric phenomena emerge, mainly storm clouds and hurricane-force winds.[42]

The blue sky is called *ostri*. In it the stars move, sinking into the "scarlet seas" (*itxasgorrieta*) at sundown in order to resume their course through the subterranean world. Thus, the sun, which during part of its course lights the surface world, shines during the rest of its journey to light the world beneath the earth.[43] The Sun and the Moon are feminine divinities, daughters of Earth, to whose womb they return every day after their journey through the sky.[44]

The day is for the men who live on the surface of the earth. But at night the earth belongs to the spirits and the souls of the dead for whom the moon shines.

Folk wisdom distinguishes in man both natural (*berezko*) and supernatural (*aidetikako*) attributes. Thus, there are sicknesses that must be cured with natural remedies and others that can only be cured by magic or through spells and prayers.

Ruperto Aurre, the sorcerer of Axanguiz (Ajangiz), who practiced his art forty years ago in the region of Gernika, told me: "There are phenomena that can be affected by science: medicine, for example. There are others that belong to the realm of the priest. And others fall within my exclusive purview. I do not advertise my art; it is people who, when the need arises, ask for my intervention; those who do not need me do not call me."

The World and Its Destiny, the Cult of *Etxe*

According to the traditional conception still prevailing among the people, a Basque person is bound to an *etxe*, "house."

Frequently the surname itself is the name of one's place of origin. The *etxe* is land and shelter, temple and cemetery, material sustenance, symbol and common center of the living and the dead of a family. It is also the community formed by those currently living in it and their ancestors. Such are the attributes of the traditional Basque home that now, with new ways of life, are being distorted and are vanishing.

Closely related to the *etxe*, the principal ways of life (which have their expression in old laws and customs) and the entire mythological and religious system that establishes and guarantees the communion of the living and the dead were developed over centuries.[45]

The conceptual world of the historical Basque, then, revolves around the *etxe*, which in turn pursues an ideal: to permit each individual to live without sorrow and without pain in harmony with those around him in communion with his ancestors in this life and the other.

The *Etxe* Is a Temple

It is of course a sacred place protected by the fire of the hearth—symbol of a spirit called *Andra-Mari*—that has supernatural virtues: sacred because of the laurel growing in the garden or kept inside the house; because of various branches of hawthorn, ash, and flowers related to the solstice; because of the flower of the wild thistle, symbol of the sun; because of the axe and the hoe that are endowed with mystical powers; because it is the dwelling of spirits of ancestors or a place frequented by them; because of the perennial offering of light for the souls by keeping the hearth fire lit according to a ritual prescription or requirement of providing light for the dead even if it is only a single straw; because of the practice of placing pious offerings of food intended for the dead members of the household on a shelf outside the windows; because of the ancient custom of constructing the houses so that the main entrance faces the rising sun; and, finally, because the house is the family cemetery.

The sacred character of the house seems to be confirmed by the *yarleku* or sacred space that each house maintains in the parish church and which is considered an extension of the house and an integral and inseparable part of it. In that space, a number of functions are performed, such as the recitation and chanting of liturgical responses, the offering of votive candles, food, and money in honor of the deceased members of the household.[46] There, just as in the home, souls are invoked to help the living members of the family with their needs. Thus, the *yarleku* seems to be a case of adaptation of an ancient indigenous custom to the requirements of the Christian liturgy and vice versa, and the cultural functions performed today in that space are a reflection of those practiced in the house itself prior to the introduction of Christianity into the country. Add to this the custom, still practiced in some places, that when the male heir of a house marries, the new bride is incorporated into the home of the husband, joining the community of his ancestors and offering candles and loaves of bread in the *yarleku* of her new house. In ancient times, apparently, this was done in the house proper, as is evident in the custom observed in Soule where the servant who comes to work in the house walks several times around the hearth of the house so that she becomes acclimated to her new dwelling.[47]

The *Etxe* Is a Tomb

Each house has—or used to have—its burial ground beside the parish church, or inside it, in which case the tombstone covering it is the corresponding *yarleku*. In either case, it is an inseparable part of the *etxe*. This is why in sepulchral inscriptions as well as in those of the *yarleku* the house it belonged to was indicated. This is how it appears in the following inscriptions from Sara: *Lecabeako thombac*, 1838, "burial grounds of the Lezabea house"; *Harizmendico yarleckhva*, 1824, "belonging to the house of Arizmendi, 1824."

But before the introduction of Christianity, the house itself had to serve as the family tomb. And the offerings to the dead were celebrated in it. There are still vestiges of this, as cited above, especially in the practice still observed in our time of burying unbaptized children beneath the eaves of the house or in the *baratz*, the "garden beside the house"; the belief, stereotyped in popular refrains, that the person whose conduct strays from Christian norms should, at death, be buried under the eaves of his own house; or the custom of lighting candles and depositing offerings (food or money) for the deceased of the house on the window frames, that is, on the *baratz* or supposed domestic cemetery, in the belief that those candles watch over the dead, actually lighting their way in their life underground and that those offerings—or the nutrition they contain—are consumed by their souls; the belief that people should not walk three times around the house, implying that this is equivalent to the parish church and cemetery, which are subject to the same beliefs, etc.[48]

The close relation between house, church, and parish cemetery is confirmed through a similar mystic process by the sacred character of the road connecting them, called *elizbide, gorputzbide, ilbide, kutzebide, erribide, andabide*, etc., depending on the town. Each house has its own which may be shared in whole or in part with other houses. Along this road—generally in a place where a crossroad is formed—they burn the straw mattress[49] of the death bed of the person whose funeral services are being observed in the church at the same time; in this rite—in front of the door of the deceased's home—they construct the ritual fire around which the funeral cortege gathers and prays on returning from the burial service, a practice still common in many towns in Lower Navarre.[50]

From the foregoing, we understand that the traditional Basque house is an institution of economic, social, and religious character held together by a family consisting of the current inhabitants in communion with the souls of ancestors, an institution responsible for continuing a tradition and carrying out indispensable religious functions. This has led to the *etxe* or house being regarded as inviolable, endowed with the inalienable right of sanctuary, to be passed on whole and undivided within the family.[51]

As the *etxes* are sacred enclosures and centers of convergence for the living and the dead, they are all considered equal, which no doubt contributed to the development of feelings of respect toward the houses and their inhabitants. In effect, all of them are equal and equally inviolable; and their inhabitants are also equally respectable, temporary representatives of equal institutions, endowed with identical rights and sacred duties in all of the houses. Anyone who violates such norms and goes against such feelings can fear being afflicted by one of the terrible diseases caused by the spirits.

These characteristics, more or less distorted by the profound transformation of life occurring in the twentieth century, which are still
apparent in Basque houses in rural areas, were even more noticeable
during the time of the *fueros* (old Basque laws). Thus, the sacred right
of sanctuary characteristic of temples in antiquity was acknowledged
for the home by Basque law. According to the Fuero of Bizkaia (third
law of Title 16), no Basque could be imprisoned for any debt that was
not directly or indirectly the result of a crime, nor could his house be
forfeited, nor his weapons and horse taken, even if by written agreement
he had renounced his noble status. And in the same Law it is forbidden
for "any executor or arbiter to come within four arm's lengths of the
house of a Basque against the will of its owner, except with a scribe and
without any weapon and for the sole purpose of making an inventory of
the executable property."[52]

The Cult of the Home

From the foregoing it should be clear that the personages to whom the
domestic cult is directed are the souls of ancestors. These are conceived
as lights and as gusts or blasts (Basque, *indar*) of wind. But in some
places, mainly in Bizkaia, they are considered to be ghosts. The word
designating this concept is *gerixeti*, used in that region. *Erio*, which is
the character that represents death, separates them from their bodies.
From that moment on their ordinary dwelling place is the underworld,
as suggested in the popular tales from the most ancient times. However,
they return frequently to the surface at night, especially to their *etxe*,
in order to help their living family members, to consume offerings, to
amuse themselves in their respective homes, and to settle accounts that
were left unresolved at the time of their death. The roads traveled by
the souls, if we go by certain legends, are certain mysterious galleries
that connect each home with the subterranean world. Certain pits and
caverns in the rural areas are considered passageways through which
the souls come and go. According to legend, such passageways surface
in hearths or kitchens, especially in the most ancient houses. Thus, it is
said that the houses of Gaztelu in San Martín de Arberua, Eiheraxaharre
or Molino in Ezpeleta, Jauregia in the same town, Ermintatxiki and
Sales in Elduayen (Elduain), Andralizeta in Ataun, Semeola in Alzola
(Altzola), Egaña in Aizarna, Agorrosin in Vergara (Bergara), Salturri in
Mondragón (Arrasate), Aldabazar in Aldaba, etc., are in communication with pits and caves frequented by souls and spirits.[53]

When the souls rise to the surface to make some request or demand, they make themselves known by appearing in the form of a light, a cloud, a shadow, a black figure, or through strange noises. A soul appearing in this way is called *argi*, "light," in Labourd and Navarre, *heotsegile*, "thunder," in Soule, *izugarri* or *izuargi*, "sacred light," in Ataun and *gerixeti* in a number of places in Bizkaia. There are places where they are called *arimaerratu*, "wandering soul."[54]

The foregoing data and observations reveal to us that among the traditional concerns of the Basque people, concern for the souls of their ancestors has high priority. It has inspired and continues to inspire much of their religious life, affecting many aspects of their economic and social life (the ownership of the house and its undivided transmission within the family) as well as their legal system.

Ministers of the Domestic Cult

The house, then, is endowed with a markedly religious significance; it is both cemetery and temple, its cult administered by those living in it.

The *etxekoandre*, "lady of the house," is the primary minister of this religion. It is she, in effect, who performs certain cult functions, such as offering candles and food to the deceased members of the house, blessing the members of her family once a year, indoctrinating all the members of the family in their obligation to maintain a communion with their ancestors, to respect their elders, and to carry out the duties imposed by the neighborhood. She represents the house in the *yarleku* it possesses in the parish church, as well as in the burial ground, presiding over the functions and sacred rituals held there on various occasions.[55]

When the *etxekoandre* or some other woman of the family cannot attend such ceremonies, she is replaced by the *andereserora*, a woman whose primary function is to perform these ceremonies in the parish church. The *andereserora*, then, is a kind of priestess who represents and fills in at church for the *etxekoandre* or other ministers of the domestic cult within the parish.

All of this has no doubt increased the appreciation and consideration in which women have been held. For this reason a woman has frequently been named heir to the house with preference over her brothers.

Regarding the status of women during the time of the *fueros*, it should be noted that in choosing the heir it was customary to follow the order of nature, and it was the first-born—male or female—who succeeded the parents in running the house, though it was possible for the parents to alter this order.[56] Here we have a situation contrary to the privileges which feudal law, in accordance with Germanic law, granted only to males in other European countries.

The esteem in which ancient Basques held women probably influenced the preeminent role a woman played in several important aspects of family life. She stayed at home, cultivated the fields, and guaranteed by her presence and her labor the continuity of the home, while her husband herded the flocks in the seasonal movement from mountains to plains, or was away from home meeting the demands of his life as a sailor or fisherman. In these circumstances it was she who was able to carry out the functions of the domestic cult, which elevated her dignity and prestige, thereby enhancing the woman's social and political condition.

The World of the Gods

Alongside the souls of ancestors, a number of mythological figures are in constant motion, more or less related to the former and almost all linked to natural phenomena of the physical world. These are spirits, numina, and names, points of convergence of images and themes. Some themes are indigenous, and others—the majority—are derived from foreign cultures and mythologies that gradually became incorporated into the tradition of the Basque people in different epochs of their historical development. Listed below are some names of spirits classified into groups, depending on the qualities and functions generally attributed to them.

> *Gauargi, Gaueko.*
> *Iruztargi, Ieltxu, Iritxu, Idittu, Iditxu.*
> *Inguma, Gaizkiña, Gaixto, Aideko.*
> *Mamarro, Galtxagorri.*
> *Saindi-Maindi, Maide, Mairi, Intxixu.*
> *Lamin, Lamiñ, Lamiñaku, Lami, Amilamia, Eilalamia.*
> *Sorgin, Belagile, Sorsain.*
> *Basajaun, Basandere.*
> *Torto, Tartalo, Anxo, Alarabi.*
> *Odei, Mikelats, Frakazar, Eate, Ereeta.*
> *Erensuge, Edensuge, Iraunsuge.*
> *Maju, Sugaar, Sugoi, Culebro.*
> *Txaalgorri, Zezengorri, Beigorri, etc.* (spirits in animal form).
> *Mari, Yona-Gorri, Lezeko-Andere.*
> *Eguzki-Amandre; Illargi-Amandre* and his mother *Lur.*
> *Ostri, Ortzi, Urtzi.*

Gaueko

Since the house is the family temple, one feels protected there, even during the night, especially between midnight and the cock's crow when the spirits rule over the earth. During the night and outside the house a person is not in his element; "*Eguna egunezkoarentzat; gaua gauez-koarentzat,*" "the day for creatures of the day, the night for creatures of the night" is a popular saying. "The creature of the day" is man; "the creature of the night" is Gaueko. The latter, then, is the night spirit or night personified, who does not allow men to perform certain actions after the ringing of the Angelus. In particular, it punishes those who pretend to be brave in the darkness of night, boasting that they are not afraid of the lack of visibility, the solitude, and the silence of those hours.

There are a number of legends related to this idea, leading to the conclusion that it is foolhardy to challenge the Gaueko.[57]

Gaueko is thought to be the devil in some folk tales, and in others to be a pagan or a pagan divinity. Sometimes it appears in the form of a cow, and in one tale from Motrico (Mutriku) it is represented in the form of a lion.[58]

Gauargi is the name used, in the region of Régil (Errezil), to designate a spirit that appears at night in the form of a light shining above prominent objects such as trees, cliffs, and houses. In its origin it was probably the guardian of the night or night itself personified as Gaueko.

Ieltxu

Ieltxu is the name given, in the region of Gernika, to a certain nocturnal spirit appearing in human form, according to some, and in the form of a bird shooting flame from its mouth, according to others. It is generally identified in the dark of night as a burning flame. It appears suddenly out of nowhere, inspiring fear. It is not evil, but takes pleasure in leading anyone who follows it out of curiosity through gullies, to the edge of precipices and other dangerous places. The usual dwelling places of this spirit are caves, chasms, and wells. The well in Busturia and a pit in Nabarrizmendi are pointed out as dwelling places of Ieltxu.[59]

Inguma

Inguma is an evil spirit that appears at night in houses when the inhabitants are asleep. It squeezes the throat of some of them, making it difficult for them to breathe, causing them unspeakable anguish.

In order to ward off attacks by this spirit, in the region of Ezpeleta it is customary to chant this magic formula upon retiring for the night:

Inguma, enauk ire bildur,
Jincoa et Andre María
Artzentiat Ingun;
Zeruan izar, lurrean belar, Kostan hare
Hek guziak Kondatu arte
Ehadiela nereganat ager.

I'm not afraid of you, Inguma,
I have God and Mother Mary
To protect me.
Stars in the sky, grasses on the ground, grains of sand on the shore,
Until you have counted them all,
Do not appear to me.

In Sara they chant this formula:

Ingumes erromes,
Ez niok ire beldurrez.
Jesús diat aita,
Ama Berjiña Ama,
Zeruko Saindu ta Aíngeru guziak guarda.

Greedy Ingumes,
I'm not afraid of you.
I have Jesus as my father,
The Virgin Mary as my mother,
All the saints and angels in heaven as my guardians.

Similar to Inguma is Aideko, thought to be responsible for all illnesses whose natural causes are unknown. Blamed also is Gaizkiñe who, by forming the shapes of a rooster's head with the feather from the pillow, causes serious illness to the person sleeping on it. Only by burning these figures can the illness be cured.

All along the Pyrenees there are beliefs related to this spirit.[60]

Mamarro

Mamarro, Galtxagorri, and other names are used to designate one or several tiny spirits in human form—in insect form, according to some—who help certain men in their work. Four of them fit inside a pincushion, and they live inside the one belonging to the person they are protecting. People who work wonders or extraordinary deeds, like the *azti*, "sorcerers," *sorgin*, "warlocks," and some healers and sages, are thought to have enlisted the help of Mamarro or Galtzagorri, whom they have invited to live inside their pincushion.[61]

Maide

Maide is also a nocturnal spirit that comes down the chimney into the kitchen to receive offerings that have been left there at bedtime by those who live in the house. In Mendive (Mendibe), they call it Saindi-Maindi, "Saint Maide."

In Soule, they attribute the construction of cromlechs to this spirit; in Mendive (Mendibe), the building of dolmens found in the region. In the region of Saint-Jean-Pied-de-Port (Donibane Garazi), they call a dolmen *Mairi-Etxe*, i.e., the house of Mairi, which must be one of the forms of the name Maide, or else Mari, the name of another spirit we will discuss later.

Intxixu is the spirit to whom they attribute the making of cromlechs in the region of Oyarzun. It is, therefore, Maide himself under a different name. The same function has been associated also with other mythical names, such as *Sorgin*, *Jentil*, and *Mairu*.

Maide is a masculine entity. His feminine counterpart is the *lamiñ*.[62]

Lamiñ

Lamiñ, *Lami*, or *Lamiñaku* is generally a spirit in the shape of a woman, except that her legs are like those of a hen. In Ceánuri (Zeanuri), Orozco (Orozko), and Elanchove (Elantxobe), she is thought to be like a tiny woman with just one eye in the middle of her forehead.

The name *lamiñ* is rarely used as the proper name of a specific spirit; in most cases it is a common name applied to all the spirits of a certain type whose characteristics are those already mentioned, such as dwelling in caves, wells, and ancient castles that have now been abandoned.

They frequently busy themselves washing and combing their hair. There are stories in which a *lamiña* angrily demands the return of a comb someone has stolen from her. A *lamiña* and two young men who were courting her appear on a tombstone in Ibernalo, as some residents of Santa Cruz de Campezo (Santikurutze Kanpezu) told me when they showed me that monument there around the year 1932.

They demand offerings. If a farmer leaves them some food on the edge of his property, the *lamiñas* will eat it during the night and, in return, plow the field or finish the work that had been left unfinished on his property.

The legend of the *lamiña* from Kobaundi (Mondragón/Arrasate) is famous: how she falls in love with a young peasant; how he succeeds in determining the age of the smitten numen; of the sorrow, sickness, and death of the young man on discovering that his beloved is not a human being; and of the sorrow of the *lamiña*, and so on.[63]

The plow, drawn by oxen, made the *lamiñas* disappear. According to others, the construction of rural hermitages was the cause of their disappearance.

Sorguiñ

This is one of the names used to designate witches. Another name is *Belagile*, very common in Soule. Another is *Sorsain*, which means protector of childbirth, no doubt because it is the spirit that presides over the birth of children. It also keeps jealous watch to see that belief in its existence is preserved by the people, severely punishing those who deny it.

Sorguiñ is also the name of the persons who used to convene in witches' sabbaths or *akelarres* in ancient times. But this meaning seems to be more recent.

In its primitive sense, *Sorguiñ* seems to be a nocturnal spirit that frequently lives in caves. Its power in the world is effective between midnight and first cock's crow.

It belongs to the family of the goddess Mari and performs certain functions under her orders, such as collecting tithes, taking them by force from people who try to cover up their wealth through lies and deception. It was they who built the most ancient bridges in the Basque Provinces.

Their disappearance has been attributed to the construction of Christian hermitages; but today it is more common to say that it was Eibar that exterminated their race, alluding by this to the introduction of firearms.[64]

Anthropomorphic stele from Saint-Michel.

Stele from Sorhapuru, on which the deceased appears to be represented.

Baxajaun

Baxajaun, lord of the forest, is the spirit that dwells in the deepest part of the forests or in caves situated in prominent places. It has a tall body in human form, covered with hair. Its long hair falls forward down to the knees, covering the face, chest, and stomach. It is the guardian spirit of flocks. It cries out in the mountains when a storm approaches so that the shepherds can move their flock into the fold. When Baxajaun is in the vicinity of the fold, there is no danger of the wolf approaching. Its presence is announced by the sheep with a simultaneous shaking and jingling of their bells. Then the shepherds can fall asleep peacefully, knowing that during that night or day the wolf, the great enemy of flocks, will not come around to bother them.

Baxajaun is sometimes represented as a frightening creature, of evil character, endowed with colossal strength and extraordinary agility. On other occasions it is depicted for us as the first farmer from whom men learned the cultivation of grains and as the first blacksmith and the first miller from whom man stole the secret of the making of the saw, the axle for the mill, and the forging of metals.[65]

Torto, Anxo

Torto, Anxo, and Alarabi are the names of a Cyclops or evil spirit with a single eye in its forehead. It usually lives in caves.

Torto, whom they call Tartalo in the Cegama region, appears in the most terrifying stories in Basque homes. It kidnaps some young person or captures someone forced by a storm to take refuge in his cave, then draws and quarters him, roasts him on the fire and eats him. There are cases, however, in which the captive manages to destroy the eye of the Cyclops or contrives a way to deceive it and escape from its control.

Because of the theme and the details of the myths related to Torto, and even because of the name Tartalo, we cannot but compare this spirit with Polyphemus, whom Homer describes in his *Odyssey*.[66]

The myth of Torto shows up in a number of places in the Basque Country. In Ataun, for example, the cave of Muskia is said to be the scenario of atrocities by the Cyclops. Another place mentioned in the legend is *Tartaloetxeeta*, "dwelling place of Tartalo," located on Mount Saadar (Cegama (Zegama)), where there is a dolmen, the supposed den of the frightening spirit.

Erensugue, Iraunsugue

In Basque mythology one of the most important spirits is Erensugue, also called Iraunsugue, Edensugue, Ersugue, etc., depending on the locale. It appears in the form of a serpent, as the second part of its name suggests: *sugue* means "snake, serpent."

In some myths, this spirit is presented with seven heads; in others, with only one.

Its most famous dwelling places are the cave of Azalegui or Ertzagania (on Mount Ahuski), the chasm of San Miguel de Excelsis (in Aralar), Faardiko-harri (in Sara); Orduña Peak, the cave of Balzola and Montecristo (Mondragón (Arrasate)).

It attracted the livestock of Ahuski and other mountains with its breath and ate them, according to the legend of Alzay (Altzai).

When it lived in the chasm of Aralar, in that of Montecristo, and on Orduña (Urduña) Peak, it fed on human beings.

In Espeleta (Ezpeleta), they say that when the seventh head forms, it bursts into flames and flies swiftly toward the region of Itxasgorrieta, or the red seas of the setting sun, where it sinks. It makes a frightening noise when it passes through the air. In Alzay (Altzai), they say that a son from Zaro Castle (now destroyed) poisoned it. Then the serpent started to burn and, wrapped in flames, flew toward the ocean, using its tail to cut off the tops of the beech trees in the forest of Itze, "Arbailles," as it passed overhead.

In Mondragón (Arrasate), they claim that a resident of that village killed it.

According to the legend of Orduña (Urduña), it was an angel who cut off its head. The legend of Teodosio of Goñi is more explicit, describing in detail how the Archangel San Miguel finished off the serpent of Aralar with his sword.[67]

Topics related to *Erensugue* led to the formation of several folk tales that were echoed by some writers, for instance, Agustín Chao [Chaho] in his description, "Le serpent du Valdextre" (in *Biarritz, entre les Pyrénées et l'océan* (Biarritz between the Pyrenees and the Ocean) (Bayonne, 1855) p. 176) and Juan E. Delmas in his *Guía histórica descriptiva del viajero en el Señorío de Vizcaya* (Descriptive Historical Guide for the Traveler in the Seigniory of Bizkaia) (Bilbao, 1864).

Sugaar

The name Sugaar means *culebro*, "male serpent." In the region of Ataun, they say that Sugaar frequently crosses the firmament in the shape of a fiery sickle. Its passage is the sign of an approaching storm.

It is believed that Sugaar lives underground, coming to the surface of the earth through the opening of certain sinkholes, like those of Agamunda and Sugaarzulo of Kutzeberri, located in Ataun. It also lives in the cave of Balzola (Dima), where it is known by the name of Sugoi.

Sugaar or other spirits that live in the sinkhole of Agamunda punish children who disobey their parents.

In the region of Azcoitia (Azkoitia) they call this spirit Maju, and say that it is the husband of the mythical character Mari, whom it joins every Friday, or whose hair it must comb on Friday evenings, as they believe in Zarauz (Zarautz).

In his *Crónica de siete casas de Vizcaya y Castilla* (Chronicle of Seven Houses of Bizkaia and Castile) (1454), Lope García de Salazar said that this Sugaar or male snake is the creature that was a devil called Culebro (snake) in Bizkaia. He was lord of the house and his union with a princess from Mundaca (Mundaka) produced the first prince of Bizkaia, Jaun Zuria.[68]

Beigorri

Of particular importance in Basque mythology are a number of spirits that take on the form of animals, mainly the horse, the bull (Zezengorri), the small red cow (Beigorri), the ram, the sheep, the male goat, the female goat, the pig, and the dog. They usually live in caverns and they have a limited function as guardians of such places.

They do not allow anyone to enter their dwelling place. In certain cases they kidnap young people who have been the target of some curse and hold them captive in their underground dens.

In the Roman period this underground mythology must have been as widespread in our country as it is today, for in the caves of Isturitz, Santimamiñe, Sagastigorri, and Covairada we have found Roman coins that, in keeping with the custom of that time, had been thrown into such places in order to win the protection of cave spirits.

It is useful to recall that the same figures that are situated by Basque mythology in caverns also appear painted or engraved by men of the Magdalenian period and earlier on the walls of some of the caves of our country.[69]

Lur

The earth *(lur)* is considered to be the mother of the sun and the moon. It is also regarded as an immense receptacle, the habitual dwelling place of souls and of most of the numina and other mythical characters.

The earth possesses the vital force that is the basis of the plant kingdom. The human organism envigorates that vital force by means of certain formulas or magical expressions and assures the conservation of livestock if some animals are offered or sacrificed to the earth.

Additionally, the earth holds treasures, according to widespread belief. Mountains and caves are identified in which a cowhide filled with gold is guarded, but the coordinates of the exact place where such a treasure can be found are never precise. How often have peasants excavated in vain in Urrezulo in Ataun, or the cave of Mairuelegorreta, or on Maruelexa peak (Navarniz (Nabarniz)) or the ravine of Larrune! Or in the caves of Balzola (Dima), or Iruaxpe (Goronaeta (Goroeta)) and Putterri!

The treasure—a golden bell, a skein of gold, a chest of gold—is in the Urbasa mountain range, in a place where the sheep graze every day. Barely beneath the surface of the earth, the hoof of a sheep grazing there touches it and will uncover it at any moment.

Gold was buried in Munoeta (a place also known as "Caesar's Camp," near Cambo (Kanbo)). There was a sword marking the spot, but it disappeared and now the gold cannot be found.

There is also treasure buried on Mount Larte, facing the Berástegui (Berastegi) church; at a spot on Mount Udalatx where the rays of the sun strike directly at noon; on Mount Ereñusarre, on Mount Goikogane (Arrancudiaga (Arrankudiaga)), on Igozmendi (Aulestia (Aulesti)); on Iruña hill (a Roman ruin); on Mount Aralar; on Mount Ariz (Leiza (Leitza)); in a cave in the Oyarzun (Oiartzun) mountains, from whose mouth can be heard the crowing of the rooster from the Berdabio farm; at a place on Mount Saibei, near Urquiola (Urkiola), from which you can see the light of the lamp from the sanctuary, etc.

The greed of those who hope to become rich digging up these treasures will not prevail. This is because of a taboo whose observance is enforced by the spirit of the earth, as occurred in the mountains of Irukutzeta and Auza and in the fields of Arranzelai (Echalar (Etxalar)).

Without a doubt, the spirit of the earth was the intended recipient of the prayers of many worshippers who in ancient times deposited their offerings (mainly coins) in the caves in hopes of winning favors from her. And apparently the origins of a number of hermitages either built in caves or converted from caves were connected to this cult, as was the practice of reciting prayers at the entrance to certain caverns in this country. In the Sanctuary of San Miguel of Aralar, at the right side of the altar, there is a hole that, according to legend, communicates with the chasm over which that church is built. Pilgrims put their heads inside it while reciting the Creed. They say this keeps them from having headaches. A similar practice is observed in the hermitages of San Esteban of Usúrbil, Our Lady of Zukiñaga (Hernani), San Juan Bautista of Orio, and San Pedro of Cegama (Zegama).[70]

Mari

There is a spirit (of feminine gender, like most of those connected with Basque mythology) that has managed to absorb many functions that have been attributed to various mythical entities in other countries. She is believed to hold sway over the other spirits. Among the components of her current names, the most ancient seems to be Mari. This word, which in some parts of the country means *señora* (lady) and in this sense, apparently, is applied to the mythical character of which we speak, is accompanied by the name of the mountain or cavern where, according to the beliefs of each town, the spirit is accustomed to appear. In Amézqueta (Amezketa), they call her *Txindoki'ko Mari'e*, "the Mari of Chindoqui"; in Ataun, *Mari-munduko*, "Mari of Muru or Mundu."[71] We will simply refer to her as Mari, as did the shepherds of Urquiola (Urkiola) in the meadow of Zabalundi at the foot of Mount Amboto who told me, while pointing at one of the caves on that mountain: *"Ara or Marijen kobia,"* "There's the cave of Mari."

It is possible that the word Mari owes its origin to the Christian name María (Mary), but we should not discard another possible origin. It should be noted that another name for the same spirit is Maya, which seems to be related to the name of her husband Maju. Judging by the functions attributed to him, this spirit must be the same one that Lope García de Salazar called *"Culebro"* or Serpent (father of Jaun Zuria), who is still called Sugaar, "Serpent," in Atáun, and Sugoi, which has the same meaning in Dima. The name Mari may also be related to Mairi, Maide, and Maindi, names used to designate other mythical characters, even though the themes linked to these spirits are different.

Forms of Mari — The legends attribute feminine gender to Mari. She is frequently presented to us in the form of an elegantly attired lady, as we are told in the stories from Durango, in which she appears, moreover, holding a palace of gold in her hands. She is presented in similar fashion in legends from Elosua, Bedoña, Azpeitia, Cegama (Zegama),

Rentería (Errenteria), Ascain (Azkaine), and Lescun. In this last place they say she wears a red gown.

She also appears in the form of a lady seated in a carriage drawn through the air by four horses (Amézqueta (Amezketa)).

In Zaldivia (Zaldibia) she has been seen in the form of a woman shooting out flames.

As a woman engulfed in fire, stretched out horizontally in the air, passing through space (Bedoña).

In the form of a woman trailing a fiery wake, sometimes dragging a broom, at other times chains, depending on the noise that accompanies her passage (Régil (Errezil)).

As a lady riding a ram (Cegama (Zegama) and Oñate (Oñati)).

As a large woman whose head is haloed by a full moon (Azcoitia (Azkoitia)).

As a woman with feet like a bird (Garagarza (Garagartza)).

As a woman with goat feet, according to the *Livro dos Linhagens* by Count D. Pedro de Barcellos.

In the form of a male goat (Auza del Baztán).

In the shape of a horse (Arano). In the shape of a heifer (Oñate (Oñati)).

Many people from Cegama (Zegama) have seen her in the form of a raven in the cave of Aketegi.

She and her companions appear in the form of a vulture in the great cave of Supelegor on Mount Itziñe, according to legends of Orozco (Orozko).

As a tree whose trunk resembles a woman, or a tree shooting out flames on all sides (Oñate (Oñati)).

At times she reveals herself as a gust of wind (Escoriaza (Eskoriatza)).

As a white cloud on other occasions (Durango, Ispáster (Ispsaster)). Sometimes they have seen her in the form of a rainbow.

She has often been seen passing through the air in the form of a ball of fire (Oñate (Oñati), Segura, Orozco (Orozko)).

She often adopts the form of a fiery sickle (Ataun, Cegama (Zegama), and Zuazo de Gamboa).

In the grotto of Zelharburu (Bidarray (Bidarrai)) she is represented by a stalagmite resembling a human torso.

Despite the variety of forms attributed to Mari in mythic accounts, all agree that she is a woman.

Mari usually takes on zoomorphic forms in her underground dens, and other forms on the surface of the earth and when she passes through the sky.

The figures of animals, like the bull, the ram, the male goat, the horse, the serpent, the vulture, etc., mentioned in mythical accounts related to the subterranean world, thus represent Mari and her subordinates, that is, the earthly spirits or terrestrial forces to which the people attribute the phenomena of the world. The changes of form mentioned in various myths confirm this idea.

Dwelling Places of Mari — The usual dwelling places of Mari are regions situated in the interior of the earth. But these regions communicate with the terrestrial surface through various conduits, which are certain caverns and chasms. This is why Mari makes her appearances in such places more frequently than in others. In this regard, a number of caverns have been identified where the numen has allowed herself to be seen on occasions that people still remember. These are, among others, the caves and chasms of Balzola (Dima), Supelaur or Supelegor (Orozco (Orozko)), Amboto, Atxorrotx (Escoriaza (Eskoriatza)), Zaldiaran, Aketegui (Cegama (Zegama)), Agamunda (Ataun), Murumendi (Beasain), Marizulo (Amézqueta (Amezketa)), Obantzun (Berástegui (Berastegi)), Odabe (Alsasua (Altsasu)), Akelarre (Zugarramurdi), Leizia (Sara), Zelbarburu (Bidarray (Bidarrai)), Azalegui (Alzay (Altzai)) and Otsibarre (Camou (Gamue)).[72]

It is commonly believed that the rooms where Mari lives are richly adorned and that they are filled with gold and precious jewels. In the cave of Aketegui the beds are made of gold (Cegama (Zegama)).

A legend from Cenarruza (Ziortza-Bolibar) tells how Mari gave one of her captives a handful of coal and that, afterwards, it turned into purest gold when it was taken out of the cave.

In the cave of Otsabio there is a young bull made of gold (Lizarza (Lizartza)). And in Zarauz (Zarautz) they say that Mari unwinds thread from a golden skein. In Amézqueta (Amezketa), too, they say that Mari keeps a skein of gold in Aralar.

The lady (Mari) of the grotto of Arrobibeltz (Ascain (Azkaine)) sits on a golden throne.

In front of the cave of Otsibarre (Camou (Gamue)), a golden comb was found which was thought to belong to a red bull (Mari) that shelters within the cave.

On the other hand, according to a legend in Zarauz (Zarautz) in the cave of Amboto where Mari appears frequently, there are objects that seem to be made of gold; but when taken outside they turn into rotten sticks.

Mari moves from place to place (Mañaria): she lives in Amboto for seven years, then seven in Oiz and seven in Mugarra. In Amézqueta

(Amezketa), they believe she lives for several seasons in Aralar, a few more in Aizkorri and another few in Murumendi.

The Family of Mari — In many Basque myths Mari is regarded as the leader or queen of all the spirits that inhabit the world.

In a legend from Azcoitia (Azkoitia) it is said that Mari has a husband named Maju, who appears in a form similar to hers. When the two come together, it causes a furious rain and hailstorm. Maju seems to be the same spirit they call Sugaar, "male snake," in Goyerri (Goierri). He is a character rarely encountered in present-day Basque mythology. In a legend from Zumaya (Zumaia) they say he visits Mari on Fridays at two in the afternoon.

Sugaar seems to be that devil from fifteenth-century Bizkaia who, according to the account in the *Crónica de siete casas de Vizcaya y Castilla* (Chronicle of Seven Houses of Bizkaia and Castile) (1454), mated with a princess from Mundaca who gave birth to a child who became the first lord of Bizkaia. In effect, García de Salazar writes that a daughter of the King of Scotland came to Mundaca with her servants and that "they established their home there and that while she was there, a devil whom they call *Culebro,* or Lord of the House, in Bizkaia came and slept with her in a dream and impregnated her and . . . the princess was impregnated and gave birth to a son, who was a very beautiful man of strong body and they named him Don Zuria, which in Castilian means Don Blanco (White)."[73]

Sugoi is the name of the serpent in the cave of Balzola (Dima), whose legend incorporates one of the themes of the account about the origins of the lords of Bizkaia.[74]

A number of legends originating in Ataun, in Villafranca de Oria, in Arano, etc., allude to the marriage of Mari with a mortal. The version from Ataun tells how, having married a young man from the farm of Burugoena in Beasain, Mari had seven sons. As she was not a Christian, she did not baptize them. But her husband tried to take her to the village church along with her sons. Then, engulfed in flames, Mari flew to the cliffs of Murumendi, saying: "*Ne umek zeruako, ta ni oaiñ Muruako,*" "My sons to the sky and now I to Muru," and she entered her ancient home through the cave in the side of that mountain.

In certain legends, two daughters of Mari are mentioned; in others, only one lives with her in her dwelling. Finally, in other legends, two sons are mentioned: Atarrabi and Mikelats—the former, good; the latter, evil.

The preceding account is a variation of a legend that was collected at the beginning of the sixteenth century by the Count Don Pedro de Barcellos, in his *Livro dos Linhagens* (Book of Genealogy, fourteenth century) about the origins of the lords of Bizkaia. Referring to Don Diego López de Haro, he writes the following:

> Don Diego López de Haro was an excellent mountain man, and one day when he was in his blind waiting for the wild boar to come, he heard a woman on a crag singing in a very loud voice; and he went toward her and saw that she was very beautiful and very well dressed, and he fell madly in love with her, and he asked her who she was, and she told him that she was a woman of very distinguished lineage, and he said to her that since she was a woman of distinguished lineage he would marry her, if she wanted, because he was the lord of that land; and she said she would, but on the condition that he would promise never to make the sign of the cross, and he agreed to that condition, and then she went with him. This lady was very beautiful and her body was in every way perfect except that she had one foot like that of a goat.
>
> They lived together for a long time and had two children, a male and a female, and the son was called Iñigo Guerra.

Count Don Pedro then adds that one day Don Diego López de Haro made the sign of the cross when he was eating with his family and that his wife immediately "jumped out the window of the palace with her daughter and went toward the mountains, so that they never saw her or her daughter again."[75]

Certain stories present Mari, in her numerous appearances, as if she were not a single numen or divinity, but one of several sister goddesses. Thus, they say in Marquina (Markina) that Marije-Kobako, who makes her appearances in the cave of Kanterazar and who has the same attributes as the goddess of Amboto, is the sister of the latter and that the two of them visit each other from time to time.

The trait of multiplying characters as a result of the plurality of their dwelling places corresponds to an elemental tendency that also appears in the case of the Virgin Mary in her various functions. Thus some popular accounts present the Virgin of Aránzazu (Arantzazu), the Virgin of Liernia, and the Virgin of Antigua of Zumárraga, etc., as sisters and not as manifestations of the same Virgin. It is not unusual to say that the Virgins are seven sisters: *zazpi aizpatxo dira euskaldun Birjiñak* (the Basque Virgins are seven sisters).

The foregoing beliefs and myths suggest that Mari and her mythical husband Maju or Sugaar fall into the category of ancestors, since they are thought to be the forebears of the house of the Lords of Bizkaia.

Mari's Female Captive — In addition to the innumerable spirits Mari has in her entourage, a female captive sometimes appears in her cave. Some legends say she is the daughter of the Irabi farm (Amézqueta (Amezketa)). Others say she is from the Iturriotz farm (Mutiloa), the Palasio farm (Abadiano (Abadiño)) or the Bixiñaa farm (Aramayona (Aramaio)).

This captive is also called Mari. She was reduced to such a condition or state for various reasons. In some accounts it was in fulfillment of some promise or agreement made by her mother. Thus, a woman from the Sarri region (Bérriz) made a vow to give her daughter to Mari, and to fulfill her promise she sent her to tend her cows in the meadow of Sarrimendi, near the cavern of the local spirit. Then the spirit captured her and took her to her den.

On other occasions she is captured because of a curse by her mother. There was a young girl [named Mari] from the Irabi farm in Amézqueta (Amezketa). One day a red calf went missing. Mari was charged by her mother with the task of finding the calf, but she refused to do so. Then her mother put a curse on her, saying: "The devil take you, if you don't bring her back." Then the young girl went out looking for the calf. A red cow appeared before her in the countryside. Mari thought it was hers, and went and grabbed it by the tail. And the supposed cow, which was really the devil or Mari of Marizulo, took her to the cave of Txindoki up on Larrunarri peak (in the Aralar mountains).

A girl from a household in Cegama (Zegama) used to spend hours combing her hair, which made her mother very angry. One day she cursed the girl, saying: "I hope a thousand lightning bolts carry you away!" The girl disappeared instantaneously. Later she appeared in the form of a human skeleton to a shepherd near a cavern in Aizkorri and explained to him how she had been captured because of her mother's curse.

In Mutiloa they also tell how a young girl was kidnapped under similar conditions. A shepherd subsequently saw a luminous gust of wind enter a cave. It was the vanished girl.

In other legends there is no mention of the curse or the promise. Mari simply overpowers a girl who comes near her cave. A girl was taken in that manner to the cave of Gabaro located near Marquina (Markina). Mari kept her there for several years, spinning thread. She trained her with great care and then let her go, giving her a handful of gold.

A young girl from Bidarray (Bidarrai) was grazing her herd of sheep on Iduskimendi Mountain. One day she disappeared. Her relatives and neighbors looked for her in vain for a long time; nothing was known about her. On numerous occasions at night, in the region of Iduski-mendi, a voice was heard crying out: "*Ago! Ago!*" "Wait! Wait!" The people were afraid. One night a luminous gust of wind appeared in the air, like a star, moving toward the cliffs of Zelharburu, and then it went into a grotto located there. The next day the neighbors went to explore the cave, and there, deep inside, they found the young girl, turned to stone. Today it is known by the name of *Arpeko Saindua*, "the saint of the cave."

Attributes and Functions of Mari — In Cegama (Zegama) they say that Mari frequently lets herself be seen in the kitchen of her cave, seated beside the fire, fixing her hair. In Oñate (Oñati), they've seen her spinning thread. Others have seen her sitting at the entrance to her cave, combing her hair. In Goyaz (Goiatz) they say she spends her time unwinding thread by the door to her dwelling in Murumendi, especially when the sun is shining and there are storm clouds in the sky. In Zuazo in Gamboa they say that Mari makes balls of yarn with golden thread in her cave of Amboto, winding it around the horns of a ram. In Aketegui (Aketegi) she does her laundry on Wednesdays and bakes bread on Fridays; a small cloud of smoke at the mouth of that cave announces those activities. The residents of Ipáster, when they see a cloud on Mount Otoyo, say that Mari has lighted her oven.

According to accounts in Oñate (Oñati) and Arechavaleta (Aretxa-baleta), when Mari is in Amboto, it always rains heavily; when she is in Aloña, there is a persistent drought. In Orozco (Orozko) they say that when she is in Supalur, there is an abundant harvest.

Mari is the forger of storms. In Oyarzun (Oiartzun) they say that she forms them on Aralar and on Trinidademendi. In Cegama (Zegama) and other villages in Goyerri (Goierri) they say she hurls them forth, either from Aketegui cavern or from Murumendi cavern. In Arano they say she sends them forth from a chasm in Muguiro, and that on those occasions she crosses the sky in the form of a horse. In Gorriti they believe that Mari pulls storm clouds out of a cave in Aralar. She draws forth storm winds from a well situated near the bridge of Mai-Mur, according to legends from Leiza (Leitza). In many towns of Araba they believe that such winds and clouds come from the chasm of Okina. In Cuartango (Kuartango) they say they come from Lake Arreo. In villages of the Rioja you frequently hear people say that they come out of the Urbión well. In the region of Lescun they say that *Yona-Gorri*—Mari—who lives on Anié Peak (Auñamendi), hurls them forth from her cave. In Tolosa they say that Mari crosses the sky seated on a horse-drawn chariot during storms, directing the clouds. The mere appearance of this spirit usually signals the next storm.

Mari rewards the faith of those who believe in her. Some travelers who wanted to cross the mountain of Atxorrotx, in Escoriaza (Eskoriatza), found themselves instantaneously at the end of their journey, a miracle that they attributed to their belief in that spirit.

Mari helps those who invoke her. If someone calls out her name three times in a row, saying *Aketegiko Dama*, "Lady of Aketegui," she perches on their head, as they say even today in the region of Cegama (Zegama).

On a number of occasions, someone asked advice of Mari and her predictions turned out to be accurate and beneficial. Thus, the ironmonger of Iraeta saw that his foundry was not working and presented himself to Mari in the cave of Amboto. She explained the cause and the remedy for the malfunction, and the ironmonger was able to get his factory working again. A similar case occurred in the foundry of Zubillaga, and thanks to the oracle of Amboto, production was able to start up again.

In the fourteenth century she must have been consulted in difficult times, as implied by an event related in the aforementioned *Livro dos Linhagens* by Pedro de Barcellos. In it, we read the following:

After some time this Don Diego López went out to do battle against the Moors, and they captured him and took him prisoner to Toledo. And his son Iñigo Guerra was very upset about his imprisonment, and he went to consult with the earth spirits about how they could get him out of prison. And they said that they did not know of any way except to go into the mountains and find their mother (the mysterious lady of the mountain whom Don Diego López de Haro had married) and ask for her advice. And he went there alone, riding his horse, and he found her on top of a peak, and she said to him: "My son Iñigo Guerra, come to me, because I know well why you have come." And he went to her and she said: "You come to ask me how to get your father out of prison." Then she called to a horse that was running free on the mountain by its name, saying to him Pardal, and she put on the bridle and told her son not to use any force to unsaddle it or unbridle it, and not to feed or give it water to drink or shoe it; and she told him that this horse would last him for the rest of his life, and that he would never ride it into any battle that he would not win, and that he should mount it and that he would arrive that very day in Toledo in front of the door of his father's prison, and that he should dismount there and, finding his father in a corral, he should take him by the hand, and pretending as though he wanted to speak with him, he should gradually lead him to the door where the horse was waiting, and that when they got there they should both climb on and before nightfall they would reach their home. And so it was.

The motif of the mysterious transporting of Don Diego López de Haro from the prison of Toledo to Bizkaia on Mari's horse appears today in the village of Dima (Bizkaia), where a soldier from the Iturriondobeitia farmstead was transported instantaneously from the faraway land of the Moors by the magic of Sugoi or Culebro that lived in the cave of Balzola.[76]

The Cult of Mari — A person who makes an offering to Mari each year will not see hail fall on his crops (Córtezubi (Kortezubi)). The best offering that one could make to her was without a doubt to take a ram to her cave. In many legends this animal appears to be Mari's favorite.

In a legend from Aya (Aia) they speak of the ups and downs that took place on a pilgrimage the shepherds made to Mari's cave in Amboto to keep hail or other storms from harming their flocks.

According to another legend, on May 3 the people of Muguiro (Mugiro) would march in a procession to one of Mari's caves located not far from there, and the village priest would celebrate Mass at the entrance. The legend adds that if Mari was in the cave during the ceremony, no hail would fall in the region during the following year.

It is also said that the priest of Isassondo (Itsasondo) would climb up to Murumendi once every seven years to celebrate Mass in front of the cavern where Mari appears.

In the grotto of Arpeko Saindua (Bidarray (Bidarrai)), every year they celebrate a pilgrimage on the day of the Trinity. The petrified young girl who is worshipped there is invoked in cases of skin and eye diseases, and she effects her cures through the water that drips along the surface of that stalagmite statue. Her devotees make offerings of candles (which are burned in front of the supposed image of the saint), coins and crosses, and even articles of clothing that were worn by the sick person, which are placed in that same cave mentioned above.

The custom of depositing coins in the caves as offerings meant for the spirit living there was widespread in pre-Christian times. As for the Basque Country, Roman coins have been found in caves in Istúritz (Izturitze), Santimamiñe, Sagastigorri, and Covairada. What the worshippers do today in the grotto of Zelharburu (Arpeko Saindua), therefore, seems to be a carry-over from pagan times.

In other places in the country as well, something similar is practiced, not in caves, however, but out in the open. Thus, in the Aralar mountains, when a shepherd loses a sheep, he offers a gift of money to

Saint Michael and puts it on top of the peak called Amabirjiña Arri, "Stone of the Virgin Mary," located near the meadow of Igaratza.

In the fourteenth century the lords of Bizkaia would deposit the entrails of a cow on a peak in Busturia as an offering to their ancestor Mari. The afore-mentioned Count Don Pedro de Barcellos attests to this in his book, *Livro des Linhagens*, as follows:

> In Bizkaia they said and still say today that the mother of Iñigo Guerra is the witch or caster of spells of Bizkaia. And as a sign of sacrifice to this spirit, whenever the lord of Bizkaia is in a village called Vusturio, all the entrails of the cows killed in his house are placed outside the village on a peak, and the next morning nothing is to be found, and they say that unless this was done harm would come during that day and night to one of the squires of his house or to something of his that would cause him great distress. And until the death of Don Juan the One-Eyed, the lords of Bizkaia always observed this practice, and some people tried to see what would happen if this were not done, and bad things happened.

Proper Behavior in the Dwelling of Mari — A person wishing to consult Mari or visit her must follow certain rules, these being:

1) You must address her with the familiar pronoun *tú* (you).

2) You must leave her cavern in the same way you entered, that is, if you entered facing inside, you must also leave facing inside (walking backward). This rule is similar to that followed, traditionally, when the soul of a dead person approaches you, to wit: always keep it in front of you.

3) You must not sit down while in the dwelling of Mari.

Commandments of Mari — This spirit condemns lying, theft, pride, and boasting, failure to keep one's word, failure to respect others, and failure to help others. Those who disobey are punished by the deprivation of loss of what they lied about, or stole, or boasted about, etc. It is a common saying that Mari supplies her pantry at the expense of those who deny what is and those who affirm what is not: *ezagaz eta baiabaz*, "with denial and with affirmation."

A shepherd was pasturing his flock of sheep in Murumendi. He got thirsty and started wandering around the mountain in search of a spring. He approached the mouth of a cave and there he saw an elegantly dressed young woman who asked him: "What are you looking for, good man?"

"I'm looking for something to quench my thirst, young miss."

"Water? You must mean cider." Immediately, that young lady held out a beautiful jug full of cider and gave it to the shepherd to drink. As soon as he tasted it, he said:

"Excellent cider. What kind of apples is it made from?"

"With the apples that Lord Montes of Ikasteguieta gave to no," answered the young girl of the cave, implying by this that they were apples whose existence their owner had denied.

There's a proverb that says: *Ezai emana ezak eaman*, "What is given to no, no takes away." *Ezai eman*, "to give to no," is to deny the truth and fail to help others.

Sanctity of Mari's Dwelling Place — Anyone who enters the caverns of Mari without being invited or who improperly takes something belonging to her is immediately punished or threatened with punishment. A boy who stole a golden canteen that was lying beside the cave of Amboto was taken from his house that same night, disappearing forever.

Some hunters who threw stones into the chasm of Gaiztozulo, which is one of the dwelling-places of Mari in the Oñate (Oñati) region, were immediately carried away by a gust of wind and a cloud that came out of the chasm.

A woman stole a golden comb from the cave of Otsibarre (Camou (Gamue)), and on that same night some property or a field belonging to her was completely covered with stones.

Punishments and Spells — Mari frequently punishes disobedience by causing the delinquents inner turmoil. She also punishes by taking something that belongs to the guilty parties. If they are shepherds, Mari takes one of their rams.

The most extravagant punishment that Mari sends to villages is hail. She herself or her son Mikelats launches storm clouds from the subterranean world, and she herself or some subordinate spirit, Odei and Eate among them, directs them from valley to valley and from mountain to mountain.

According to several legends, to avoid hailstorms and other disasters, in ancient times people resorted to the celebration of masses and casting spells beside the mouth of certain caverns.

If you cannot prevent the formation of the storm, there remains the tactic of counteracting it through gestures and magical formulas. When a man from Ipiñizar (Ceánuri (Zeanuri)) saw a storm cloud approaching, he rolled into the palm of his left hand an herb called *uztai-bedar*, "rainbow herb" or *Rumex Crispus*, and with his right hand he signaled to the storm the direction it should take. In this way, like others who practiced the same spell in other regions, he kept the hailstorm from falling in his neighborhood.

There are some people who believe they are endowed with magical powers and who use certain phrases consecrated by tradition to address the storm spirit (Mari or her subordinates Odei and Eate), sometimes using gestures to signal where rain should fall and where it should hail.

Lightning and thunder are phenomena attributed to Mari or her subordinates. To keep lightning from striking a house, it is customary to place an axe in the doorway with the blade facing up. It is thought that lightning is a polished stone (Neolithic axe) or a piece of flint hurled by the storm spirit. The name *oñeztarri*, "lightning stone," used to designate lightning in the Gernika region, is derived from this belief. This stone or Neolithic axe is considered a symbol of lightning that protects the house where it is found against the harmful effects of the fearsome meteor. But since the Neolithic axe is not well known, today the steel axe is used as an antidote against lightning.

The sickle is the symbol of Mari. It is known that Mari crosses the sky in the form of a fiery sickle, according to certain legends and beliefs. Therefore this instrument is considered a shield against lightning in some regions of the Basque Country and is affixed to the end of a pole in front of the house during storms, to keep lightning from striking there.

From everything we have said about Mari, it can be ascertained that this spirit constitutes a thematic nucleus of or point of convergence for numerous mythic themes of different origins: some of Indo-European origin, others of pre-Indo-European origin. But if we consider some of her attributes (the control of terrestrial forces and of subterranean spirits, her identification with various terrestrial phenomena, etc.) we are inclined to consider her as a symbol—perhaps a personification—of the earth.[77]

Akerbeltz

Among the representatives or substitutes for the subterranean spirit Mari, there exists a figure and a name who managed to concentrate around himself a fairly important group of beliefs and practices. We refer to the figure of the male goat and his name Aker.

In addition to his general characteristics which include living in subterranean regions, having power over many spirits, causing storms, etc., the numen called Akerbeltz has healing powers and a beneficial influence on animals commended to his care or protection, an influence he exercises through his mortal symbol, the male goat.

Therefore in some houses, in an effort to prevent the livestock from being stricken by some disease, they raise a male goat in the stable, and it must be black, that is, *akerbeltz*, "black male goat," in order to enhance its beneficial effect.

Basque witchcraft, which had such great resonance in the sixteenth and seventeenth centuries, endowed this ancient representation of the subterranean numen with particular notoriety. Undoubtedly, within the Basque mythological system, this was merely an episodic event, blown out of proportion through the focus on witchcraft simmering in every country at that time, more intensely in the minds of intellectuals, inquisitors, trial judges, and judges of *autos da fe* than among the simple village people of Sara and Zugarramurdi. But in the statements of those accused of witchcraft, there are frequent allusions to Akerbeltz, a black male goat, and to the *Akelarre*, where the goat presided over covens of witches.[78]

Akerbeltz or a spirit in the form of a male goat was worshipped (or thought to be worshipped) in the *Akelarre* by male and female witches on Monday, Wednesday, and Friday nights. Those attending danced and offered loaves of bread, eggs, and money to the numen. Judging by the description of certain actions and beliefs attributed to them in *autos da fe*, it could be said that they represented a clandestine movement constituting a crystallization of the opposition against Christianity as well as against the reigning social order officially recognized in the country, though this may have been little more than an attitude planted in the minds of the supposed witches by the questions of their judges.

A number of sites have been identified as places for the gathering of witches: the *Akelarre* in Zugarramurdi, Larrune (Larrun), Jaizkibel, Irantzi (Oyarzun (Oiartzun)), Pullegui (Pullegi) (Oyarzun (Oiartzun)), the *Mairubaratza* (cromlech) of Ameztoia (Oyarzun (Oiartzun)), Mandabiitta (Ataun), the *Akelarre* of Mañaria, Garaigorta (Orozco (Orozko)), Petralanda (Dima), Eperlanda (Múgica (Muxika)), Akerlanda (Gautéguiz of Arteaga), Abadelaueta (Echagüen (Etxaguen)), Urkiza (Peñacerrada (Urizaharra)), etc.

The *Akelarre* of Zugarramurdi is a plain located in front of the entrance of the cavern called *Akelarren-Leze*, "cave of the meadow of the male goat." It is believed that in that site and in that cavern witches gathered in ancient times. In the vestibule of the cave, slightly above the level of the floor, there is a small opening in the wall like a window which, according to legend, is the seat where, in the form of a male goat, the devil received the male and female witches.

The same cavern has on the eastern side another wider entrance called *Sorginen Leze*, "cave of the witches." Here, each year on the fourth day of the festival of the village's patron saint (August 15) they celebrate a traditional ceremony organized by the elders of the community. For this ceremony, two of the elders buy one or two rams on the morning of that day, slaughter them inside the cave, and roast them on a bonfire which they light on the spot. At noon the old people of the village gather in the cave and distribute the roast meat and eat it with bread and wine. Each one pays for his fair share. Afterwards, linked together by their hands or by handkerchiefs, they all form a long file and leave the cavern. They continue in this way until they reach the home of the priest, where they dance, and then they move to the town square where they dance the *sokadantza* (a line dance).

The numen Akerbeltz, who appears mainly as a protector of cattle and a leader of witches, may have an antecedent in the pre-Christian Pyrenean spirit Aherbelste. Sacaze, in his work *Inscriptions antiques des Pyrénées*, says of the latter: "D'après un linguiste, Aherbelste signifierait *bouc* dans son radical, et *noir* dans sa terminaison" (According to a linguist, Aherbelste would mean "mouth" in its root, and "black" in its ending).[79]

Ekhi

In Basque, the sun is called by the names *eguski* (Tolosa), *iguzki* (Sara), *eguzku* (Roncal), *ekhi* (Liguinaga (Liginaga)), and *iki* (Bardos (Bardoze)).

In Ataun, they call the solar light *euzki* and the star *euzkibegi*, "eye of the sun." In Berástegui (Berastegi) they call the star *Jainkoaren-Begi*, "eye of God."

In some villages they greet the sun by saying *agur*, "goodbye," when she is in the West. In the region of Vergara (Bergara) they address it, "*Eguzki amandrea badoia bere amangana*," "Grandmother Sun is going home to her mother," implying that she is retiring into the bosom of the earth. The sun is regarded, therefore, as the daughter of the earth.

In the region of Mañaria they say that the mother of the sun is Andre Mari, meaning the Virgin Mary. But earlier in that region the name Andre Mari may have been used to refer to the earth herself personified, that is, to the numen Mari, as is still the case in several villages in Gipuzkoa and Navarre.

The epithets "blessed" and "holy" are applied to Grandmother Sun. In Rigoitia (Errigoiti), when she is about to go down in the West they say to her, "Eguzki santa bedeinkatue, zoaz zeure amagana" (Holy, blessed sun, go to your mother).

In addition to her natural attributes, the sun possesses the ability to frighten away evil spirits that exercise their power in the world at night. Certain kinds of witches are frozen in place if they are surprised by the sun before they put away the tools of their trade. There are categories of *lamias* that lose their power and their influence on men as soon as they are touched by the rays of the sun. One *lamia* left her golden comb at the entrance of the abyss of Mondarrain. A shepherd picked it up and carried it away. The *lamia* followed him down the mountain, demanding her comb. She almost had him in her hands when the first rays of the sun peeking over the horizon touched the clothing of the shepherd. Then the *lamia* said this to him: "Eskerrak emaitzok Iuzkiari" (Give thanks to the sun), and she withdrew into her cave.

Beliefs and Rituals of the Solstice — Given the sacred character of the sun in the conceptual world of the Basques, it is not surprising that many beliefs and customs of Indo-European solar mythology have become associated with the idea and with the word used to refer to the diurnal star in the Basque Country.

Thus, certain solstice festivals here have the characteristics of a solar cult. It is said that the sun comes up dancing on Saint John's morning; that baths taken on this morning and the morning dew on this day keep you from getting sick during the year; that branches of hawthorn, ash, hypericon, flowering fern, etc., placed in the doors and windows, and flowers and herbs laid down as a carpet at the threshold of the main door to the house on that day protect the home against lightning; that flowers gathered for Saint John, used to make an infusion, serve to cure certain illnesses, etc. Belonging to the same group of customs is the practice of making bonfires in front of houses and at crossroads on Saint John's Eve; the practice of jumping through these fires to avoid skin diseases; the practice of all the members of the family chanting prayers together while circling the fire, always with the fire on their left; the custom of taking handfuls of herbs lit in these fires to sown fields in order to frighten away evil spirits and avoid plagues and infestations in crops; the practice of planting the so-called tree of Saint John in the public square, a tree that must not be reclaimed by its owner even when it has been dug up against his will; the wearing of crowns of evergreens and herbs by pilgrims visiting certain hermitages of Saint John; the custom of passing people with hernias three times through a split formed in an oak tree to heal the condition, etc.

Other rites are still practiced at the winter solstice by the Basque people. Among these are the fires that are still lit at the end of the year in some villages; the *Gabonzuzi*, or Yule log, the trunk that is burned in the fireplace at Christmas; the purification of domestic animals by making them walk over that log; the ritual blessing of bread on Christmas Eve by the father of the family; the gathering of the first moisture that falls after midnight on New Year's Eve.

Circles, Swastikas, Thistle Flowers, and Other Symbols — On monuments of popular Basque art we frequently see certain signs that seem to represent the sun and that probably had their origin in the solar cult: signs in the form of a simple circle, concentric circles, wheels with rectilinear and curved radii, pentagonal stars, swastikas, oviform signs, rosettes, etc.

The most ancient of these monuments discovered so far date from the Roman epoch. Examples are the funerary stone of Urbina in Basabe on which is engraved a wheel with curved radii; those of Ibernalo (Santa Cruz de Campezo (Santikurutze Kanpezu)) and of the Institute of Vitoria with rosettes; the *tetraskelion* or *lauburu* [traditional Basque symbol] in the Pamplona museum, the stone of Santa Cara, etc.

Although in historical periods these signs have been used frequently as mere decorative elements, there are cases in which they have represented the sun in the consciousness of their sculptors, even in our day. We could offer no other interpretation to the figures of wheels, rosettes, circles, etc., associated with figures of the moon or which are paired with the moon on various monuments from the Middle Ages as well as from modern times.

Here it is reasonable to ask what is the value and precise meaning of the solar symbol in the Basque cultural environment or traditional way of thinking. In many cases it is a simple decorative motif; such is the lot of all symbolic figures. But the fact that they are sometimes substituted for the radiated circle of the monstrance (*Iduski-Saindu*, "holy sun"), whose religious meaning cannot be questioned as it is the receptacle used to expose the consecrated Host to veneration by the faithful, leads us to attribute sacred meaning to the solar symbols in Basque art.

The character of the solar symbol that the Basque peasant of our day places over the main door of the house may also contribute to our understanding of the meaning of these emblems. We refer to the flower of the wild thistle (*Carlina acaulis*). It is designated by several different names, one of which is *eguzkilore*, which means sunflower, and it represents this star in the mind of those who use it. Placed in the same location occupied by the circle of the monstrance or the rosette or the solar wheel in some ancient houses and regarded by the current inhabitants as a representation of the diurnal star, it performs the same mystical functions attributed to the sun. It is believed, for example, that the sun frightens away evil spirits, and a certain kind of witches, a certain category of *lamias*; the same power is attributed to its symbol, that is, the flower of the wild thistle. That is why this flower is nailed above the door: to prevent the intrusion of evil spirits, witches, and the numina of disease, storm, and lightning.

Through what has been said, then, we can glimpse the sacred character and meaning of this symbol in its different forms of natural flower (thistle), rosette, cross with petal-shaped arms, etc.

Considerations based on solar mythology must have influenced the genesis of the custom, practiced even in our day, of orienting buildings so that the principle façade faces east, a custom whose traces are still seen in old houses in Sara, Ataun, and other regions. The huts of shepherds are oriented the same way in many sheepfolds, and in Ataun we have heard it said that this is healthier for the shepherd.

In medieval tombs, the east-west orientation (head facing west and feet facing east) is common. And in Neolithic dolmens we find the same custom, which in this case must correspond to the same solar beliefs and myths as in other countries.[80]

Ilazki

The moon is called *illargi, iratargi, iretargi, idetargi, ilazki, argizai,* and *goiko*, depending on the region.

It is possible that the name *illargi*, which according to some means light of the dead (from *il*, "dead," and *argi*, "light"), is related to the belief that the moon illumines the souls of the deceased. It is also believed that wax, whose name *argizai* coincides with one of the names of the moon, provides light for the ancestors in the family sepulcher. On the other hand, it is possible that the names *iretargi* and *idetargi* are etymologically related to the names of the nocturnal spirits Ireltxu, Iritxu, Iruztargi, and Idittu, whose apparitions are mentioned in several legends of Bizkaia. But these linguistic speculations do not yet allow us to reach firm conclusions in the area of our mythology.

According to popular belief, the fate of souls of the dead is related to the moon. This seems to derive from the belief that dying during the waxing moon is considered to be a good omen for the soul in the afterlife. But it is problematic whether the name *argi*, used to refer to the souls of the dead, has any relation with the names of the moon.

The moon is of feminine gender and is referred to that way in phrases addressed to her. She is called grandmother, as is the sun. When she rises over the eastern mountains, they say: "*Illargi amandrea, zeruan ze berri?*" "Grandmother Moon, what news from the sky?" In Mañaria, they told us that, according to popular belief in that region, the mother of the moon is the earth.

She has, in a certain way, a sacred character, since in some places they teach the children that the moon is the face of God, and in others they pray a *Salve Regina* when they see her rise.

In Ceráin, they greet the moon, saying: "*Illargi amandre santue, Jainkok bedeinkautzala; nere begi ederrak gaitzik ez deiola; ikusten duen guzik ala esan deiola,*" "Holy Grandmother Moon, may God bless you; may my astonished eyes bring no harm to you; may all who see you speak to you in the same way."

It seems that one day a week—Friday—was consecrated to her: *Ostiral* (from the root *Irargi*, "moon") which means Friday, pairs up with *Ostegun* (from *Egu*, "diurnal light") meaning Thursday. One of the names for Monday—*Ilen*—seems to be also related to the name of the moon, as is Sunday—*Igande*—which corresponds to the full moon.

The magical objects that may have belonged to bewitched persons must be burned on Friday in the moonlight at a crossroads. Friday is the day of choice for gatherings of male and female witches.

In certain villages, it was customary to go out into the moonlight to dine on soups made from millet.

As in many other countries, here too they attribute to her an influence over plants and animals, different influences according to the phases of the satellite. Thus, it is thought that the tree cut down when the moon is waxing (especially at low tide) gives good combustible wood, while one cut down in the waning moon gives off little heat; that people or animals conceived when the moon is waxing are of the masculine sex, and those conceived when the moon is waning turn out to be female; that when the moon is waning you should cut trees whose wood is to be used for constructions and the making of furniture and tools.

Regarding the effects of the cutting down of trees, Friday (on occasion, also Wednesday) is equated with the waning of the moon. For other cases it is equated with the waxing.

Wheat, corn, and potatoes should be planted while the moon is waning. If these are planted when the moon is waxing, the plant grows larger but the grain is smaller and less abundant. This drawback can be avoided, however, by making sure that the planting is done at low tide.

Certain operations are contraindicated on Fridays as well as on holidays. For example: starting an important job, taking the flock to the mountain, extracting honey from the hives, hiring servants or persons for permanent service and bringing them into the home, getting married, cutting fingernails, going to mass or carrying out a purification ceremony.[81]

Urtzi, In

Among the myriad of Basque names, beliefs, and myths there are numerous elements from Indo-European mythology, for example, those referring to the celestial divinity—that is, the deified firmament.

According to the itinerary of Aymeric Picaud, contained in a twelfth-century codex from Santiago de Compostela, in that period the Basques used the word *Urcia* to refer to God. It is possible that in this case Picaud misinterpreted what the Basques said to him and that *Urcia* no longer had the meaning he attributed to it. But that term seems to be an element, as the name of a divinity, in several words that have maintained their religious content down to the present day. I refer to words used to express the light from the sky, the firmament, lightning, thunder, and the dawn, such as *urzondo*, "dawn," *orzondo*, "dawn," *iurtziri*, "noise from the sky, thunder," *ortzi*, "brightness in the sky," *ortziri*, "thunder," *ostiri*, "firmament," *ihuzturi*, "lightning, thunder," *ozkar*, "thunder." In these words, the roots *urz, urtz, ortz, ost* mean the light from the sky or the deified firmament to which they dedicate a day of the week—Thursday—as derived from its Basque name *Ortzegun* (from *ortz*, "sky" and *egun*, "day"). In this the Basques followed the procedure of the ancient Indo-Europeans, not only because they too came to identify the divinity *Dyeus*, "sky," with the spirit of thunder and lightning, but also because they dedicated the day Thursday to the sky or to the light from the sky, which was the supreme divinity.

From the above we can deduce that a divinity called Urte, Orte, or Ost, the personification of the sky or celestial light, was worshipped by the Basques. They attributed the formation of storms to that divinity, as is seen from the Basque names for thunder, lightning, lightning-bolt, and hail. Thus, several names come to mind, such as *ortziri* and *ortzantz* (the sound of *ortz*); *ozme*, "lightning," *ihuzturi*, "lightning-bolt, thunder," *ozti, osti*, "storm."

It is possible that another name for this divinity was *Egu*, since in several regions of the Basque Country, Thursday is called *Eguen*, which seems to mean "from celestial light" or "from the sun."

From some of the names for lightning, thunder, and hail it can be inferred that the sky was also referred to by the word *in*. Thus, the word for "thunder" in Ataun, *inusturi*, corresponds to *ortziri*; "thunder" is *ozkar* in Arratia, *ozkarri* in Zumárraga, but *iñar* in Esteribar, while "lightning-bolt" is *inhar* in Labourd and *inhaza* is "lightning" in Tardets (Atharratze). Belonging to this circle of names are *inhazü*, "lightning, lightning-bolt," *iñetasi*, "hailstone," *iñistue, iñizitue*, "lightning bolt," *iñatazi*, "hail," *iñastura*, "lightning, lightning-bolt, rain of stars," *indriska*, "cloudburst," *intz, inontz*, "dew." In each of these the root *in* occupies the place that the roots *ortz, urtz*, and *ost*, all of which mean "sky," occupy in words with analogous meanings. It is possible that this old root served to form the name *Inko*, which is used today in some regions of the Basque Country for the name of God.

Probably the use of the name *odai* to express "sky" is more recent, as is the use of Odei to refer to the storm-spirit; these are words that did not spread to many topics, but were only used to convey certain beliefs that had previously belonged to to the circle of *in* and *urtz*.

The beneficent rains of springtime, called *ostebi*, "rain from heaven," are attributed to this divinity. Collected at the top of Mount Ereñusarre, this rain is used to cure skin diseases.

Certain names for lightning, such as *oneztarri, tximistarri*, and *ozpinarri* (probably *ozkar, ozkarri*, and *inhar*, as well) which mean "lightning stone," correspond to an ancient myth known widely in European countries in which lightning is a special stone (Neolithic axe, knife, or point of flint) that sinks down to the depth of seven states or levels upon falling to the earth. After seven years it slowly begins to rise one state per year until after seven years it reaches the surface. From then on it protects the house where it is found against evil spirits or *Aide-Gaizto*, which is lightning itself. This myth includes the Indo-European idea of Thor's hammer and Jupiter's arrows.

In some places in the Basque Country, however, it is thought that lightning is made of bronze; in others they say it is made of iron. The current custom of placing steel axes with the sharp edge facing upward on thresholds during storms in order to protect houses from lightning derives from the veneration of the stone axe and belief in its supernatural powers. Before the discovery of steel axes, those made of bronze must have served the same function: in the entrance to the cave of Zabalaitz (in the mountains of Aizkorri), an axe from the bronze age was found stuck in the floor of the cave with the blade facing up.[82]

KIXMI, OR THE TWILIGHT OF THE GODS

The myths and their characters respond to the demands of human logic as it seeks to explain the world and its phenomena.

Basque myths can serve as data for anyone trying to reconstruct the world of representations of the ancient people of the Pyrenees. But our main purpose has been to describe a fraction of the contemporary mentality.

In this brief treatise we have collected data, whether or not it has been inspired by ancient Basque mythological conceptions, that has come to us on the margins of Christian beliefs or joined with them through historical congruence. But not all. For example, we have not taken the time to consider certain numens, such as those grouped together with Eate, Odei, and Mikelats, because many of the themes referring to them fluctuate among one group of characters and another and overlap, moreover, with thematic areas already described or sketched. Even these are dispersed and found today in fragmented condition, as incoherent elements of one or more systems dismembered over time. That is why it is so difficult to achieve restorations that can be considered valid.

The data documented in the preceding chapters appears to be endorsed by tradition and, furthermore, to be linked to the most wide-spread thematic nuclei in the country.

The modern Basque speaks of these themes and characters as belonging to a world that disappeared with the coming of Christianity, although in certain backwaters untouched by the tide of the last few centuries many vestiges of ancient times have survived.

In Zamakola (Dima, Bizkaia) they told me that the old spirits were banished by the bells of Christian hermitages. My informants from Sara (Labourd) assured me that the dominant subterranean spirits of the ancient world were exterminated when the churches and hermitages were built.

The introduction of Christianity and the consequent disappearance of the pagan myths form the central theme of a legend that is widespread among the Basque people. According to one of its versions originating in Ataun, where I heard it many times during my childhood, the pagans were enjoying themselves one day on Argaintxabaleta Hill in the Aralar mountains, when they saw a luminous cloud moving toward them from the east. Frightened by the phenomenon, they consulted a wise elder and took him to that site so he could contemplate the mysterious cloud and tell them what it meant. The old man told them, "The *Kixmi* is born and the end of our race has come; throw me over that precipice." *Kixmi*, which in their language meant monkey, was the name the pagans used to refer to Christ. Then, followed by the miraculous cloud, they all ran toward the west, and when they came to the small valley of Arraztaran, they hurriedly entombed themselves beneath a huge gravestone, that has been called *Jentillarri* (stone of the pagans) from that day forward, the very dolmen of that name that I explored years later in the company of Drs. Aranzadi and Eguren. Thus did paganism come to an end, according to legend.

The introduction of Christianity was, undoubtedly, a slow process. It did not destroy all the elements of the ancient religion. In some cases it preserved the old forms, filling them with a new spirit, as we have had occasion to observe in the preceding chapters. But later the new religion was accepted and zealously practiced for centuries until the present day. Now that the Basques are being faced with new modes of economic, social, and political life, they seem also to be disconnecting themselves from the Christian ideal and elaborating a new world of representations, a new concept of life associated with these new ways, relegating the old values to the marginal zones of their existence.

Notes

1. José Miguel de Barandiarán, *Fragmentos folklóricos. Paletnografía vasca*, 12.

2. Ibid.

3. Ibid., 13.

4. Ibid.

5. Ibid., 57–58.

6. Ibid., 58.

7. Ibid., 13.

8. Ibid., 12.

9. Ibid., 13

10. Ibid., 13–14.

11. J. M. de Barandiarán, "Creencias," *Anuario de Eusko-folklore* 1:86.

12. J. M. de Barandiarán, *Fragmentos folklóricos*, 14.

13. Ibid.

14. Ibid.

15. Ibid., 22–23.

16. Ibid., 26.

17. Ibid., 28.

18. Ibid., 25–26.

19. Ibid., 27.

20. Ibid., 26–27.

21. Ibid.

22. Ibid.

23. Ibid., 27

24. Ibid., 28.

25. Ibid., 31.

26. Ibid., 33.

27. Ignacio María Barriola, *La medicina popular en el País Vasco*, 82–83.

28. J. M. de Barandiarán, *Fragmentos folklóricos*, 39–40.

29. Resurrección M. de Azkue, "Los santos," *Euskalerriaren yakintza*, I. Madrid, 1935, 299–301.

30. Leopold von Schroeder, *Arische Religion*, Vol. 1, 457. Alluding to the oak, he says: "Dem Donnergott gehört dieser Baum auch sonst bei den arischen Völkern; so bei den Römen, so bei den Germanen, bei den Kelten, bei den alten Preussen und wohl auch bei Slaven. Es ist nicht unwahrscheinlich, dass dies schon in der Urzeit der Fall war."

31. Barriola, *Medicina popular*, 26–27.

32. J. M. de Barandiarán, *Fragmentos folklóricos*, 54–55.

33. Ibid., 40.

34. Ibid., 9–10.

35. Ibid., 42.

36. Ibid., 29–30.

37. Ibid., 53–54.

38. von Schroeder, *Arische Religion*, Vol. 2, 339.

39. See pages 54, 61, 62, 91, 130, 143, 165, 168, and 274 of Seligmann's work.

40. *Eusko-folklore* (Vitoria) no. 1 (1921): 1–2. In traditional tales the earth is thought to extend infinitely far in all directions. Legends are told in which the protagonists attempt to reach the end of the world, a vain undertaking, according to popular belief, which assumes the surface of the earth to be without limit. Because of this, those who undertook such projects traveled over vast distances without achieving their goals. Strange adventures or events bring such expeditions to an end, inevitably awakening a feeling of sympathy and wonder in the audience.

Not even the Sun touches the limits of the world when, at the end of its journey, it reaches the western or "scarlet" seas (*itxasgorrieta*) where it sinks down into the womb of its mother the Earth (according to an informant in Elosua), from which it would rise in the morning.

The traveler who journeyed through the worlds (*munduz-mundu*) with his rooster, whose crowing announced the dawn, did not get any farther than the country in which men managed to make the Sun rise every morning by pounding on the rocks with their sticks (*Relato de Atáun* (Story of Ataun)).

41. *Eusko-folklore* (Vitoria), no. 13 (1922): 1–2. According to beliefs we have compiled in towns in Gipuzkoan Goyerri (Goierri) and in Abadiano (Abadiño, province of Bizkaia), the mountains are growing.

We have heard peasants from the Vitoria region say that the hill on which the towns of Arechavaleta (Aretxabaleta) and Gardélegui (Gardelegi) are built has been gradually growing even in our times, to such an extent that the elders have been able to perceive the phenomenon. This seems additionally plausible to them because this hill is crowned by an alluvial terrace similar to the one that appears at its foot, forming the bottom of the valley.

The geologist Ramón Adán de Yarza, in his work *Descripción física y geológica de la provincia de Alava* (Madrid, 1885), says: "The old men of Salvatierra [Agurain] assure us that from their village today they can make out the bell towers of some towns of the region, in particular that of Audicana [Audikana], which were formerly hidden by the intervening hills." He adds that, according to references published in the *Acts* of the Spanish Society of Natural History, in 1847 the citizens of Salvatierra could barely see the tip of the weathervane of the belltower of Zalduendo (Zalduondo), whereas twenty-three years later they could see the entire village.

There have been many crags moved by giants, as can be seen in numbers 26 and 27 (1922) of *Eusko-folklore*. Among these: Leziako-Aitza in Placencia (Soraluze); Txoritekoa, in Ceráin; Aitzorrotza, in Ursuarán; Arrabiola, in Segura; Sansonarri, in Tolosa; the crags of Ondarraitz, in Hendaya (Hendaia); the mountain called Peña de Aya, in Oyarzun, and Arraspia, in Ainhoa.

42. *Eusko-folklore*, no.1:2; *Eusko-folklore*, no. 2: 6–7. Popular narratives indicate different mountains as the origin of many storm clouds. The most famous are: Gorbea, Amboto, Arreo, Urbión, Beriaín, Aizkorri, Muru, Txindoki, Aralar, Apanize, and Ori. In such places there are pits or wells from which the spirit of the storms (Odei, Eate, or Mari) sends out storm clouds heavy with water and hail, accompanied by lightning and thunder.

Inside the earth, many spirits of Basque mythology have their dwelling, especially those that take anthropomorphic and animal forms (*Eusko-folklore*, 2nd and 3rd series, Sare, 1947–1949; San Sebastián, 1954–1959). Hoping to make their way to Escoriaza (Eskoriatza), some shepherds tried to get past an anthropoid inhabiting the mountain of Atxorrotx. A strong gust of wind, which was Mari (the principal figure of subterranean mythology) blew them from one end of the cavern to the other (*Eusko-folklore*, 3rd series, no. 3). In a legend of Amézqueta (Amezketa) it is said that a furious storm always accompanies the spirit Mari when she emerges from the subterranean regions or goes from one mountain to another (*Eusko-folklore*, 3rd series, no. 3).

We will return to this matter of Mari and the storms when we discuss the functions of this character.

43. J. M. de Barandiarán, "Contribución al estudio de la mitología vasca," in *Homenaje a Fritz Krüger*, vol. 1 (Mendoza, 1952), 104–05. [See also] J. M. de Barandiarán, "La religion des anciens Basques," in *Compte rendu analytique de la IIIe session de la Semaine d'Ethnologie religieuse*. Enghien, 1923.

44. When the Sun sets, they would say "*Agur*" (a form of greeting) in Mañaria when I visited that region in 1929 and 1930 to explore Silibranka, Atxuri, Salleunta, and San Martín, caverns with archeological remains that are mentioned in a number of legends. And in addition they addressed a few words to it, calling it "Santa Clara," which in Basque, according to the songs dedicated to Santa Clara in Ondarroa, means *Argi*, "light," and affirming that it went to its rest in its mother. In Elosua, they understood this to mean the earth; but in Mañaria they said it was the Virgin Mary. In this regard, it should be pointed out that in some towns they use the name Andra Mari, "Lady Mary," for the Virgin as well as for the other Mari, spirit of the earth or simply earth personified (in Oyarzun (Oiartzun) and in Arano).

45. There are beliefs and legends that link the house to the temple and the cemetery. In many Basque communities they believe it is dangerous to walk around a temple. A woman from Elorrio did so, carrying a child in her arms. Afterwards she heard these words: "Give thanks to the child you're carrying in your arms; if not for that, you would not have lived long." A woman from the Jaulei farmhouse (Berástegui/Berastegi) was turned into a witch because she walked around the church of that town

three times. In Oñate (Oñati) it is believed that if a person walks around a church three times, he will be taken away by the devil. Or anyone who does this will see the dead, as they say in Zaráuz (Zarautz).

The same beliefs apply to cemeteries, according to what I was told in Garay (Garai). Concerning the act of walking around houses, similar beliefs prevail. The act of walking three times around the cemetery or the church seems to be connected with the souls of the deceased. It is they who object to this behavior. Now, the house, or to put it more clearly, the yard around the house, is also regarded as a cemetery; and this was the case in an earlier time. In "Pueblo de Cortezubi. Barrios de Basondo y Terliz," *Anuario de Eusko-folklore,* vol. 5, 1925 (Vitoria), p. 62, I compiled the following data from Cortézubi (Kortezubi, province of Bizkaia): "*Itxusuria* is the name of the gutter around the roof and the strip of soil onto which it empties. This is where they bury children who die without being baptized: this is something all informants have heard. Twenty-five years ago, one of these, Lorenzo de Bengoetxea, witnessed the burial of a child in the *itxusuria* on the left side of the Andikoetzeta house. Another informant, Matías de Aranaz, saw them bury two children in the *itxusuria* of two homes in Rigoitia [Errigoiti], fifty-five years ago.

"People believe that you should not walk around the house three times after the *Aremetako* (Angelus bell), that is, after the ringing of Animas, which is nine o'clock at night in summer, eight o'clock in winter. They say that a man made a bet he could walk around the house three times, but it didn't turn out well for him." (Data from Cortézubi [Kortezubi])

"The custom of burying the unbaptized (children who are not Christian) beneath the eaves of the roof must have been widespread in earlier times, because even in our period we find it, though in a somewhat decadent state, in towns quite distant from each other. In addition to the above-mentioned cases in Cortézubi [Kortezubi] and Rigoitia [Errigoiti], we know of analogous ones in Oyarzun [Oiartzun] (*Anuario de Eusko-Folklore,* vol. V, p. 126), Berriatúa, Motrico (Mutriku), Mendaro, Arecha-valeta [Aretxabaleta, province of Gipuzkoa], Sara, etc.

"A resident of Santa Agueda (Arechavaleta) asked the priest of that parish if there was a place in the cemetery set aside for the cadavers of the unbaptized. He told him there was not. Then the man said that, following an ancient custom, he would bury a child of his who had just died in the *ittukiñpean* or *tellapean* beneath the gutter of his house, and he did so.

"They say in Abadiano that you cannot walk around your house three times at noon; but you can do so if there is a laurel bush planted beside one of the walls of the house. The second part of this superstition is undoubtedly related to another in Oyarzun [Oiartzun], according to which if you don't place a laurel branch on the roof of a newly constructed house, some misfortune will befall the building. For this reason in that same town when something bad happens to a house they say: *Erra-murik gabea duk itxi au* (This house has no laurel).

"In Ataun it is said that you cannot walk around a house at night; but you can if you carry a laurel branch in your hand. Every night a group of spinners met in the farmhouse next to the spa of Erremedio. One night, one of them, named Kataliñ, bet the others she could walk around the house three times. She actually walked around it twice; but the third time she disappeared. After a while, on a bridge now named *Katalinzubi* (Catalina Bridge) which is near the Ertzillegi farmhouse, they heard these words: '*Kataliñ deabruk eaman din*' (The devil took Catalina away). Nothing was ever heard of her again." (From *Eusko-folklore* (Vitoria), series 1, nos. 69 and 70, 1926.

46. Anuario de la Sociedad de Eusko-folklore (Vitoria) Vol. 3, 1923. In this book, describing the funeral rites practiced during the first quarter of this century in different Basque towns, the significance of the tomb each house has in the parish church is frequently mentioned. Here is what we said therein describing the funeral rites of Ataun: "Each house in the parish has its tomb in the church, which is a section of the pavement inside the church itself." Although today there is a common cemetery outside the church, the bodies belonging to the corresponding house or household in an earlier time were buried in that section or area. For that reason each family lights votive candles on their tomb for their ancestors and chants prayers to their souls and dedicates offerings to them. During some church functions they burn candles wound in spiral patterns on the tombs, which is why they are called *eskubillo,* "wax wheels." At other times, especially when the candle is thick or long, they roll it around a square tablet which is supported on four legs. In earlier times the surface was lengthened into a rectangle without legs and imprinted with shapes which, viewed all together, represented a clearly anthropomorphic design: it was called *argizaiola,* "wax board."

47. Alain Fougères. *Les droits de famille et les successions au Pays Basque et en Béarn d'après les anciens textes* (Family Rights and Successions in the Basque Country and in Béarn, According to Ancient Texts) (Bergerac, 1938), p. 89. [See also] J. M. de Barandiarán, "Materiales para un estudio del pueblo vasco: en Liguinaga" (Materials for a Study of the Basque People: in Liguinaga (Liginaga)), *Ikuska* 1 (1947): 126–31 and 177–84; 2 (1948): 9–24 and 78–84; 3 (1949): 33–49; 4 (1950): 2–36.

In Ataun the wife, on moving into her husband's house when she marries, carries offerings and votive candles to the tomb corresponding to her new home on the first Sunday after the wedding. Thus she takes possession of the house, associates herself with its ancestors, and incorporates herself into the family of her husband.

48. "Contribución al estudio de la casa rural y de los establecimientos humanos. I," *Anuario de Eusko-folklore* (Vitoria), Vol. 5, 1925: 25, 62, and 126; and *Eusko-folklore* (Vitoria), 1st series, no. 48 (1924): 47–48.

Concerning the lights and offerings that are placed on the tombs, there exists a very vague belief that they are a tribute made to God in honor of the dead, as I noted in "Creencias y ritos funerarios: Cortezubi," *Anuario de Eusko-folklore* of 1923 (Vol. 3, p. 40). But alongside this belief there is another quite different, as can be observed in the following occurrence that my informant from Cortézubi (Kortezubi), Matías de Aranaz, described to me in the year 1921. I copy it from my lecture, "La religion des anciens Basques," read in session 3 of the Semaine d'Ethnologie Religieuse, celebrated in Tilburg (Holland) in September of 1922:

"There are people who say that the souls of the dead need physical light just as mortals living in the world do (Larrabezua). This is what I was told in Cortézubi (in Bizkaia). Once, the roof of a mine tunnel collapsed in Somorrostro (Ezkerraldea) near Bilbao. The miners were buried beneath the rubble. After a long time the rubble was removed and a miner from Axangiz (Ajangiz, in Bizkaia) was found alive in a hollow. Asked how he had survived for so many years under the rubble, the miner said that during his long existence in that prison, he had only been without light for a single day. That was the day when his mother, blocked by a storm, had been unable to go to the church and light a candle on the family tomb."

The following report from Berástegui (Berastegi) was published In *Eusko-folklore* (1st Series, (1926): 42): "In Berástegui, there are those who believe that the dead need light in order to get to heaven. For this reason it is customary to place lighted candles on the tombs in the church. Today, most people offer such lights only to the Lord. Even so, one of the women questioned told the informant: 'Not long ago in a mine tunnel (I think it was in Bizkaia) a cave-in trapped a group of miners. The mother of one of them lit the candle on the tomb in the church every day; only once did she fail to light it. After a few days, her son was brought out alive from beneath the earth and he said that he had only gone without food, water, and light on a single day. It was the day when his mother had not lit the candle on the tomb.'"

In Ataun, the same belief exists.

I wrote the following about Liguinaga (Liginaga) in *Ikuska* 1949: 35: "For funerals, they no longer take offerings to the church; but until a few years ago, they took two or three loaves of bread. They say that during the funeral service, the loaves lost all their nutritional value, which according to popular belief had been eaten by the soul of the deceased for whom the funeral rites were celebrated. It is also said that the lights burning in the church on such occasions lighted the way for the deceased in the other world."

According to reports from Oyarzun (Oiartzun), Andoain, and Axpe, in these towns it is believed that the souls of the deceased actually eat part of the loaves that are placed as an offering on the tombs during the funeral service and mass. In conformance with this belief, they say in Arachavaleta (Gipuzkoa) that the bread of the offering, after having been left exposed on the tomb, weighs less than before (*Eusko-folklore*, ibid., 43).

49. This is hardly practiced at all now, because straw mattresses are rare.

As for the *andabide* or path that connects the tomb with the home, it is a sacred object traditionally linked to the home, as is the tomb, even if the latter belongs to only a single house whereas the former can be common to several houses.

Regarding this matter, tradition, which is in a state of decay today, has been scrupulously observed throughout the country until very recently. On a certain occasion when the body of a man from Basondo (Cortézubi (Kortezubi)) was taken to the parish church on the occasion of his funeral and to bury him, the poor condition of the road obliged the funeral cortege to cross the property of another household. The owner came out to meet the priest and those carrying the cross and the coffin preceding it to stop them and make them return to the *andabide*. After a brief struggle and argument between the two parties, the cross, the priest, the pallbearers and the entire cortege had to give in and go back through the quagmire they had gone around. According to tradition and belief, the passage of the corpse through a private property creates servitude.

A case similar to this occurred in Ataun, as noted in *Anuario de Eusko-folklore* (Vitoria) 3 (1923): 117.

Bonifacio de Echegaray, "Significación de algunos ritos funerarios del país vasco" (The meaning of certain funeral rites of the Basque Country), *Revista Internacional de los Estudios Vascos* 16 (1925): 94–118, 184–222.

50. After the funeral, it is the custom in many towns for the group of people forming the mourning party to return to the house of death. So it was in Uhart-Mixe, as I was able to verify in 1937 and published later in the following words: "The next-door neighbor, the pallbearers, the children who accompanied the coffin with candles,

the relatives who live far away, and finally, all those who took part in the different activities and services occasioned by the death move on toward the house of death. When they arrive at the door, a neighbor puts some straw on the ground and lights the fire there. Everyone sits around it and recites the Our Father, the Ave Maria, and a Requiem. Then they go in to eat." ("Matériaux pour une étude du peuple basque. A Uhart-Mixe," *Ikuska* (Sare) nos. 6–7 (1947): 174–75).

51. Bonifacio de Echegaray, "La vida civil y mercantil de los vascos a través de sus instituciones jurídicas" (Civil and Mercantile Life of the Basques through Their Juridical Institutions), *Revista Internacional de los Estudios Vascos* 13 (1922): 582–613 and 14 (1923): 27–60. [See also] P. Luis Chalbaud, "La familia como forma típica y transcendental de la constitución social vasca" (The Family as the Typical and Transcendental Form of the Basque Social System), *I Congreso de Estudios Vascos*, 43–64 (n.p., 1918); [and] Nicolás Vicario y Peña, *Derecho consuetudinario de Vizcaya*, 30ff (Madrid, 1901).

52. *Fuero Nuevo de Vizcaya*, article XVI, laws III and IV.

53. "La Tierra," *Eusko-folklore*, 1st Series, no. 2:6–7.

In Ataun, it is believed that the cavern of Agamunda is connected to the kitchen of the Andralizeta farm.

The Moors use a subterranean road to go back and forth between the kitchen of the Ermintatxiki farmstead in Elduayen (Elduain) and another farm in Berástegui (Berastegi), as it is customary to say in those towns.

A cat that was thrown into the cave on Mount Malkorbe (in Elduayen (Elduain)) came out through the kitchen of the Sales farmstead (*Eusko-folklore*, ibid.).

A goat went into a cave in the region of Oyarzun (Oiartzun) and stuck his horns through the kitchen wall of the Bainketa farmhouse (in Baringarate), according to information sent to me by Don Jesús Elósegui.

They say in Ispoure (Izpura) that a subterranean road connects the fortress of Saint Jean Pied de Port (Donibane Garazi) and the Larrea house in that area.

In Ezpeleta they say that there exists a subterranean corridor that goes from the Elizalde house to the mill called Elizaldeko-eyhara.

In the same town they say that between the Meatze pit on Mount Mondarraín and the old building or Juareguí fortress, there's an underground passageway.

In Aizarna, they say that the Amalda cave extends as far as the stable of the Egaña farm.

Not far from Alzola (Altzola) there is a chasm. They say that a sheep that fell into it appeared in the kitchen of the Semeola farm.

It is a traditional saying in the region of Vergara (Bergara) that stones thrown into the chasm of San Marcial fall into the kitchen of the Agorrosin farmhouse.

They told me in Albistur (Albiztur) that the kitchen of the Aldabazar farm is connected with the cave of Arrobigañ located in that town. Aldabazar is an old house with five rooms, at the foot of Intxurre peak, where you can still see the ruins and excavations of an ancient fortress or fortified campground.

We should add to these legendary cases that of the Salturri farm in Mondragón (Arrasate), in the stable of which there is the entrance to a deep cavern.

54. *Anuario de Eusko-folklore* (Vitoria) 3 (1923), passim.

55. J. M. de Barandiarán, "Matériaux pour une étude du peuple basque: à Uhart-Mixe" (Materials for a study of the Basque people: Uhart-Mixe), *Ikuska*, no. 4 ff.

"Materiales para un estudio del pueblo vasco: en Linguinaga," ibid. *Anuaro de Eusko-folklore* 3 (1928). In almost all the towns whose funerary rituals are described in this book, women play an important role in the ceremonies related to the cult of the ancestors.

56. Marcel Nussy Saint-Saëns, *Contribution à un essai sur la coutume de Soule* (Contribution to an Essay on Customs in Soule), 69 (Bayonne, 1942).

57. Regarding the topic of the attributes and functions of Gaueko, here is what we published in "Las iglesias: Rodeo de las iglesias," *Eusko-folklore*, 1st series, no. 70, 1926, translated from Basque:

"They say that in ancient times a large group of spinners would meet every night in the Lauzpeltz farmhouse (now destroyed) in Ataun.

"On one occasion the girl from the farm made a wager with her companions that she would bring water from the spring that exists on the mountain where the Iturriotz farm is located.

"Indeed, the girl took a pitcher and set off toward the spring, while the other spinners stood watching her from the Lauzpeltz doorway in the moonlight.

"From time to time her companions would shout to her: 'Where are you now?'

"'In such and such a place,' she would respond, naming the place where she was.

"'Where are you now?' they would shout from the doorway over and over.

"'I'm in such and such a place,' she would answer again; but her voice sounded weaker and weaker as she moved away.

"'Where are you now?' they repeated.

"And the girl no longer answered.

"The spinners became afraid at the thought that something bad was happening to their friend.

"At that moment a gust of wind blew through the doorway of the Lauzpeltz farmhouse and you could hear these words: *Gaue Gauekontzat eta eune eunezkontzat,* 'The night is for Gaueko (the night spirit) and the day is for the creature of the day.'

"And nothing was ever heard from the girl from Lauzpeltz again."

* * *

A legend from Berástegui (Berastegi) is somewhat similar to the last part of the previous account. It goes like this:

"They say that on Mount Akerkoi there is a chasm where pagans lived in previous times. The people were very much afraid of them.

"On the Elaunde farm lived a young girl whose name was Kattalin. She had the custom of spinning thread in the moonlight.

"One night when the young girl was working beside a window of her house, the pagans came and kidnapped her, crying out these words: 'Night for Gaueko, the night spirit, and the day for the creature of the day; Kattalin of Elaunde belongs to us.' In this way Gaueko used his pagans to punish the spinner."

* * *

A young girl from a farm in Oyarzun (Oiartzun) made a wager that, after the ringing of the Angelus, she would bring water from the spring. And, in fact, she went; but she didn't come right back. Her family members were apprehensive about her long delay. Later on, some drops of blood and the empty pitcher the girl had been carrying fell down through the chimney. She was never heard from again.

* * *

The sad adventure of the daughter of Inhurria in Beyrie is related in many popular stories of Lower Navarre, a devil carrying her away in some versions, while in others it was the Basajaun, the representative of Gaueko who punishes those who make wagers at night (J. M. de Barandiarán, "Matériaux pour un étude du peuple basque: à Uhart-Mixe," in *Ikuska* (Sare), nos. 10–13 (1948): 85–86).

58. "Las iglesias: Rodeo de las iglesias," *Eusko-folklore*, 1st series, no. 70:38; *idem*, 40; "Tradiciones y leyendas. Lurpeko eremuetan: Genios en figura animal," *Eusko-folklore*, 3rd series, no. 2:12.

59. "Las grutas: Animales y monstruos que habitan en las grutas," *Eusko-folklore* (Vitoria) 1st series, no. 11, 1921.

In Bermeo they spoke of the nocturnal spirit called Iditxu or Iritxu who would appear in the form of a small pig that seems to be just within reach of people who travel at night. Anyone who follows him will be fooled because Iditxu leads him through forests, mountains, and caves and finally leaves him in the same place from which they set out, without the traveler gaining anything but disappointment and a weary body.

60. J. Romeu Figueras, "Mitos tradicionales pirenaicos" (Traditional Myths of the Pyrenees), *Pireneos*, nos. 16–17:171.

61. "Brujería y brujas," and "Prakagorri (genio familiar)," *Eusko-folklore* (Vitoria), 1st series, no. 24, 1922. "The extraordinary powers attributed to witches are thought to come either from the magical force of certain ointments and phrases or from certain insects or tiny men who help and serve them in everything.

"These mysterious beings, genuine familiars of the witches, are called *famerijelak* (in Cortézubi) [Kortezubi] . . ., *mamarroak* (Zaráuz) [Zarautz] . . ., *bestemutilak* (Gernika) . . ., *galtxagorriak* (Zaráuz) [Zarautz] . . ." In Orozco they call them *bearreztanak*, in Albistur (Albiztur), *mozorroak* and in Sara, *aidetikako*.

62. "Los monumentos prehistóricos," *Eusko-folklore* (Paris), 1st series, no. 42 (1924): 21ff.

63. Wentworth Webster, *Basque Legends*, 48 (London, 1879); Jean Barbier, *Légendes du Pays Basque*, 27 (Paris, 1931); Resurrección María de Azkue, "Los santos," 363; Julio Caro Baroja, *Algunos mitos españoles*, 47 (Madrid, 1944); J. M. de Barandiarán, "Genios de figura humana o semihumana. Lamin," *Eusko-folklore*, 3rd series, 56ff.

Lami is a thematic nucleus in which numerous motifs of Basque mythology have been concentrated. The representation of the *lamia* as a human figure, except for the feet which are those of a bird, is the predominant one in the Basque Country.

The memory of the *lamias* has left numerous vestiges in the toponymy: Lamindania (the Lacarry (Lakarri) mill), Laminenziluak (caverns of Camou-Cighi), Laminosin (a well in Juxu), Lamuxaín or Lamusin (a ravine in Sara), Lamien-leze (cave of Zugarramurdi), Lamiarri (a crag in Arizcun (Arizkun)), Lamiako (in Vera (Bera), Lamiarrieta (stones in Arizcun (Arizkun)), Lamirain (a ravine in Arano), Lamiarriaga (a place in Endarlaza (Endarlatsa) where *lamias* keep their stones), Lamitegi (a house and property in Bedayo), Lamiategi (a mill in Oñate (Oñati)), Lamiñosín (a well in Ataun), Lamiñeneskátza (a grotto in Mondragón (Arrasate)), Lamiñategi (a ravine in Motrico (Mutriku)), Lamikiz (a household in Marquina (Markina)), Lamindano (a section of Dima), Lamiñerreka (a river in Ceberio (Zeberio)), Lamiñapotsu (a well in Ceànuri (Zeanuri)), Laminazulo (a cavern in Amboto), Lamiaran (a place in Usansolo), Lamiako (a neighborhood near Algorta), etc.

Belief in *lamias* has been common until our times in culturally backward zones or levels of the population. The clash between the traditional and new trends produced an attitude of compromise that appears in the following account:

"My father was from Mendive [Mendibe]. When he was a boy, he would go early in the morning to catechism. Once he saw *lamias* in the road, as he was crossing a river. He told the priest what he had witnessed, and the priest told him: 'All creatures that have a name exist; but keep the secret to yourself, it is not necessary to say that they exist.'" (*Eusko-folklore*, 3rd series, p. 60).

Another attitude of compromise, similar to the former, appears in this other recommendation: "*Direnik ez da sinistu bear; ez direla ez da esan bear*" (You should not believe they exist; you should not say they do not exist).

Lamias live in caves, like that of Maltsoenborda (Urepel (Urepele)), Arrikolezia (Iriberri), Laminazilo (Saint-Martin d'Arberoue (Donamartiri)), Mondarrain (Ezpeleta), Osoloko-koba (Marquina (Markina)), Oarri (Guizaburuaga (Gizaburuaga)), Karkabeta (Ceánuri (Zeanuri)), Supelegor (Orozco (Orozko)), Santimamiñe (Cortézubi (Kortezubi)), etc. They also lived in the rocks of Xeruenborda (Ascain (Azkaine)). More frequently they appear living in the backwater of rivers, in springs and pools, like Laminosine in Juxu, the bridge of Utsalea (St. Pée (Senpere)), the ravine of Irimategui (Marquina (Markina)-Echevarría), called Altzibar, the pond near the grotto of Lezao (in the Encia mountains), etc.

The motif of the theft of the comb from *lamias* is frequent. Here is a formula collected in Ataun, which they use to threaten the thief:

> *Andra Geazi,*
> *Ekatzu nere orrazi;*
> *Bestela galduko ittut*
> *Zure ondorengo azkazi.*

(Lady Engracia, give me my comb; if you don't I'll destroy your future descendants.)

The *lamias* went to houses to ask for or demand food, especially grease, the leftovers from stews, flour, and crumbs from cornbread.

In their relations with human beings, the *lamia* often appears in love with some young man from the neighborhood, a motif that in some versions forms part of the cycle of Mari.

A legend of the *lamia* in love and the young man who plan to get married but can't carry out their plan exists in several versions in different parts of our country. The one set in the Kobaundi cave of Garagarza (Garagartza) (Mondragón (Arrasate)), follows:

"A young man from the Korrione farm went to Kobaundi. There he saw a *lamia*: a beautiful woman, more beautiful than the Christian women on this earth. He fell in love with her.

"The *lamia* gave him her word that she would marry him on the condition that he could guess how old she was.

"The boy explained the situation to a woman from his neighborhood and she promised to find out the age of the young woman of the cave.

"The neighbor went to Kobaundi. She stood at the mouth of the cave with her back to the entrance. She bent over, lowering her head to the level of her knees and stood looking back between her legs.

"The *lamia* came out, and alarmed at seeing this spectacle, she said: 'I'm one hundred and five years old but I've never seen anything like this.'

"Then the neighbor of Korrione went home and told the enamored young man the age of the *lamia*.

"The boy climbed up to the cave and said to the *lamia*: 'You're a hundred and five years old.'

"The *lamia* agreed to marry the boy from Korrione.

"The young man declared his intention to his mother. Fearing that the bride was not a human being, she told her son to go back and look at her feet.

"The young man did so and saw that his fiancée had duck feet. This frightened him and he got sick. Then he died.

"The *lamia* attended the funeral of her fiancé, walking alone up to the door of the Garagarza [Garagartza] church."

* * *

The motif of the *lamia* asking for a man's help seems to be an isolated element, scarcely integrated into the body of legends related to these spirits. In the most frequent case the *lamias* ask the men to send them a woman to help them in childbirth, as in the version from Yábar (Ihabar) collected by D. Resurrección María de Azkue (*Euskalerriaren yakintza*, 2:425), which follows:

"A *lamia* solicited the service of a midwife. The latter agreed to help her and went to the cave of the *lamias*. They told her she should take nothing away from that place and that, on returning home, she should not look back. Her work completed successfully, the midwife picked up a piece of bread; but she could not leave that cave until she had put down what she had stolen. Then the *lamias* gave her an entire loaf and presented her with many precious objects from which she could choose the one she wanted most. She chose a golden comb for carding wool. On returning to her house she had to cross a river, and the *lamia* who was accompanying her made it dry up by striking it with a branch from a tree. Then the midwife looked back to see if the river was still dry. Immediately half of her golden comb went back into the den of the *lamias*."

The preceding legend appears in many places in Vasconia. Versions collected in Esquiule (Eskiula), Lacarry (Lakarri), St. Martin-d'Arberoue (Donamartiri), St.-Pée (Senpere), Zugarramurdi, Ituren, Abaurrea, Yábar (Ihabar), Guizaburuaga (Gizaburuaga), Elanchove (Elantxobe), and Cortézubi (Kortezubi) have been published by a number of ethnographers, as can be seen in *Eusko-folklore*, 3rd series, no. 11, 1958.

Sometimes the *lamia* appears asking a man to rescue her from the cave where she is held prisoner (Ibid., 104–5). In St.-Pée (Senpere) the *lamias* asked for a prayer for one of her companions who was dying (Ibid., pp. 115–16).

The peasants would make an offering of bread, milk, cider, corn, and bacon to the *lamias*, who would show their gratitude by helping them in their work in the field, as can be seen in accounts published in *Eusko-folklore*, 3rd series, no. 11 (1958): 117–20, and in "Matériaux pour une étude du peuple basque: à Uhart-Mixe," *Ikuska* , nos. 10–13 (1947): 87.

* * *

Lamias also appear helping men in different ways: giving them gold or building bridges, like those in Bidarray (Bidarrai), in San Martín de Arrosa (Arrosa) and in Licq (Ligi), or churches in San Martín de Arrosa, in Espés (Ezpeize) and in Arros (Arroze), houses in Larramendi (Juxue) and in Latsa (Ostabat), castles in Gentein (Ordiarp) and in Donamartiri (San Martín de Arberua), the palace of Laustania and the dolmens of Mendive (Mendibe) (*Eusko-folklore*, 3rd series, nos. 11–13).

It should be noted that in the westernmost regions of the country, the building of old bridges is not attributed to *lamias*, but to devils (a change of numen or name in the thematic cluster), and sometimes to pagans or Moors. So is the case in legends related to the bridges of Azalain (Andoain), of Torre-Auzo (Oñate / Oñati), of Urkulu (Salinas de Léniz / Leintz Gatzaga) and Castrejana (Ibid.).

Another aspect of *lamias* is their struggle with men: the latter are at times kidnapped and reduced to slavery by *lamias*, as *lamias* are by men. Finally, men succeed in exiling the *lamias* through religion, with prayers and litanies; the building of Christian hermitages brings an end to the former dominance of the *lamias*. Now it is more frequent to say that the *lamias* and other spirits of traditional mythology were sent into exile by Eibar, that is, by firearms made in that industrial city (*Eusko-folklore*, 1st series, nos. 63 and 64).

64. "VII: Brujería y brujas," *Eusko-folklore* (Vitoria), 1st series, nos. 18–24, 1922. "*Sorgin*" [*Sorguiñ*] is rarely used as the proper name of a specific spirit; it is almost always a generic name designating certain spirits, to which the people attribute different supernatural functions. By extension this name has also been applied to men and women whose conduct seemed extravagant and mysterious to their neighbors.

In Ataun, they say that a conflict arose among some seamstresses about whether or not *sorgines* existed in the world. All were inclined to believe that they did except for one who expressed her incredulity on this matter. She was returning to her house at night, when suddenly some mysterious beings appeared before her, shouting: "*Ez geala, baño bagaittun; Maripetraliñ ez beste guztik emen gaittum*" [sic] (We don't exist, but we do; we are all here, except for Maripetraliñ). On saying this, each *sorgin* pulled one hair from her head, so that the poor seamstress was left completely stripped bald.

The character of these spirits also appears in the following legend from Elorrio:

On a certain occasion a young woman was returning to her house when she heard a cry or *irrintzi*. She answered with the same cry. Then she heard the *irrintzi* again. She answered a second time. And she also replied to a third *irrintzi*. Then the *sorgines* attacked her; nothing was left of her but a few hairs and pieces of clothing.

65. Vinson, Julien, *Folk-lore du Pays Basque*, 43 (Paris, 1883); "II. Los genios y los gigantes," *Eusko-folklore* (Vitoria), 1st series, no. 14 (1922).

In Ataun, they say that the *baxajaun* grew wheat on Muskia mountain, situated in that town. A brave man—San Martinico—went to visit them in their cavern. Arguing with those spirits, he deliberately fell onto a pile of wheat that was there, filling his *albarcas* or Basque shoes with grains of wheat. Thus, on returning to his town, he carried in his shoes the seeds of the precious cereal. On discovering this, the *baxajaun* threw his axe at San Martinico, but he missed and could not prevent the growing of wheat from spreading throughout the world.

They tell the same legend in Albistur (Albiztur), in Cegama (Zegama), and in Cortézubi (Kortezubi).

* * *

Thanks equally to the use of a trick, San Martinico managed to steal from the *baxajaun* (from the devil according to other versions) the secret of the making of the saw, the soldering of iron, and the axle of the mill wheel.

The *baxajaun* was making the saw, according to a certain legend from the region of Oyarzun (Oiartzun); San Martinico could not do it because he lacked a model for it. Wanting to know the secret, he sent a servant to announce in the town that San Martinico had constructed a saw. On hearing this, the *baxajaun* asked him, "Has your master seen the leaf of the chestnut tree?"

"He hasn't seen it but he will," answered the servant, who later told San Martinico what had happened.

This is how the technique for making the saw was spread throughout the world.

With the same trick, San Martinico succeeded in learning how the *baxajaun* soldered two pieces of iron together, according to a legend from Cortézubi (Kortezubi). He ordered the herald to announce that he had discovered the process for soldering iron. The *baxajaun* asked the herald, "Did San Martinico sprinkle the pieces of iron with water from potter's clay?"

"He didn't, but he will," was the reply. And as a consequence of this new secret stolen from Baxajaun or the devil, the technique of soldering iron was spread throughout the world.

A legend from Sara explains that the axle for St. Martin's mill was made of oak and that when it was used to turn the wheel it burned up. But the axle of the *baxajaun's* (or the devil's) mill lasted for a long time. San Martín had it announced that his mill now functioned without any interruption.

"That means that he has used an axle made from an alder tree," replied the *baxajaun*.

"He is going to use one," replied the herald. And thus, thanks to San Martinico's trick, men were able to benefit from the use of the mill all over the world.

66. "La Tierra: Tartalo," *Eusko-folklore* (Vitoria), 1st series, no. 8 (1921): 29; M. Cerquand, "Légendes et récits populaires du Pays Basque," *Bulletin de la Société des Sciences, Lettres et Arts de Pau*, 1874–75, 252.

"After supper, the cowherds of Esterenzuby [Ezterenzubi] would leave a piece of bread for Anxo, who came every night after they had gone to sleep. One time, however, only the youngest of them left his share; the others did not. Anxo made off with the clothes of those who had not left their offering. They sent the young man to Anxo's cave to ask for their clothes, promising to give him a calf for doing so. Anxo returned the clothing and ordered the young cowherd to hit the calf ten times with a stick. The cowherd did so, and the calf gave birth to 101 sheep."

67. Agustín Chaho, *Biarritz entre les Pyrénées et l'Océan* (Biarritz between the Pyrenees and the Ocean), Vol. I:176; J. Vinson, *Basque Legends*, 20–41; R. M. de Azkue, *Euskalerriaren yakintza* 1:360; 2:131–35; Julio Caro Baroja, "Notas de folklore vasco" (Notes on Basque Folklore), *Revista de Dialectología y Tradiciones Populares*, vol. 2 (1946), 3rd Notebook; J. M. de Barandiarán, "Traditions et legendes. Lurpeko eremuetan (Dans les régions souterraines): Serpent," *Eusko-folklore* (Sare), 2nd series, no. 7 (1949): 6ff; J. M. de Barandiarán, "Ele-zaar: Herensuge," *Euskojakintza* 4 (1950): 259; J. M. de Barandiarán, "Contribución al estudio de la mitología vasca," *Homenaje a Fritz Krüger*, vol. I:126 (Mendoza, 1952).

The names of this spirit that are most commonly known among the Basque people are the following: Erensuge (in Sara and in Zugarramurdi), Herensuge and Lerensuge (in Ezpeleta), Errensuge (Camou (Gamere)), Hensuge (Laguinge (Liginaga)), Herainsuge (Ezpeleta), Edensuge (Sara), Edeinsuge (Saint-Esteben (Doniztiri)), Edaansugue (Uhart-Mixe), Egansuge (Rentería (Errenteria)), Igensuge (Zaldivia (Zaldibia)), Iraunsuge (Ataun), Ersuge (Manuscript of Otxandiano, according to the *Diccionario* of R. M. de Azkue), Sierpe (Lequeitio (Lekeitio) and Zubiri) and Dragoi (Mondragón (Arrasate)).

Some of the themes concentrated around this spirit have overlapped with those of Sugaar or Sugoi, another spirit that takes on the form of a serpent. In certain cases, it seems that the former have replaced the latter which have a more traditional air in the country. In fact, the areas where Sugaar holds sway appear to be surrounded by those where Erensuge is popular, fragmented and confined to the most scattered locations, which is indicative of its greater antiquity in the country.

68. "Traditions et legendes. Lurpeko eremuetan (Dans les régions souterraines): Serpent," *Eusko-folklore* (Sare), 2nd series, no. 7 (1949): 3ff.

Sugaar usually appears in the form of a sickle or fiery half moon moving acoss the firmament (Ataun). In Dima he is called Sugoi and lives in the cave of Balzola, attended by the *lamias* ("Las grutas: Animales y monstruos que habitan en las grutas," *Eusko-Folklore*, 3rd series, no. ii:121).

Sugoi sometimes appears in the form of a serpent, at other times as a man. It is one of the spirits closely linked to the cycle of Mari. There are characteristics that assimilate him mainly with Sugaar or Maju, Mari's husband; other characteristics assimilate him to Mikelats, Mari's son.

Two brothers, neighbors of a farm in Bargondia (Dima) saw Sugoi in the form of a serpent inside the cave of Balzola. The younger one threw a stone which cut off his tail. The elder son, more compassionate, did not approve of this conduct. Later on, when he was far away from home and feeling sad with nostalgia, the elder son was transported instantaneously to the cave of Balzola by an unknown man. On bidding him farewell at the mouth of the cave, the mysterious benefactor gave him a chest full of gold for himself and a red sash for his brother. The latter did not want to put on the sash, and they tied it to a walnut tree in front of their house. The tree burst into flames, leaving nothing in its place but a deep pit. (*Eusko-folklore* (Vitoria), 1st series, no. 11, 1921.

The last part of the preceding legend also appears in Sara, forming part of the cycle of Axular, in which Sugoi is replaced by Mikelats.

J. M. de Barandiarán, "Axular'en itzala," a lecture given at the Sorbonne on September 28, 1956, and published later in *Gure Herria* 29, no. 2.

69. "Traditions et legendes. Lurpeko eremuetan (Dans les régions souterraines) . . . [various topics]," *Eusko-folklore* (Sare), 2nd series, nos. 1–7, 1947–49.

In the oral literature of the Basque people there are frequent allusions to spirits that inhabit caves. The cavern of Obantzun (Berástegui (Berastegi)) appears in the following story:

"On a farm in Berástegui (Berastegi), called Etsoinberri, every night the servant and the maid of the property would stable a mare which they sent up to the mountain every day to graze. Whoever found the mare first would return home on her back. One day when the maid was the first to see the mare, she said to the servant: "Here's our black mare back," and she ran up to pet her and then mounted her.

Immediately, the mare headed toward the chasm of Obantzun and entered it with her rider. The servant approached the edge of the abyss, but didn't see anything. He said to himself: 'What mare could that have been?' He was returning home terrified, when he found his mare in a deep hole, the real Etsoinberri mare.

"A long time passed after the Etsoinberri maid disappeared. Nothing was known about her until one day her ring and earrings were found in the Iturran fountain." ("La tierra: Sima de Obantzun. La yegua de Etsoiberri," *Eusko-folklore* (Vitoria), 1st series, 1921: 7).

70. *Eusko-folklore*, 1921, pp. 4 and 22; *Eusko-folklore*, 1923, pp. 13 and 14; Ibid., 1924, pp. 29 and 30.

J. M. de Barandiarán, "Ele-zaar, 4, Mendiko urrea," in *Eusko-jakintza* 2 (1948): 345.

Based on the popular belief regarding the existence of a golden bell buried at the top of Irukutzeta, beside the boundary stone dividing the lands of Vergara (Bergara), Azcoitia (Azkoitia), and Elgoibar, some men began to dig up the burial site of a dolmen located there. But then they had to abandon their plan and leave because they were threatened by a monster that came out of the ground. (*Eusko-folklore*, 1924: 29).

On Larrun peak there was a stone resembling a tombstone. It was near the chapel, which is no longer there. There was an inscription on it: "The person who turns me over won't be sorry." Some boys who climbed up there on the second day of Pentecost for the festival or pilgrimage celebrated there on that date turned it over, expecting to find the treasure of Larrun. And on the other side they saw this inscription: "I was fine before; now I'm better."

Cases like this one on Mount Larrun are repeated at Arano, Aizkorrondo (Cegama (Zegama)), on Piñuri (Vergara (Bergara)) and on Mount Oiz (*Eusko-Folklore* (Vitoria), 1st series, no. 28 (1933): 13.

71. J. M. de Barandiarán, "Mari, o el genio de las montañas" (Mari, or the Spirit of the Mountains), *Homenaje a D. Carmelo de Echegaray*, 5 (San Sebastián, 1923); "Resumen de la mitología mariana," *Eusko-Folklore* (San Sebastián), 3rd series, nos. 5 and 6 (1955 and 1956): 46–47.

72. Ibid.

73. Lope García de Salazar, *Crónica de siete casas de Vizcaya y Castilla* (Chronicle of Seven Houses of Bizkaia and Castile) (n.p., 1454).

74. Sugoi is one of the spirits closely linked to the cycle of Mari. He shares some characteristics with Sugaar or Maju, Mari's husband, and others with Mikelats or Atarrabi, Mari's son and companion of Axular in Lezia, which is a cavern in Sara. He is the master of the *lamias* and punishes with a magic sash, like Mikelats ("Genios de figura humana o semihumana," *Eusko-folklore* (San Sebastián) 3rd series, no. 11 (1958): 121.

75. J. M. de Barandiarán, *Die prähistorischen Höhlen in der baskischen Mythologie*. In *Paideuma*, vol. 2, notebooks 1–2. [See also] Don Pedro de Barcellos, *Livro dos Linhagens*; Carmelo de Echegaray, "Vizcaya," *Geografía del País Vasco-Navarro*, 794–96.

76. "Animales y monstrous que habitan en las grutas: Baltzolako sugoia," *Eusko-folklore* (Vitoria), 1st series, no. 11 (1921). See the legend above, in note 68.

77. In some villages, like Sara and Ayerre (Aiherra), it is customary to place a scythe affixed to the end of a stick planted vertically in front of the house at or near the doorway. It is thought to be a protection against lightning.

78. Pierre de Lancre, *Tableau de l'Inconstance des Mauves Anges et Démons, ou il es amplement traité des sorciers et de la sorcellerie* (Tableau of the Inconstancy of the Bad Angels and Demons, with a Thorough Discussion of Sorcerers and Sorcery) (Paris, 1612). An edition of the parts of this book that are most relevant to our case appeared in *Bulletin du Musée Basque* (Bayonne), 2nd series, no. 15 (1938).

79. P. Gaston Sacaze, *Inscriptions antiques des Pyrénées* (Toulouse, 1892), 432.

80. J. M. de Barandiarán, "De la vida tradicional vasca: Valores de algunos símbolos" (Of Traditional Basque Life: the Meaning of Some Symbols), in *Homenaje a don Luis de Hoyos*, vol. 2, 41 (Madrid, 1950).

81. Julio Caro Baroja, "Sobre la religión antigua y el calendario del pueblo vasco," in *Trabajos del Instituto Bernardino de Sahagun*, vol. 6, 47 (Madrid, 1948). (Reprinted in *Vasconiana* 2. Madrid: Minotauro.)

82. J. M. de Barandiarán, "Contribución al estudio de la mitología vasca," 134–35.

Selections from
Prehistoric Man in the Basque Country

by José Miguel de Barandiarán

MESOLITHIC

The end of the Paleolithic era coincides approximately with the end of the last glacial period. Afterwards, the climate becomes more benign, and this change leads to the extinction of some species of the glacial fauna and obliges others (the reindeer, the blue fox, the seal, etc.) to emigrate to distant countries. As a result, the means of subsistence that had been common until then begin to grow scarce. Man has to adapt to the new conditions of life, nourishing himself poorly on the species that remain, and on mollusks especially in the coastal zones. This apparently leads to the decline of industry and the disappearance of Magdalenian art.

The way of life continues to be fundamentally the same as in the previous period, that is, the trapping of animals and the gathering of plants and fruits, and it continues in this manner until the beginning of the third millennium before Christ. It is the Mesolithic period, which in the Basque Pyrenees is comprised of two stages: the Aziliense and the Asturiense.

AZILIENSE — In almost all the Basque prehistoric strata in which levels of the Upper Paleolithic have been discovered there is a layer whose content is similar to the Aziliense strata of other countries. This occurs in Isturitz (Izturitze), in Berroberia, in Urtiaga, in Ermittia, in Lumentxa, in Bolinkoba, in Balzola, and in Santimamiñe. Only in Silibranka (Mañaria) and in Laminen-eskatza (Mondragón (Arrasate)) does it appear isolated, without the presence of more ancient archeological strata.

Man — The human remains of the Aziliense period discovered so far in the Basque Pyrenees are those from the cave of Urtiaga that are now preserved in the Museum of San Telmo in Donostia-San Sebastián. Of these, two craniums have been studied. The two are identical or coincide almost completely with the present-day Basque type in a number of indices, leading us to conclude on another occasion[1] that, in light of these coincidences, these craniums can be considered the first examples of the Pyrenean or Basque type.

If, as seems likely, the man from Urtiaga is the result of a local evolution of the Cro-Magnon with whom he is identical in a number of traits and characteristics, the question about the origin of the Basques as a people who emigrated from another country is meaningless. The question to ask would be, from where did Cro-Magnon man come?

Food — The remains of horses, less abundant in Aziliense dwellings than in preceding ones, reveal that this species was still hunted, as were ruminants, mountain goats, deer, and wild boar.

There are also bones of bear, fox, mountain lion, and badger, although their presence in this period can be due to causes other than the hunt and the need for nourishment.

There are also remains of birds, particularly pheasant, geese, thrush, falcon, mockingbird, and mountain dove (*Columba livia*).

There are vertebrate fish of different sizes, both circular and elliptical, which leads us to think that fishing was practiced.

Among the shellfish there are limpet, *Mytilus*, *Nassa reticulata*, *Turbo*, *Dentalium* and *Monodonta* (*Trochus*), this latter a species that comes to replace the periwinkles in Lumentxa during the final stage of this period.

The change of climate, the disappearance of several species of animals that had been the choice for hunting during the Paleolithic and the emigration of others to Nordic regions, the increased number of shellfish, fish, and birds used for food, and a considerable abundance of vegetable nourishment oblige us to imagine that Aziliense man ate a diet that was quite different from that of the hunters of the Magdalenian period.

Industry — Man in this period used stone and bone tools similar to those of the preceding period, sometimes differing only in minor details.

Thus, in many of his dwellings he left us stone instruments such as stone disks with carvings, stone tips with different shapes, engravings and points with smooth backs, others with smoothed edges, disk-shaped scrapers with chipped edges, chisels with half-point and lateral point, triangular punches and tips, whose forms, as well as their small size, make it impossible to mistake their use. Alongside this industry, mostly microlithic, he also fabricated large stone instruments such as a stone hammer with a slot in the center for a handle, and he used numerous cylinders of different sizes (figs. 1 and 2).

From bone he fashioned points, compressors, spatulas, chisels, and flattened harpoons provided with an orifice and a row of teeth (fig. 3).

Art — Already at the end of the Magdalenian period there is an obvious decline in art. Its manifestations are cruder than in the preced-

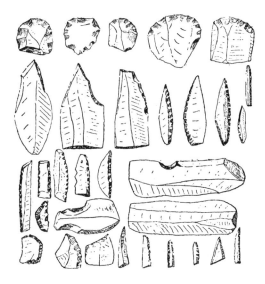

Fig. 1.—Aziliense stone work from Urtiaga. The objects in the bottom row are from Ermittia.

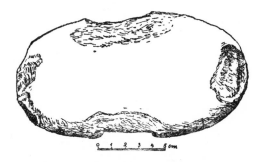

Fig. 2.—Pounder or hammer, or a weight for a fishing line, from Urtiaga.

ing stages and stylization tends to replace naturalistic art. This process is further accentuated during the Aziliense period. We find no parietal figures [cave drawings] in this period in the Basque Country, and the bone carvings consist of indecipherable incisions that may be merely decorative. Beads made of jet, perforated deer teeth and small shells of the type *Nassa reticulata* found in the Aziliense period may have been used for bodily decoration, though it is likely that they were also used as amulets for magical beliefs (fig. 4).

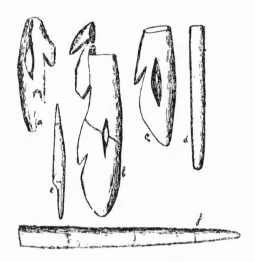

Fig. 3.—Aziliense bone artifacts: *a)* tip of a harpoon from Lumentxa; *b)* harpoon from Ermittia; *c)* harpoon from Urtiaga; *d, f)* punches from Ermittia; *e)* tip from Urtiaga.

Fig. 4.—Aziliense pendants from Urtiaga: *a)* deer teeth; *b) nassa*; *c)* jet.

Also, ochre and hematite rouges were probably used for body painting.

Way of Life — The remains of food items that we mentioned above, and the tools of stone, bone, and horn conserved in the strata of this period, lead us to speculate that Aziliense man lived primarily from hunting, like his Paleolithic ancestors. Apparently, then, man was adapting his preferences and the orientation of his economy to the new situation created by the change of climate, the disappearance of some game animals, and the increase of vegetation.

His spiritual concerns continued, in part, as before. The same amulets were still used. But other manifestations disappear from the scene; he is no longer interested, for example, in the representation of animals; the artist's interest has shifted to other areas. Most likely, there have been changes in the spiritual structure and in the conceptual world that parallel the transformation that has taken place in his economic way of life. We do not know the full meaning and extent of these changes, although there are those who speculate that the decline in hunting as the dominant form of economy determined the disappearance of certain aspects of upper Paleolithic magic with the resulting abandonment of the former depiction of animals as art on walls and domestic objects, giving way to the predominance of animist concepts and the cult of the dead. This is possible; but we should not dismiss the idea of a fundamental continuity of the Paleolithic religion and magic expressed through symbols more fleeting in material and form than those of the previous period.

ASTURIENSE — In the diggings explored so far in the Basque Country, typically Asturiense remains are rare. But after the Aziliense age, a lengthy period with specific fauna and industry still elapses before the first manifestations of the Neolithic.

The fauna indicates a moderate climate. Undoubtedly, the flora was being enriched by new species that offered man more advantageous possibilities than in former periods.

The Basque site in which this age is best represented is that of Santimamiñe, where there is an extensive deposit of shells. An Asturiense strata with industry typical of that era has been discovered near Biarritz, on the Mouligna beach, beneath carbonaceous strata with Neolithic ceramics.

Outside our country the Asturiense period is represented in different locations in Santander, in Asturias, in Galicia north of Portugal, and in the area northwest of Catalonia.

Fauna — In general, Asturiense sites are characterized by the extraordinary abundance of shellfish, especially in those sites situated in coastal regions. In Santimamiñe, 94 percent of the food remains are made up of shellfish, 5.5 percent of game animals, and the rest of other species, including fish, represented by numerous vertebra. Wild boar, deer, roe deer, kid, mountain goat, bull (rare), and horse (even more rare) were hunted. Keeping in mind that most of the bones of each example of these hunted species are missing, probably because the carcass was dressed outside the cave, it can be affirmed that the edible volume of flesh from game animals was no less than that from shellfish.

Among the latter, 76 percent are oysters (*Ostrea edulis*, especially); 17 percent, baby clams (*Tapes*), 2 percent, *Scrobicularia plana*; 0.8 percent mussels (*Mytilus edulis* and *M. minimus*); 0.6 percent other mollusks (*Helix nemoralis*, *H. adspersa* and *H. quimperiana*); 0.4 percent limpets (*Patella vulgata*, *P. aspera* and *P. lusitanica*); 0.3 percent *Monodonta lineata*, *M. sagittifera*, and *M. reticulata*. There were also periwinkles (*Littorina littorea*) in small numbers, *Cardium edule*, *Murex erinaceus*, *Nassa reticulata*, *Triton nodifer*, etc.

There are several species of birds: doves (*Columba palumbus* and *C. oenas*), partridges, thrush, blackbirds, water hens, ducks, geese, eagles, kites, mockingbirds, owls, etc.

Man — We do not yet have documents sufficiently explicit to inform us about the type of man that inhabited our country during the Asturiense. The human remains found in the Santimamiñe shell bed could not tell us much in this regard, even if they were contemporaneous with that deposit of shellfish, because their fragmentary condition does not permit us to make useful measurements for a serious study. It can be assumed, however, that the characteristics of the man who lived at the time in this part of the Pyrenees would not be incompatible with those of the preceding population that already exhibited a number of traits common to the historical Basque.

Industry — Hard stone picks considered typical of this period were found in the strata beneath the lignite of Mouligna, near Biarritz. Three similar picks were also found in Lumentxa, at a level situated between the upper part of the Aziliense and the base of the Neolithic. In the layer beneath the shell deposit of Santimamiñe some flint artifacts also appeared that were similar to those very instruments, though, despite such pieces, it is difficult to justify the attribution of the strata of shell-fish of that deposit to the typical Asturiense period (fig. 5).

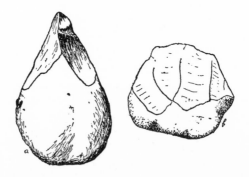

Fig. 5.—*a)* Asturiense pick from Mouligna; *b)* from Santimamiñe.

There are also other types of instruments, mainly flint, such as knives, flat stones with notches, adzes, disk-shaped or keel-shaped scrapers, tips and leaves with filed backs, small triangular stones, etc. (fig. 6).

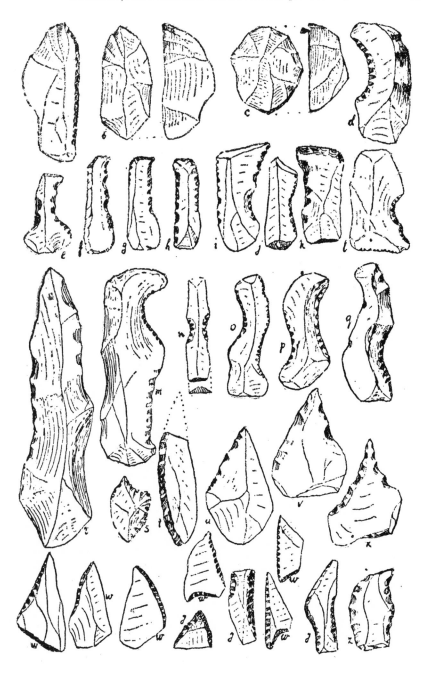

Fig. 6.—Asturiense stone-work from Santimamiñe: *a, b, c),* scrapers; *d, g)* notched flat stones; *r)* finished stone plate; *s, u, v, x)* stone punches; *t)* point with back filed down; *w)* triangular and trapezoidal points; *y)* chisels; *z)* engraver's chisel.

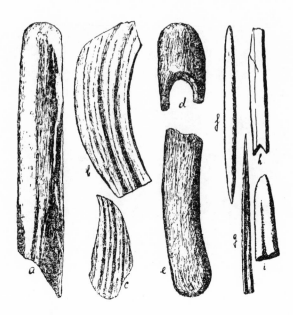

Fig. 7.—Asturiense bone-work from Santimamiñe: *a)* bone scraper or spatula; *b, c)* boar-fang knives; *d)* small fork or perforated piece of a cane; *e)* bone spatula; *f, g)* bone awls; h) carved bone; *i)* scraper.

Fig. 8.—Asturiense pendants from Santimamiñe: Cardium, *Nassa* shell, and stone ring.

There are instruments made of bone, such as tips, gouges, and chisels, surfaces with a sharp edge carved from the tooth of a wild boar, and lamps or perforated horns (fig. 7). A stone ring, quartz crystals, perforated *Nassa* and *Cardium* from Santimamiñe must have been used as jewelry (fig. 8).

Way of Life — The hunt continued to be an important occupation of the man of our country, even in regions near the coast, as can be deduced from the quantitative and qualitative analyses of strata that contain remains of food in shelters or human settlements of that period.

The wild boar, which until the end of the last century lived in the wooded mountains around Santimamiñe, must have been trapped with great frequency.[2] After wild boar, the most frequently hunted animal was the deer, followed by the mountain goat; then the roebuck; then the goat.

Since hunting parties consisted of many individuals working together, the spoils must have been divided up in the camp, each hunter taking the portion of meat due him with the fewest possible bones. This explains why many bones, especially those without marrow, are missing from the diggings.

The presence of bones of doves, partridges, and other birds in Santimamiñe suggests that these birds were also hunted at that time.

Because success in hunting was uncertain, the gathering of shellfish in certain periods provided a reliable source of food for the people living in areas close to the sea. In dwellings of the Asturiense period we find remains not only of species that are eaten today on the Basque coast, such as oysters, baby clams, sea mussels, *Monodonta*, limpets, and cockles (*Cardium*), but also those eaten in other places on the Cantabrian coast, such as jackknife clams (*Solen*), sand gapers (*Scrobicularia*), small scallops (*Chlamys*), *Mya*, bay scallops (*Pecten*) and periwinkles (*Littorina*).

Fishing was also practiced in the coastal regions, as evidenced by the bones of fish that were relatively abundant in Santimamiñe and in Lumentxa.

We do not know what method was used for fishing, nets, hooks, or something else.

As for the procedure used in the gathering of shellfish, we do not believe that picks from the Asturiense period were used much on our coasts; for catching oysters, mollusks, etc., bone chisels, and wedges made from boar's teeth were more suitable, as we can see from those who currently engage in that work.

The collection of fruits and plants provided another source of food; but we have no direct evidence, nor do we know of objects that presuppose the existence of this way of life.

Stone jewelry and sea shells no doubt were involved in magical or religious beliefs; but we lack specific evidence revealing anything about the conceptual world of the Asturiense man of our country.

Much of what we observe in the way of life of this second Mesolithic Basque period comes to us from preceding periods. But not everything: their stone work (quartz picks and small flint objects) coincides with Asturiense and Tardenoisiense work from other countries and shows that the inhabitants of Santimamiñe, Lumentxa, and Mouligna did not live in isolation, but maintained relations with different peoples, particularly with the people of northeastern Cantabria and Asturia. They also maintained local Paleolithic tradition, and had relationships with people from the South and East whose Mediterranean cultures demonstrated Tardenoisiense traits.

NEOLITHIC

The age of polished stone has not been studied in the Basque Pyrenees as a distinct stage of the Eneolithic, even though some of the diggings explored in this country allow us to recognize it as a cultural complex situated in the strata between the Mesolithic and the age of metals. In Santimamiñe, for example, the strata comprised of the first ceramic forms and the first traces of copper with types of vessels similar to those of the Basque dolmens is nearly one meter thick over a great expanse of that dig. Therefore, it will be useful to describe below some of the features of this period.

The climate was still the same as in the Asturiense, as can be ascertained by the fauna living in the region at that time. The preponderance of *Monodonta* over periwinkles and the abundance of mussels along the Basque coasts are perhaps a sign of an average temperature higher than during the preceding epochs.

The Neolithic sites discovered so far in the Basque Pyrenees are those of Santimamiñe, Lumentxa, Bolinkoba, Urtiaga, Ermittia, Uriogaina, Isturitz, and Mouligna (fig. 9).

Fig. 9.—A drawing of Mount Lumentxa of Lequeitio, seen from the highway of Mendexa. At the foot, a stream. The arrow marks the entrance to the famous cave.

Fauna — Among the species that inhabited the Basque Country during the Neolithic were cows, horses, deer, mountain goat, roebuck, chamois, wild boar, fox, mountain lion, the weasel, and the martin. Deer and especially wild boar were the animals most hunted by man.

Sheep already existed in Bizkaia, as we know from their remains in Santimamiñe; this is an indication that the practice of domesticating and using them had already reached this part of the Pyrenees.

Among the birds that, in one way or another, ended up in the diggings of this epoch, we find goose, pheasant, thrush, white partridge, falcon, crow, mockingbird, and owl.

There are abundant shellfish: *Monodonta*, oysters, baby clams, limpets, and mussels; less abundant are *Scrobicularia, Solen, Cardium, Dentalium vulgare, Pecten, Unio, Nassa reticulata*, etc.

The remains of different fish—hake, *Belone vulgaris*, *Labrus* and others—also appear in Neolithic diggings.

Man — In the Neolithic strata of Lumentxa, human remains were found that, like others found in different prehistoric Basque sites, showed no sign of having been buried when they were deposited in the cavern. They must have been simply placed on the ground. Therefore, they should not be considered to be more recent than the Neolithic strata in which they lie.

Through such remains we were able to reconstruct almost completely the cranium of an infant, which, compared to the recent Basque type, scarcely differs at all from the average Basque of today.

Industry — Man made a number of artifacts in stone, some of which copy older forms, such as flint points and disks with smoothed backs, tips from Gravette, disks with notched stone leaves, saws, scrapers and knives; others are new, such as the axes of polished ophite from Santimamiñe, polished hammers, picks, mallets, files, and arrows (fig. 10).

In the Neolithic layer of Lumentxa there was a grinder, that is, a pair of stones the larger of which has a smooth concave surface, the other slightly rounded for rolling easily over the first (fig. 11).

There are also a number of round stones with orifices which must have been used in necklaces, perhaps as amulets (fig. 10), like rock crystals. As in previous periods, ochre dyes were used.

Hole punches and needles were made from bone and horn (fig. 12).

Ceramics appear during the final stage of the Santimamiñe shell bed, associated with new kinds of arrows (foliaceous), polished axes, and sheep bones.

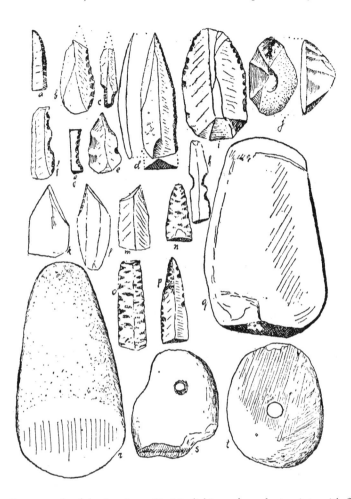

Fig. 10.—Stone-work of the Santimamiñe Neolithic: *a, b, c, d, e)* points with finished backs and sides; *f, g, h)* flat stones with notches; *i, j)* scrapers; *k, l, m)* chisels; *n, o, p)* points with designs on the face; *q)* hammer of polished ophite; *r)* axe of polished ophite; *s)* pendant of fired clay; *t)* stone pendant.

Fig. 11.—Neolithic grindstone from Lumentxa.

Fig. 12.—Hole punch of bone and needle of horn from Santimamiñe.

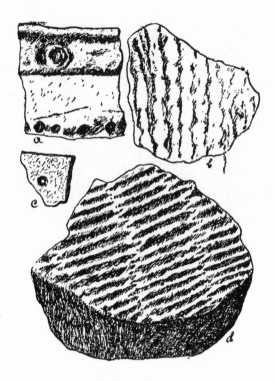

Fig. 13.—Neolithic ceramics from Santimamiñe: *a)* ceramic with circles, furrows, and surface incisions; *b)* ceramic with digital impressions; *c)* shard from a vessel with a hole for hanging; *d)* the base of a pot with the imprint of weaving.

The first of these are crude clay vessels with grooves on the surface left by fingers. There are also some with crater-shaped decorations, others with rolls of clay in relief, with furrows and impressions from the woven surface on which they were made (fig. 13).

Way of Life — The remains of food and industry of the Neolithic Basque man lead us to think that he was dedicated mainly to hunting, an occupation that he alternated with those of fishing and gathering shellfish along the coast. But the grindstone from Lumentxa and the appearance of the sheep in Santimamiñe reveal the beginning of new economic forms: the herding of sheep and the probable use of grains.

Undoubtedly, bovids were the first animals to be domesticated in the Basque Country. The bovine species that has traditionally been exploited in the Pyrenees is identical to that which lived in a wild state in ancient times in this country, indicating that the Basque domesticated the very type of cow that he had previously hunted.[3] The same was true with the goat and the horse.

The domestication must have been very incomplete at first. It consisted of a kind of appropriation of the offspring of animals which were then set free on the mountain where they grazed during all seasons. When the flesh of one of these animals was needed, the owner would capture it, hunting it as had been done in former times. Probably the animal was divided up among several individuals or families, just as in former times when it was hunted by organized parties during the Paleothic.[4]

We do not know which cereals man ate; but the mill of Lumentxa leads us to consider the milling of edible grains, a probable indication that farming was being practiced in the country, limited no doubt to small parcels or gardens.

The remains of fish found in Neolithic sites indicated that fishing was practiced at the time. They probably sailed in small one-piece canoes (trunks of trees hollowed out), similar to those found in the lake sites in Switzerland, like the small canoe discovered in the dig of Adur (depicted in the Museum of the Sea in Biarritz in 1937), a probable example of the survival of Neolithic models of our country, used even today in the Nive River.

We know of no basketwork from this period in the Basque territory; but the ceramics of Santimamiñe, the kind molded on wicker mats, reveal that this type of vessel was in use, woven with reeds or strips of ash.

Social life within the confines of each valley, according to the requirements of the rudimentary development of herding bovids, goats, and pigs, was affected mainly by the demands of the herding life in the mountainous regions. In the lower regions and on the plains, agriculture and sheep herding had already taken their first steps and their first battles had begun as well.

Without any doubt, the Neolithic population practiced some kind of religion. The use of ochre as a rouge and pendants of stone and quartz crystal could have been intended for decoration of the body; but it is more likely that they served some magical or religious function. There was also the belief in a future life. The clay vessel found beside the infant bones in Lumentxa must have been placed there with offerings for the deceased. Most likely, their former beliefs and rituals regarding religion and magic remained the same, since later in recorded history they still formed the background of the conceptual and mystical world of the people of the Pyrenees, though their most characteristic expression from earlier times—the naturalistic figures of the Paleolithic—had been replaced by simple signs and by symbolic objects and expressions.

The Neolithic, then, was a period of great transformations in our country as it was in others.

The introduction of the sheep and the domestication of other animals constituted events of extreme importance. On the other hand, geographic conditions of the Pyrenees imposed a regimen of transhumance on those initiating the development of livestock here. This must have led to the periodic practice of great displacements of the shepherds of the Pyrenees who, establishing regular contact with different populations, became the conduits of different practices, such as ceramics, leaf-shaped arrows, polished axes and hammers, hand mills, etc. Such displacements continued until the present, though today they represent only a fraction of what they were in the past (fig. 14).

Although these transformations do not necessarily require the migration of peoples, we cannot preclude the possibility that groups of shepherds from outside the Pyrenees might have come this far in their back-and-forth movement of transhumant life, bringing new cultural elements with them. But their presence in this part of the mountains has not been definitively established by anthropology; rather, it seems that there were no significant changes in the composition of the people, because the same traits of the men who lived in these regions during the Mesolithic period continue to characterize those of later periods.

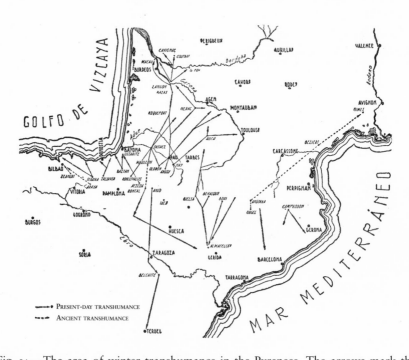

Fig. 14.—The area of winter transhumance in the Pyrenees. The arrows mark the outermost limits of herd movements.

ENEOLITHIC

After the Neolithic period, which properly speaking ends around two thousand years before Christ, the natural landscape of the Basque Pyrenees continued largely unchanged. In addition to cows, goats, sheep, horses, pigs, and dogs, all of them domesticated by then, the fauna consisted of the same wild species as in the preceding period. Nor are we aware of any important alterations in the flora.

On the other hand, the human occupation of the Pyrenees landscape was greatly intensified and extended. Many zones, scarcely inhabited earlier, were occupied by man. The high mountains, especially, were inhabited by a relatively large population and were now traversed by flocks of sheep, goats, and cows. This was so in the mountains of Gibijo, Arrato, Gorbea, Oiz, Aizkorri, Entzia-Urbasa, Ataun-Burunda, Elosua-Polpol, Aralar, Orin, Belabieta, Larrun-Atxuri, Artzamendi-Iuskadi, Urrixka-Berdaritz, Sorogain-Astakarri, Lindus-Atalosti, Irati Abodi, and Ahuski, where the sites of numerous dolmens exist. These are generally found in pastures and on the hills and in the passes leading to them (fig. 15).

As would be expected, human settlements also existed in lower regions; proof of this lies in the dolmens of Añes, la Rioja, the valley of Cuartango, la Llanada of Vitoria, Elgea, Altzania, Kalamua, Gorriti, Belate, Landarbaso, Jaizkibel, Ibardin, Abarratei, etc. and the Eneolithic digs of Mairuelegorreta, Surbi, Santimamiñe, Lumentxa, Urtiaga, Jentiletxeta, El Castellar, Isturitz, and others.

The climate is similar to that of today, and the diversity of zones at all altitudes complement each other to assure pasture during all seasons of the year. This forced the herbivores to migrate often, resulting in the transhumance of flocks, which would constitute one of the most original features of the economy of the Pyrenees from that time on.

Clearly, then, the animals and, with them, the men exploiting them, were spread throughout the country, depending on the abundance of pasture in its valleys and mountains. The placement of their sites provides a guide to indicate the roads that crossed our land at the time (fig. 15).

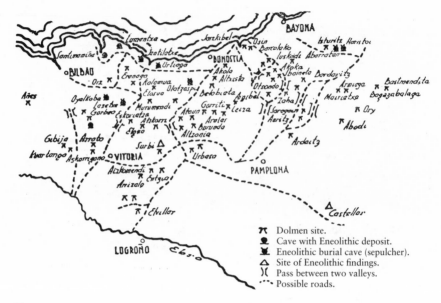

Fig. 15.

Taking into account the number of dolmens we know about and those we can estimate from the toponymy and from the tradition in the regions of the country that have been studied thus far, as well as the burial grottos and the average number of dead deposited in them and in the dolmens, we estimate the approximate number of individuals making up the shepherd population of the Basque territory to be five thousand.

In and around the pasturage and by virtue of contacts with different peoples brought about by transhumance, a relatively prominent culture developed in the Pyrenees and bordering areas that had no parallel since the good times of the Magdalenian epoch.

Man — Our Eneolithic population presented anthropological features congruent with those of the present-day Basque. This fact has been revealed to us by the human cranium discovered in the Eneolithic layer of Santimamiñe, by the one from Urtiaga (infantile) and, above all, by the craniums found in the dolmens in the elevated pasture lands, that is, in those of Aralar, Aizkorri, and Urbasa.[5] This means that the prehistoric transhumant shepherds of our mountains were of the same physical type as their successors, the historical Basques. The characteristics of their race, denominated "Western Pyrenean race" by the Belgian anthropologist Víctor Jacques, are the following: predominantly mesocephalic; bulging temples; occipital orifice with the surface very inset or sunken, causing the chin to recede slightly when the neck is held erect; lower jaw narrow and chin protruding; nose somewhat long and pointed, etc.

In the countries around the Pyrenees, where in former times the Cro-Magnon type predominated in the higher Paleolithic (craniums from Camargo in Santander, from Parpalló in Valencia, from Duruthy in Les Lhandes), there were now different types of men, such as this one from the Basque Pyrenees (Western Pyrenean race) situated between the Acro-cephalic from Catalonia and the Brachicephalic from western Cantabria. Professor Alcobé, who recognized it in the valley of Arán, says that the discovery of the Western Pyrenean type in Arán, naturally more or less altered by interbreeding, is a new argument in support of the ancient geographic dispersion of the type far more extensive than the current residence of its most characteristic representatives.[6]

Dwellings and Sepulchers — Caves were still being used as dwellings and as sepulchers. In those of Santimamiñe, Lumentxa, Bolinkoba, Mairuelegorreta, Arratandi, Jentiletxeeta, Urtiaga, Ermittia, Urio, and Isturitz their inhabitants occupied the entrances with hearths on the inside a short distance from the entrance. The hearth had the form of an open shallow circular pit dug into the ground and surrounded by stones, as has been observed in Santimamiñe, in Lumentxa, and in Urtiaga.

In addition to the caves there were dwelling places out in the open, rustic constructions without doubt; but we have no knowledge about them or their form. It can be assumed, however, that in the pasturages such generally temporary dwellings would have been similar to present-day shepherds' huts.

The only type of construction from this period that we know about in our country is the dolmen. This is a sepulchral monument large enough to hold some or many cadavers. It is formed with several unfinished stone blocks arranged vertically on the ground so that they form a flat enclosure frequently rectangular in shape, and on other occasions with more than four sides. On top of these blocks is the roof; one or more large, flat stones. The stone that closes the enclosure on the East is usually lower than the others, so that there's a space between it and the roof: this is the entrance to the dolmen. The major axis of the floor of the dolmen is oriented approximately from east to west, with the entrance stone on the east side. The whole structure is almost always surrounded and at times covered by a catafalque or mound of earth and irregular stones (fig. 16).

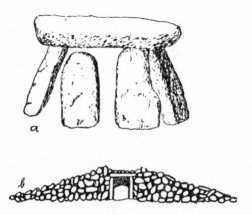

Fig. 16.—*a)* Dolmen of Aizkomendi (in Eguilaz, Araba); *b)* vertical view of the dolmen of Artekosaro (Urbasa Mountains).

Fig. 17.—Dolmen of Mokua.

There are dolmens whose catafalque is surrounded by a circle of stones placed on the ground, to form a cromlech, as can be seen in figure 17.

Those of Mokua, Iragorri, Iuskadi, and Atalosti are of this type.

The simplest dolmen has a single chamber shaped in a rectangle: it is the most common type in the country. There are some that have two contiguous chambers, like that of Jentillarri, Arzábal, Berdaritz (with covered galleries); others have a corridor in front of the entrance, like that of Aizkomendi, the "Witch's Hut," of Elvillar (figs. 18 and 19), the one in western Igartza, and that of Artekosaro. In addition to the chamber, this last one has an antechamber and a corridor, and its catafalque

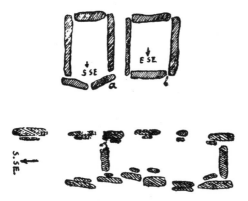

Fig. 18.—Above: sketch of the floorplan of the dolmens of Miruatza (*a*), in Ataun and Ausukoi; (*b*), in Aralar. Below: Sketch of the floorplan of the covered gallery of Jentillarri (Aralar).

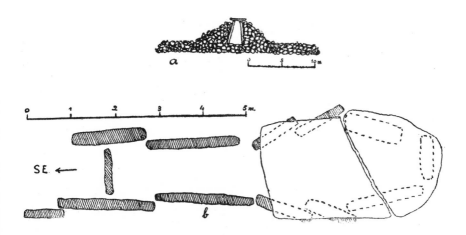

Fig. 19.—"Witch's Hut," dolmen with corridor situated on the Lanagunilla end of Elvillar (Araba): *a)* vertical cut NE-SW of the catafalque in two concentric levels and of the chamber; *b)* sketch of the floorplan of the chamber, the antechamber, and the corridor. Only the roof over the part corresponding to the chamber is preserved.

is formed in two concentric laddered levels, an example unique so far in the country.

Dolmens are usually found in pastures, on hills, and in passes leading to such places. In other places the types described so far are rare.

The theories that attribute different origins to these dolmens, based on the different types observed in the Pyrenean region, do not seem well founded to us. Such differences do not exceed probable variations in the manifestations of one element within a cultural cycle.

Clothing — We know little or nothing specific about the clothing of the Eneolithic Basque. He probably wore garments made of materials close at hand. As cattle and sheep herding were the most important occupations of a large part of the population, we can say that sheepskin, goatskin, and cowhide must have been used as elements for clothing, as they have been until recent times among the shepherds. The discovery of items among Eneolithic household furnishings that seem to be adapted for the sewing of animal skins (awls, needles, scrapers, chisels) confirms our hypothesis. Skins were also used to make footwear, that is, the *albarkas* (leather sandals), a practice that has continued through the present day.

Wool and also certain vegetable fibers were probably used for making thread and weaving items of clothing. Although we have not found clear evidence of this in our territory, contacts with other countries where vestiges of such craft have been found undoubtedly made it possible for the transhumant population of the Pyrenees to acquire this skill.

We do not know if painting played an important role in bodily adornment. The ochre found in Jentiletxeeta and in the dolmens of Askorrigana, Artekosaro, etc., could have been used for this purpose.

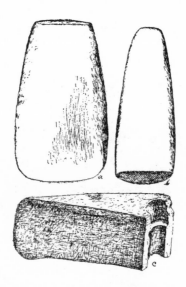

Fig. 20.—Eneolithic industry: *a)* polished stone axe from Apodaka; *b)* small stone hoe from the dolmen of Bidarte; *c)* stone axe from the dolmen of Balenkaleku.

Industry — In the inventory of artifacts from this period, the forms inherited from the previous period constitute the highest percentage. Beside them appear new objects which, if not the most important in the repertory of the period, do characterize the complete array of Eneolithic crafts.

Most of the instruments that have come down to us are made of stone. A number of pieces were carved in flint, such as knives, files, scrapers, drills, planes or plates with notches, points from La Gravette, and arrowheads with leaves or wings. Polished axes were made of ophite and other hard materials; sometimes, from limestone. Drills and grinders were made from sandstone or quartz. There were also pendants of sandstone, quartz crystal, jet, alabaster, slate, and fired clay (figs. 20 and 21 A, B, and C).

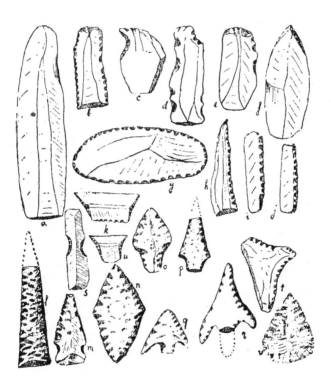

Fig. 21 A.—Stone craft from the Eneolithic: *a)* plate from Lumentxa; *b, c, d)* plates with designs and notches from Santimamiñe; *e, f)* scraper and chisel from Urtiaga; *g, h)* scraper and point with marginal designs from Santimamiñe; *i, j, k)* plates with smoothed back and trapezoid from Lumentxa; *l, n, o, q)* arrowheads from Santimamiñe; *m, r)* arrowheads from Lumentxa; *p)* same, from Urtiaga; *s)* plate with side notches from Santimamiñe; *t)* same, from Urtiaga; *u, v)* trapezoid and point from Bolinkoba.

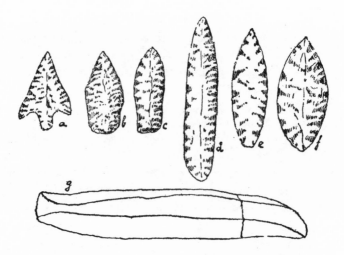

Fig. 21 B.—Different kinds of flint arrowheads of the Eneolithic: *a)* arrowhead from the dolmen of Ueloguena (Aralar); *b)* same, from Ermittia; *c)* same, from Jentil-etxeeta; *d)* same, from the dolmen of Pagobakoitza (Aizkorri); *e)* same, from the dolmen of Oiduegi (Aralar); *f)* same, from Jentiletxeeta; *g)* knife from Gorostiaran (Aizkorri).

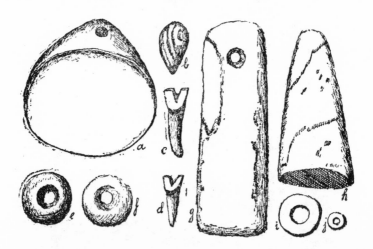

Fig. 21 C.—Eneolithic pendants and amulets: *a, b)* cardium and *nassa* from Jentil-etxeeta; *c, d)* human incisors carved in V-shape from the dolmen of Argarbi; *e, f)* amulets of jet; *g)* slate plaques from the dolmen of Balenkaleku; *h)* a small votive torch from the dolmen of Keixetako-egiya; *i, j)* bone rings from the dolmen of Igaratza.

The first metal (copper) objects appear, such as awls, arrowheads, chisels, axes, rings, and bracelets (fig. 22).

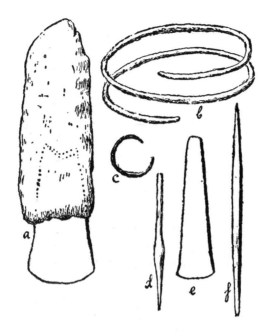

Fig. 22.—Eneolithic industry: copper objects: *a)* copper chisel with deer horn handle from Santimamiñe; *b)* bracelet from the dolmen of Debata (Aralar); *c)* ring from the dolmen of Argarbi; *d)* awl from Santimamiñe; *e)* axe from Iruzubieta; *f)* awl from the dolmen of La Cañada (Urbasa).

The ceramics copy old forms, but also include novelties that place them in particular relationship with forms situated in other countries.

There are vessels with smooth, lustrous surfaces and others that have incisions made with fingernails or with bivalves of mollusks; parallel grooves, circular and oval depressions, plain nipples, and others with an orifice or several tubes (Urio).

In Santimamiñe, in the layer characterized by the presence of copper objects (chisel, punch, and other shapeless artifacts) and Eneolithic arrows made of silica, the oldest ceramic pieces seem to be made of ordinary mud with series of hemispherical holes on the perimeter and with leaf and flower shapes on the edges, associated with vases with smooth surfaces with or without nipples on the top. These are followed by ceramic pieces with parallel grooves, incisions made with fingernails, and bands that resemble the ornamentation found on bell-shaped vases. Finally there are examples of ceramics with lines cut in the shape of parallel crowns, or with lines in a zigzag shape. But this sequence needs to be confirmed before it can be accepted as the norm.

In dolmens we frequently find the type of ceramic made of mud with a smooth surface, vases with S-shaped profiles, some decorated with incisions or protruding dimples, some unadorned, and occasionally (in Urbia) bell-shaped vases (figs. 23 and 24).

Fig. 23.—Detail of the Eneolithic ceramics of Santimamiñe.

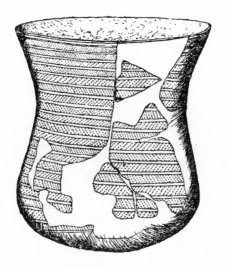

Fig. 24.—Bell-shaped vase from the Pagobakoitza dolmen (Aizkorr*i).*

Many of the elements that constitute the production of artifacts by Basque Eneolithic man that differentiate him from the preceding period, such as megaliths, arrow types, axes of stone and copper, slate pendants, and the new forms of ceramic craft came, apparently, from countries where they originated during different stages of this period. This and the stratification of the ceramics of Santimamiñe, even if we know little about it, have allowed us to attempt a chronological ordering in the process of Basque Eneolithic culture.

Thus, the first stage, that of crudely made ceramics, either smooth or with crater-shaped holes and crudely decorated edges found in Santimamiñe, seems to correspond to dolmens with the same ceramic associated with microliths of geometric form from the hill of Ataguren, from Santa Engracia, from Askorrigana, and from Lindus. They were probably contemporary with the first style of bell-shaped vase from other countries.

Ceramic pieces with series of parallel grooves, with the marks of fingernails and with bands of incisions similar to those of the bell-shaped vase, correspond to the second stage, represented by the examples of the second Eneolithic strata of Santimamiñe, as do the foliated arrowheads of the funereal grottos of Jentiletxeeta and of the dolmens of Artekosaro, La Cañada, and Pamplonagañe. They were probably contemporary with the second style of the bell-shaped vase.

To the third stage we assign ceramics of the final Eneolithic period of Santimamiñe, decorated with lines cut in zigzag shape and in the form of parallel crowns, and the dolmens of Pagobakoitza and Gorostiaran with bell-shaped vases of the third style, those from Debata, Zurgaina, and Ueloguena with arrowheads with barbs or tongues in the style evolved in Almería, and the one from Balenkaleku with its axe of hollowed ophite and an interior furrow which has parallels in northern Europe.

But this classification or chronological ordering based on comparisons of counted objects and on stratigraphic considerations that have not yet been confirmed is of little proven value and may not reflect the true process of Eneolithic culture.

Ways of Life — If we compare the area of recent pastoral communities of the Pyrenees with that of the sites of dolmens in the same region, it will be easy for us to appreciate the coincidence of the two in their general configuration and even in details such as the absence of dolmens in those places with insufficient pasture for cattle and the fact that the contemporary shepherd's hut has sometimes been built over a dolmen or Eneolithic catafalque. This suggests that at least part of the Basque

Eneolithic population extended throughout the territory and adapted to it as if in response to the demands of the lives of the shepherds.

Indeed, almost all the Basque dolmens, for example, are found in pasturages and in ports and on hills that have access to them. Thus, the dolmens of Gibijo, Arrato, Gorbea, Entzia, Urbasa, Aizkorri, Aralar, Lindus, Abodi, and others occupy the high pastoral regions known by those names. And those of Ataguren, Arane, San Román, Berjalarán, Zudaire, Bakedano, Baiarrate, Belate, Pittarre, Bordaundi, Urateka, Ibaineta, Otsondo, Iuskadi, Berdaritz, Abarratei, Arrizabala, and Murenxillo are found on hills and passes contiguous to such regions (fig. 15, p. 154).

We can, then, affirm that the herding of sheep, which had already begun to appear in the Neolithic period in our country, succeeded in occupying a large part of it during the following period. And since the high pastures to which the dolmen culture extended could not have been used for grazing or inhabited except during the summer, the population must have practiced transhumance, which was, as we know, quite common in the zone around the Pyrenees, between the Dordogne and the Ebro, between the Ariège and the Gallic region.

The most significant fact in the lives of the Eneolithic population of the Pyrenees was this transhumance of sheep. It obliged man to displace himself periodically with his flocks from one region to another and to establish his temporary dwellings and burial grounds in those regions, bringing men and peoples of different races and cultures into contact with each other. This transhumant movement was, no doubt, what caused the unification of the bovine species and of the ovine species that has been observed in the southwestern part of Aquitaine and the northern part of Spain as far south as Portugal.[7] And along with this came also the currents of cultural unification of the entire Pyrenean region with the introduction of different customs and techniques mentioned above. The shepherds who herded their flocks through different countries in autumn to their winter camps and who traveled back through them in the spring to their summer sheepfolds were the sustainers and conduits of a culture that featured new elements from different origins built on a traditional foundation.

There are those who, basing their conclusions on such novelties, have thought that a foreign people had come to occupy our country at the beginning of the Eneolithic. This opinion has not been confirmed by anthropology; rather, it seems that there were no significant changes in population, as we noted above in discussing the Neolithic, since important characteristics of the man who inhabited these regions during the Mesolithic still characterize the man of the following epochs.

On the other hand, not all of the population was transhumant. Nor were all of them shepherds. Household items found in the Eneolithic strata of Santimamiñe, Lumentxa, and Urtiaga, and the remains of food accumulated in them, prove that hunting was practiced and that fishing provided some food for the coastal population. Of all the bones of mammals that we extracted from the Eneolithic layer in Santimamiñe, more than 60 percent are from wild animals. The remainder belong to species (cow, horse, sheep, goat, dog) that might have been domesticated or semi-domesticated. Of the wild animals, 28 percent are deer and 30 percent wild boar. Following these, in very small percentages, are the roebuck, the mountain goat, and the fox. Although the significance of these figures must be considered provisional (a rigorous and meticulous study of the material from Santimamiñe documented in the Archeological Museum of Bilbao has not yet been undertaken), it can be affirmed that hunting continued to be the common and most important source of food for most of the population.

Without a doubt, the land was cultivated, though in small sections of our plains. The small hoe from the dolmen of Bidarte is perhaps proof of this. But the role of agriculture must not have been of great importance yet in the economy of the country, judging by the rarity of its vestiges.

The sites of this non-transhumant or sedentary sector of the population were located in the lower regions and in the intermediate zones between the high pastures and the plains of the sub-Pyrenean regions (Santimamiñe, Jentiletxeeta, Aizkomendi, Elvillar, Urio, Isturitz, El Castillar). It was this sector especially that practiced hunting and the use of wild cattle, cultivated the land, and used ceramics, and despite the importance of herding sheep, it can be said that their way of life constituted the important center of Eneolithic culture in the Basque Pyrenees.

The Basque Eneolithic is somewhat enigmatic, unless studied in connection with the cultures that flourished in neighboring countries at the time. Contact with these and the suitability of the natural Pyrenean landscape itself were sufficient cause for the propagation of the pastoral life all along the sierra, the populating of the elevated pasturages, transhumance, the megalithic constructions, the new ceramic forms (bell-shaped), new weapons (northern axes and southern arrows) and metals. These facts were not confined to present-day Vasconia, but formed part of a wider cultural circle that covered a vast territory, including all of the Pyrenees and extensive lower zones, both in the valley of the Ebro and in the Aquitaine region—a territory whose coincidence with the area of Pyrenean pastoral transhumance and, in large part, with

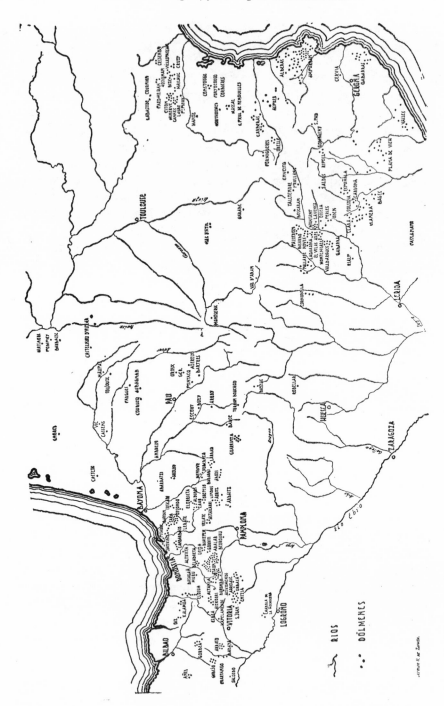

Fig. 25 A.—Rivers; Dolmens.

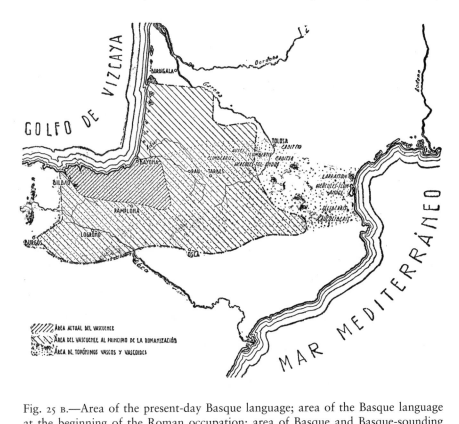

Fig. 25 B.—Area of the present-day Basque language; area of the Basque language at the beginning of the Roman occupation; area of Basque and Basque-sounding toponymy.

Basque toponymy, constitutes a phenomenon of particular importance in Basque archeology and linguistics (figs. 14 (p. 152) and 25 A and B).

The Pyrenean zone, then, was the center of convergence for techniques and customs that, originating in different adjoining countries, were grafted onto the traditional indigenous life. In this way, a culture was formed in a very natural landscape consisting of the mountains and their complementary regions.

Language — The Basque names for certain instruments reflect the materials from which they were made during the Neolithic and Eneolithic: for instance, *aizkora* "axe," *aitzur* "hoe," *aizto* "knife," and *zulakaitz* "chisel," in which the component *aitz* means "stone." This is an indication that the Basque language preserves elements from the vocabulary of the Stone Age.

The fact that *urraida* (from *urre*, "gold" and *aide* "similar") and *zirraida* (from *zillar* "silver" and *aide* "similar") are the Basque names for copper and tin and that their formation accurately reflects the order of the historical appearance of these metals was probably also an indication that the Basque vocabulary preserves words—*urre* and *zillar*—that existed before the diffusion of copper (Eneolithic) and tin (Bronze Age).

Another indication of the same phenomenon are the names *ozme* "lightning, thunder," (from *oz*, *ortz* "sky" and *me*, "stone" or "mineral"), *ozminarri* "thunder," *ozkarri* "thunder" (from *ortz* "sky" and *arri* "stone"), *tximistarri* "lightning bolt," and *oneztarri* "lightning bolt," which express mythological ideas widely diffused throughout Europe during the expansion of the Indo-Europeans (late Neolithic).

On the other hand, the coincidence of the area of Basque-sounding toponymy with that of culminating events of the Pyrenean Eneolithic reveals a probable connection of these with the Basque language. It is therefore likely that it was spoken during the Eneolithic period by the population that occupied the Pyrenean valleys and some of the neighboring countries.

The relationship that several contemporary linguists (Trombetti, Marr, Dumézil, Uhlenbeck, Lafon, Bouda) find between the Basque language and the languages of the Caucasus could be explained by their derivation from a primitive Basque-Caucasian culture and language. Since the latter was apparently related to the primitive Indo-European language spoken during the final Neolithic in the regions to the east of the Ural mountains, and with the Fino-Ugrian languages spoken in the region of the middle Volga, it would be reasonable to place the cradle and center from which the languages of the Basque-Caucasian family radiated within the confines of Europe and Asia. This probably occurred around the third millennium before our era. If such hypotheses were confirmed, the Basque language, Asiatic in origin, would have been imported some four thousand years ago by a migrating people or would have been associated with a cultural movement that introduced new ways of life into the Pyrenean population at the beginning of the Eneolithic. But it is still too early to formulate a categorical solution to this question, which is undoubtedly reserved for future research in prehistoric anthropology and archeology and in comparative linguistics.

Religion — There are reasons to believe that the old religion, characterized by the cult of spirits in animal form, and by magical rites connected to the ancient ways of life still evident—dominated by the hunt—continued to weigh upon the man of this age. We have already seen that the hunt continued to be an important occupation of a large part of the population. The changes in primary materials and the appearance of some new techniques may not have profoundly

E.SE.

Fig. 26.—Roof of the dolmen of Ezkiregi (Ardaitz-Navarre) with a groove carved into the surface.

altered their spiritual orientation. It is likely, then, that the old religious-magical background continued, though stripped of the naturalistic art of earlier times. But a new element entered into it with the movement of shepherds and the contacts they made.

The megalithic burial stones that began to appear in all the sites in the Pyrenees where the sheep were pastured, in an area ultimately covering the entire Basque Country, are the material documents or visible signs of a world of beliefs, concepts, and purposes.

The same east-west orientation of the dolmen and the placement of the corpses within it, laid out in the direction of the sun's path, seem to be inspired by a cult dedicated to that star. It could be said, then, that the sun, or the solar divinity, was the object of religious veneration.

Abundant remains of bonfires have been found beside certain dolmens (Intxusburu, Beotegi, and Igartza), suggesting offerings of fire, sacrifices, and offerings of food at funerals.

The grooves found on the roofs of the dolmens of Olaberta and Ezkiregi (fig. 26) also seem to be related to funeral sacrifices, serving to channel the blood from the animals that were sacrificed on top of the dolmens.

Pieces of animal flesh were deposited near the corpses of humans, probable offerings made to the deceased.

In most of the dolmens that have been explored, we have also found ceramics, pieces of pots in which libations were offered to the deceased.

Other items found in the dolmens are weapons and instruments of stone (axes, arrows, knives) and metal (copper arrows, punches or awls, bracelets, necklaces), amulets and pendants (rock crystal, beads made of jet, alabaster, jadeite, and the fangs of boar and bear, bone earrings and slate plaques, rings made of horn and bone, fish vertebrae).

There are also tiny stone votive axes, sacred instruments whose character has been preserved until our times.

Dyes, such as hematite and ochre, have been found in the dolmens of Askorrigana and Artekosaro.

Of particular interest for their rarity are two fork-shaped human incisors found in the dolmen of Argarbi, but the current state of our knowledge of the Eneolithic does not allow us to interpret them.

The orientation of the bodies and of the megalithic sepulchers, the offerings deposited in them, the amulets and utensils provided for the dead, the solidity of the dolmenic constructions which have come down to us through centuries and millennia, the sacrificial offerings suggested by certain remains, the surviving residue of bonfires, and the very placement of the dolmens in sites probably occupied by shepherds' huts or folds, provide clear indications of the existence of a religion and domestic cult in which ancient elements appear in association with new forms and beliefs.

THE BRONZE AGE (1200–600 B.C.)

Following the formation of the Pyrenean culture of the Eneolithic, especially considering the techniques and ways of life of the population, it is important to acknowledge a period in the Basque Country characterized by the use of certain bronze weapons (axes, arrowheads, daggers) and tools. On the other hand, neither the natural landscape, nor the fauna, nor the human type ("western Pyrenean") experienced any appreciable differences.

The vestiges of man and human culture of this age are found in a number of sites, such as those of Santimamiñe, Goikolaua, Oyalkoba, Lezetxe, Lamikela, and Esterlocq, and in dolmens such as Obioneta (Aralar). Isolated objects have been found in Iruzubieta, Kutxiñobaso (Cenarruza), Arceniega, Faardiko-harri (Sara), Zabalaitz (Aizkorri), Orkatzategi (Oñate (Oñati)), etc.

Industry — Almost all of the instruments that have come down to us are made of stone. But we are not yet in possession of sufficient material to allow us to identify their particular character and style.

There are also objects of bronze: axes, tips for arrows and spears, awls and bracelets. Among the axes, some, like those of Arechabala (Aretxabala) (in Iruzubieta) and Castellar, which are flat, probably belong to the first period of this age. Those from Zabalaitz and Faardiko-harri, with decorated edges, seem to be from the second period. From the third period, perhaps, are the twisted bracelet and the slotted axes found in Kutxiñobaso. The tubular axe, from Arceniega, is from the fourth period (fig. 27 A).

As for ceramics, we know of only a few funeral urns, all handmade. Urns from Obioneta and from Lamikela: some with a flat base, others convex; some saucer-shaped, some bi-conic; with or without nipples; some with a smooth surface, others with bands of vertical incisions. Their style and form, generally crude, are reminiscent of more ancient ceramic types that survived in the Basque Pyrenees until the Bronze Age (fig. 27 B).

Dwellings — Some natural caves were inhabited by man; in Santimamiñe, Lumentxa, and Harixtoi, ceramics and stone artifacts from this time were found.

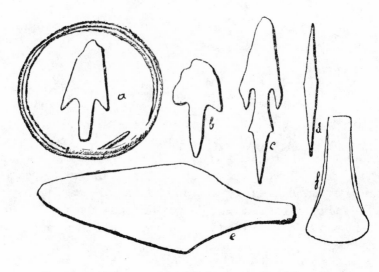

Fig. 27 A.—Bronze-age industry: *a)* bracelet and arrowhead from the necropolis of Lamikela (Contrasta); *b, c)* arrowheads from the dolmen of Obioneta; *d)* awl from the dolmen of Ueloguena; *e)* lance tip from the dolmen of Obioneta; *f)* axe from Zabalaitz (Aizgorri).

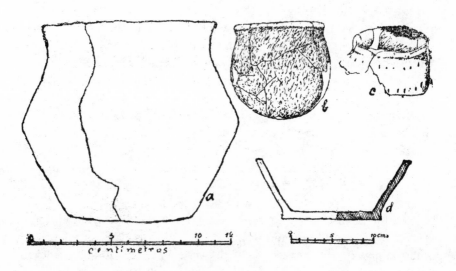

Fig. 27 B.—Ceramics from the dolmen of Obioneta: *a)* based on the Memoir published by Aranzadi and Barandiarán; *b, c, d)* from reconstructions done by J. Elósegui (*Ikuska*, 3, 1).

Probably many of the man-made caves in the south-southwest region of Araba were also inhabited during the Bronze Age; some, even earlier. On June 28, 1928, we excavated the earth that covered the floor of an artificial shelter located on the right side of the grottos on the hill called "El Montico" (in Albaina). We examined four superimposed layers. The top two contained varnished ceramics and unshaped slivers of flint; the next layer produced very crude black ceramics along with slivers and small finished chips of flint and a stone for pounding; the fourth layer held no ceramic remains, only some small flint pieces with carvings on the edges that resembled craft from the Mesolithic. Since the shelter had been carved in the rock before it began to fill in, that is, before the layers into which we were digging had formed, it would be safe to attribute it to an epoch prior to the Bronze Age, perhaps Neolithic or Mesolithic. Although the other shelters and artificial grottos of the region have produced no objects that could help us date them with certainty, the result of the excavation of "El Montico" and the similarity of these structures with other analogous ones in other countries that have been attributed to the Eneolithic or the Bronze Age lead us to think that they must have been inhabited at least since the latter period (figs. 28 A and 28 B).

Fig. 28 A.—The cliffs of Uriatxa beside the plain called Busturia (county of Treviño). On the cliff to the right, a black mark indicates the entrance to an artificial grotto several meters above the base of the cliff.

Fig. 28 B.—Entrances to three artificial grottos of Santorcaria (Laño).

We have not discovered any remains of dwellings out in the open, but it can be assumed that they outnumbered those in caves. The artifacts discovered in Salbatierrabide (near Vitoria-Gasteiz) reveal that there was a prehistoric site there, probably inhabited by humans since the Bronze Age.

Sepulchers — One part of the population followed the old custom of depositing corpses inside natural caves. Human remains have been found alongside ceramics and beads or pendants from that age in Oyalkoba, Lezetxe, Isturitz, Harixtoi, and Goikolaua. In this last cave, a cadaver had been placed above the stalagmite level of the floor. Since it had not been moved during subsequent periods, the skeletal remains, though quite scattered and broken, had remained in the same place alongside broken pieces of pots and tiny pierced disks of white stone when we visited the cave on September 12, 1935. Several bodies were also buried in the shelter of Lamikela (Contrasta).

Another part of the population deposited corpses in dolmens. The southern dolmen of Obioneta can be assumed to have belonged to this

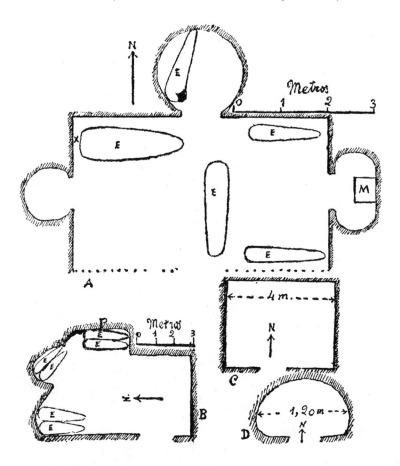

Fig. 28 c.—Floor plans of four artificial grottos in Araba: *A)* one of the burial grottos of El Montico (Albaina); *B)* burial grotto on the western slope of Kanas (Urarte); *C)* one of the grottos of Txarronda (Marquínez); *D)* one of those found on the western slope of Engua Hill (Marquínez). Sepulchres opened on the floor are marked with the letter *E)*. At (*M*) (sketch *A*) there is a podium, possibly a pedestal or altar. On the wall marked with an *X*, there is the engraving shown in figure 31 *A*. On the wall marked with a *P* (sketch *B*), above the tombs, there is another engraving, shown in figure 31 C.

age because of the items found inside. It is unusual in that the floor is paved with stones, like the dolmens of Portuzargaña and one in Landarbaso that may be contemporary with it.

Finally, the artificial grottos of Araba may have served also as cemeteries, since in many of them there are tombs dug into the rock of the floor. But the fact that these are completely empty deprives us of data that might have given us information about their period.

It is possible that the custom of incinerating corpses may have been introduced in some parts of the country. In 1918, in the sand pit of Salbatierrabide (near Vitoria-Gasteiz) I discovered a site formed by a stratum with human remains that covered another thicker layer with objects from the Iron and Bronze Ages. Underneath the latter there were several burial pits for incineration: hemispherical holes one meter in diameter and 0.65 meters deep dug into the gravel bed of the recent Pleistocene terrace. The only one I was able to explore completely was formed from top to bottom by three layers of blackish soil separated by other layers of yellowish soil, made of sand and gravel. In addition to soil, the blackish layers contained ash, carbon, segments of burnt bones, broken pieces of crude ceramic vases (pots with nipples and orifices for hanging), knives made of flint, arrowheads of flint and ophite and tiny axes of polished stone. The alternating layers were archeologically sterile[8] (fig. 29).

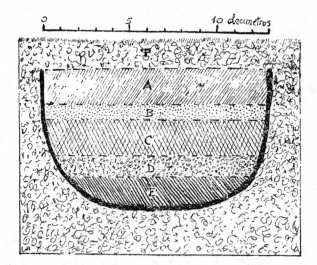

Fig. 29.—Incineration urn from Salbatierrabide: *T)* gravel layer beneath soil with vegetation; *A)* blackish clay with stones, coal, pieces of burnt bone, shards of clay pots, flint, spear point, polished arrow, boar fang. 16 centimeters thick. At the bottom, a limestone urn measuring 40 centimeters in length and width and 6 centimeters thick. *B)* sandy yellow soil with no archeological remains. 9 centimeters thick. *C)* loose blackish soil with shards from clay pots, pieces of unformed flint, two silex knives, an arrow point, two polished stone axes, coal, ash, and pieces of charred bone. 20 centimeters thick. *D)* a gravel layer, with no archeological remains. 10 centimeters thick. *E)* compact blackish soil with shards from clay pots (rough, blackish substance similar to the ceramics of the upper level), coal, bits of flint, and a quartz scraper. 10 centimeters thick.

Religion — Only in tombs do we find archeological data related to the religion of the Bronze Age. But these do not reveal any significant change after the Eneolithic, except for the cremation of cadavers which to date has only been acknowledged at one site. This ritual is connected to specific ideas about the destiny of man after death and probably to a new religion. It constitutes a novelty in the later periods of this age which subsequently, during the Iron Age, attained considerable extension throughout our country.

The artifacts found in burial sites consist of weapons of stone, copper, and bronze, amulets of stone and bone, perforated fangs of wild boar and bear, bracelets of bronze, bi-conic and saucer-shaped ceramic vases.

Perhaps we should also attribute to this age the figures carved deeply into the rock beside the door of one of the artificial grottos of Santorkaria (in Laño), which seem to represent three axes with handles. The engraving that I discovered on the face of a wall in 1917 in a sepulchral grotto of Urarte may also be from that period (figs. 30 and 31).[9] We can say the same about the vase or urn engraved with the figure of a star from Goikolaua.

Such customs or rites, objects and images that have paradigms in the Eneolithic culture and in the Bronze Age of other countries of West-

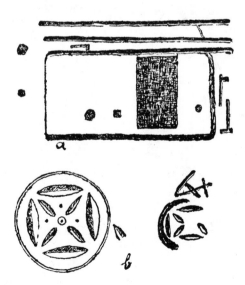

Fig. 30.— *a)* Entrance to a cave in Santorkaria (in Laño); *b)* engravings on the inside of the same cave.

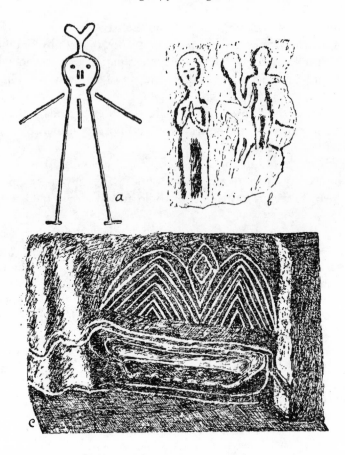

Fig. 31.— *a)* an engraving from El Montico (a cave in Albaina); *b)* a sculpture in the cave of Santa Leocadia (Marquínez); *c)* an engraving in the artificial cave of Kanas (Urarte).

ern Europe are proof of the influences that continued to arrive in the Pyrenees from different directions.

These archeological facts naturally confirm the persistence of the Pyrenean culture of the Eneolithic and also reveal the influences of a nature-based religion that constitute a religious stratum in which we can discern the cult of a celestial divinity, linked to the cult of the axe (votive axes from the dolmens and images of axes from Santorkaria), and the solar cult brought to mind by the east-west orientation of the dolmens and the radiated images on the ceramics from Goikolaua and Ermittia. These cults must have existed in connection with the cult of the ancestors.

In the environment of this naturist religion, certain beliefs and rites must have evolved relative to the phenomena and forces of nature that traditional Basque culture and the vocabulary of Euskara have preserved until today. Such are the beliefs in a celestial divinity denoted by the names *ortzi, urzi* (sky, thunder, God); *ortzegun* (day of the sky, of the celestial divinity); *eguen* (day of the sun or celestial light, Thursday); the veneration of the sun and its symbols (circles, swastika, pentagonal star, ostensorium or *iguzkisaindu* "holy sun" and the flower of the wild thistle, called *eguzkilore* "sunflower"; the greetings to the sun and moon; the custom of building houses and shepherds' huts so that the main façade faces east; the festivals of the solstice and the names *Ekhaina* (month of the sun, June) and *Eguberri* (new sun, Christmas); the belief in the spirit of storms, called *Odei*, and in the spirit of the fire of the hearth; the attribution of a mystical power to the axe, the hoe, and to solar symbols, as agents that protect the house during storms; the custom of placing candles and food in tombs as offerings to the dead and the belief that they use them and eat them in the afterlife, etc. This entire religious complex, in accordance with the archeological suggestions mentioned above, the elements and names of which apparently pre-date the Celtic and Roman influences of our proto-history, must have its origin in the Eneolithic and Bronze Ages of the people of the Pyrenees.

THE IRON AGE

After the end of the Bronze Age, numerous movements of populations are recorded in Western Europe, making it possible for the people of the Pyrenees to establish contact with different people and cultural currents. One of these, probably of Celtic origin, imported or diffused by an immigrant people, spread over a large part of the Pyrenees, especially in the northern pasturages. Another current, also Celtic, was propagated in the regions to the south, forming small groups and fortified settlements at different points in the Basque Country.

Monuments of the first wave are the *baratz* (one of the names by which they are known to the people) or circles of stones like cromlechs, that in many cases circumscribe small tombs with incineration urns with an area that extends the full length of the mountain range from the Ariège to the borders of Navarre and Gipuzkoa. Their principal sites in the Basque Country are the *baratz* or groups of *baratz* of Elorta (in Askonobi), Irati, Ocabe, Lindus and Atalosti, Zaho, Baigura, Iuskadi, Artzamendi, Ezurreta, Mailarreta and Goizamendi, Ibaineta, Gorostiarria, Mandale, Pittare, Lerate, Oyarzun (Oiartzun), Elazmuño and Olegi, Aramo, Unamuno, Etzela and Oentzun (in Berástegui (Berastegi)), and Altxista (above Urnieta) (figs. 32 and 33).

We are speaking of a modality of Celtic culture that some believe to have originated in Bohemia and in Bavaria. It spread to the Pyrenean regions by moving through Switzerland and Northern Italy, where it was propagated mainly in the Ariège, Upper Garona, Upper and Lower Pyrenees, and in an extensive zone of the Basque Country, especially on its oceanic slope.

The landmarks of the Celtic wave from the south, known even today, are found in Castejón (near Arguedas), in Etxauri, La Hoya (Laguardia), Iruña, Kutzemendi, Salbatierrabide, Oro, and Arrola.

Vestiges of this age have been found also in caves such as Harixtoi, Urio, Goikolaua, and El Bortal (Carranza).

Very few serious excavations have been carried out yet in the principal sites of the Iron Age in the Basque Country. For that reason and, in part, due to the lack of material contained in the excavations that

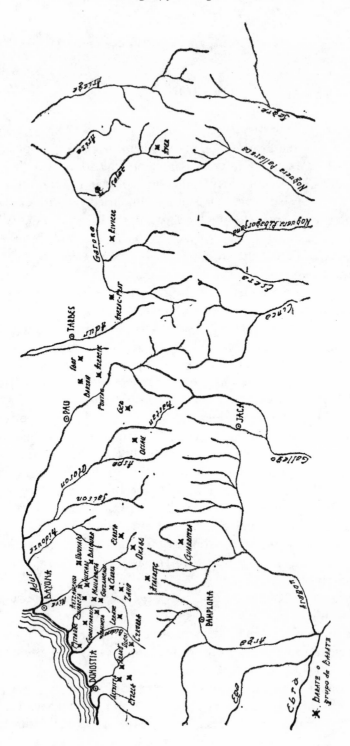

Fig. 32.—Area of the *baratz* or Pyrenean cromlechs.

Fig. 33.—Cromlech of Ataloste (Mount Lindus).

have been explored, it is not possible to arrive at clear chronological conclusions.

Dwellings and Sepulchers — The caves must have been less inhabited than in preceding periods; but in some, ceramic remains have been found, revealing that they were occupied during the Iron Age. The cave of Harixtoi (in Donamartiri) contains, apparently, a stratum with ceramics of the Hallstattic type. The ceramics found on the surface at Goikolaua (in Berriatúa) are analogous.

However, most of the dwellings must have been out in the open, located in sites more convenient to the transhumance and pastoral life of one part of the population and to the agricultural life of the inhabitants of the lowlands. Dwellings with rectangular floors and walls of adobe and interlocking strips of wood have been discovered in the Castejón excavation. In Iruña there were dwellings with rectangular floors, with walls made of stone without mortar. In Kûtzemendi and Salbatierrabide as well, remains of walls of the same kind were found that could have been for dwellings. In the last-named site there was also a circular pit one-and-a-half meters deep and one meter in diameter, similar to those that have been recognized in other communities of this period.

At the very least, tombs for cremation were generally used in one sector of the population. The *baratz* in the eastern parts of their area of the Pyrenees contained vases with ashes and offerings. The corpses were placed on the fire with their adornments and personal items. Their ashes and charred bones were then enclosed in pots, which were covered by a mound of earth and irregular stones surrounded by a circumference of stones partially buried in the ground. At times the ashes were deposited in the tomb without any receptacle. The few excavations that have been undertaken in these monuments in the country have produced no archeological material, except for those at Okabe, where several broken pieces of pottery have been found.

Another funeral custom was, undoubtedly, that of depositing the ashes of cadavers in large urns in caves. This is the purpose of the pots found in the cave of Bortal (Molinar de Carranza), Uriogaina (Sara), and those that were found in a secondary gallery of the cave of Harixtoi (fig. 34). The one in Uriogaina must have been sealed with a sandstone lid that lay over the broken pieces of the pot when it was found. The pot had been broken open and its contents spilled out.

Fig. 34.—Vases from Harixtoi.

Industry — In Salbatierrabide, in the stratum beneath the one containing crafts of the Roman epoch, saucers and pots of the Hallstattic type were found, as well as pins and needles made of bone and bronze, a ring, a brooch, a belt buckle, etc.

In Kutzemendi, at the very top of the hill commonly called "Castillo de Oralizu" today, situated in Mendiola to the south of Vitoria, there are the remains of an ancient community with an abundance of clay vessels with ornamentation engraved on them and in relief, similar to ornamentation from the Iron Age. The clay weights found there reveal that the craft of weaving was practiced there (fig. 35).

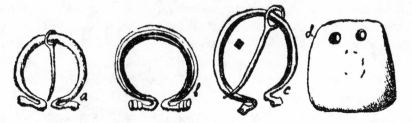

Fig. 35.—*a, b, c)* buckles from Salbatierrabide, La Hoya (Laguardia), and Iruña; *d)* weight for a loom from Kûtzemendi.

At the top of the mountain where the sanctuary of Our Lady of Oro sits, there are also remains from an ancient community, whose area includes the hills of Atxabal, Santa Marina de Gitabé, Losobraus, Arriaga, Eskotilla, and the hill of Uribiarte and its northern and northeastern slopes. Judging by the ceramics and hand mills that were taken from a thick blackish stratum at the site, an Iron Age community existed there.

In La Hoya, which is a low hill located near Laguardia, I also collected ceramic pieces from all along the crest. Their existence convinced me that there was a community there at the end of the Iron Age.

But it is in Etxauri, especially, where a necropolis from the second Iron Age was discovered, with an antenna-like sword, a bridle for a horse, a sickle, and a bar from a plow providing a good sample of the contents of the site (fig. 36).

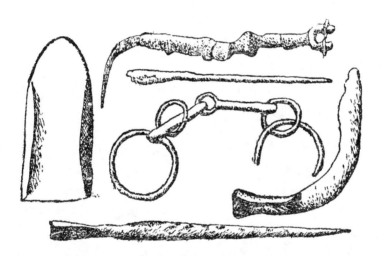

Fig. 36.—Iron objects (Celtic) from the necropolis of Etxauri.

The scarcity of the remains of crafts does not preclude us from considering that the Iron Age was well represented in the Basque Country. The considerable number of sepulchers, communities, and sites with strata from this age proves that different movements of peoples and cultures intersected here and that a systematic exploration would reveal abundant material to describe the life of the Basque population of those periods.

Ways of Life — The location of the *baratz* or incineration sepulchers in the Basque territory—generally in high pasturages—is a fairly certain indication that a large sector of the population herded sheep, practicing transhumance. The shepherd of the Iron Age followed the tracks of his Eneolithic ancestor, exploiting the possibilities of the natural landscape. For this reason, the sites of both Ages frequently coincide in the same places.

But in the western region of the Basque Country—Araba, Bizkaia, and most of Gipuzkoa—no *baratz* have been discovered; they have been found only in the eastern part, their area of diffusion extending as far as the Ariège.

In Araba and southern Navarre, the settlements of Oro, Kûtzemendi, Iruña, Salbatierrabide, La Hoya, Castejón, Arguedas, etc., reveal another culture and probably other ways of life based on agriculture and cattle, as can be concluded from their locations themselves, an opinion that seems to be confirmed by the discoveries—plow and sickle—in Echauri (Etzauri).

Notes

1. José Miguel de Barandiarán, "Exploración de la cueva de Urtiaga," *Euskojakintza* (Bayonne), vol. 1 (1947): 686.

2. On August 12 of 1919, as I was going from Santimamiñe to the cavern called Kobaederra, less than a kilometer from there I saw alongside the path on which I was climbing, a deep open pit in the ground; it was a trap for catching wild boar, according to my guide.

3. Adolf Staffe, "Beiträge zur Monographie des Baskenrindes," *Revista Internacional de los Estudios Vascos* 17 (1926): 34.

4. This conclusion seems reasonable, since the existence of such rudimentary livestock development in use down through the ages in the mountainous zone of the Basque Pyrenees cannot be explained unless it proceeded from primitive herders or is considered a carryover of their method. Also, the division of an animal among several individuals or families, allotting each a share (right half, left thigh, etc.), appears to be a vestige of the ancient sharing of the hunted animal.

5. T. de Aranzadi, J. M. de Bandiarán, and E. de Eguren, *Exploraciones de la cueva de Santimamiñe* (Explorations of the Cave of Santimamiñe), 2nd memoir, 33 (Bilbao, 1931). Aranzadi and Barandiarán, "Exploración de la cueva de Urtiaga, II," *Eusko-jakintza*, Vol. 2 (1948): 321. Aranzadi and Ansoleaga, *Exploración de cinco dólmenes del Aralar* (Exploration of Five Dolmens from the Aralar) (Pamplona, 1915); *Exploración de catorce* [fourteen] *dólmenes del Aralar* (Pamplona, 1918). Aranzadi, Barandiarán, and Eguren, *Exploración de nueve dólmenes del Aralar guipuzcoano* (Exploration of Nine Dolmens from the Gipuzkoan Aralar) (San Sebastián, 1919); *Exploración de seis* [six] *dólmenes de Aizkorri* (San Sebastián, 1919); *Exploración de seis dólmenes de Urbasa* (San Sebastián, 1922). Aranzadi and Barandiarán. *Exploración de ocho* [eight] *dólmenes de la sierra de Aralar* (San Sebastián, 1924).

6. Alcobé, "Antropología de la población actual de las comarcas pirenaicas" (Anthropology of the Present-Day Population of the Pyrenean Region), *Pirineos* 1:114.

7. Henri Cavaillès, *La Transhumance Pyrénéenne et la circulation des troupeaux dans les plaines de Gascogne* (Pyrenean Transhumance and the Circulation of Flocks on the Plains of Gascogne), 11–12 (París: Colin, 1931).

8. Workers who were extracting the sand in the area caused all of these pits and a large part of the site to disappear in a few days.

9. J. M. de Barandiarán, "El arte rupestre en Alava" (Cave Art in Araba), in *Boletín de la Sociedad Ibérica de Ciencias Naturales* (Zaragoza), March–April 1920. T. de Aranzadi, J. M. de Barandiarán, and E. de Eguren, *Grutas artificiales de Alava* (Artificial Caves of Araba), San Sebastián, 1923.

Selections from
An Ethnographic Sketch of Sara

by José Miguel de Barandiarán

HUMAN ESTABLISHMENTS AND THE RURAL HOUSE

Temporary Dwellings

The rural houses located in valleys and in the zones below the mountain ridges, whether they are farmhouses or not, are generally permanent family dwellings. But when they are devoted entirely or partially to sheepherding, these houses possess one or more temporary shelters deeper in the mountains where the family member in charge of watching the sheep dwells for days or entire seasons. Such shelters are called *etxola* (hut) or *artzain-etxola* (shepherd's hut) (see fig. 1).

The *etxola* is generally a square or rectangular structure with dry walls of unworked stones and a pitched flagstone roof (in Basque, *gaina*) supported by wooden trestles. Beneath the ridge of the roof and facing east is the principal façade and in it the doorway. Sometimes the side walls protrude a few decimeters past the façade, as does the roof, thus forming a shelter like the open portal of houses. In some huts there is a window in one wall, or an open space in the interior parameter of the wall, where the wooden vessel that holds milk (*kaiku*) is placed after milking until it is used or transported to another location (fig. 1: 1 and 4).

In *etxolas* built for sleeping overnight, there is a ramshackle bed where the shepherd sleeps across from the entrance. It consists of a platform of poles placed horizontally on two parallel beams laid on the ground a meter and a half apart. This holds the platform twenty centimeters above the ground. On top of this platform tree branches are laid and over them a thick layer of ferns serving as a mattress. A blanket is the final addition (fig. 1: 3).

In some cases the shepherd's hut is adjoined to the side of a barn or stable (fig. 1: 2); there are others built inside the barn in one of the corners close to the entrance.

The old shepherd's huts were larger than those built today and had two compartments: in the first were the fireplace and the bed, and in the second different kinds of equipment and shelves for cheese. In these the

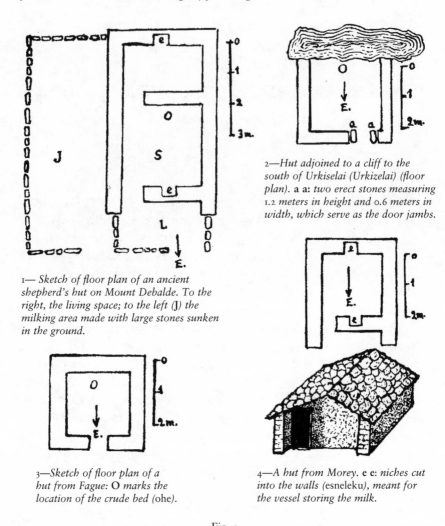

1— *Sketch of floor plan of an ancient shepherd's hut on Mount Debalde. To the right, the living space; to the left (J) the milking area made with large stones sunken in the ground.*

2—*Hut adjoined to a cliff to the south of Urkiselai (Urkizelai) (floor plan).* a a: *two erect stones measuring 1.2 meters in height and 0.6 meters in width, which serve as the door jambs.*

3—*Sketch of floor plan of a hut from Fague: *O* marks the location of the crude bed (ohe).*

4—*A hut from Morey.* e e: *niches cut into the walls (esneleku), meant for the vessel storing the milk.*

Fig. 1.

shepherd remained on the mountain during the entire season of summer pasturage.

There are shepherd's huts in Muy, Altsaan, Erkaizti, Fage, Urkizelai, and on the slopes of Ibantelli, Saiberry, Atxuri, etc.

Ardiborda —This is the word for the rustic fold where the shepherd keeps the flock while it is pasturing on mountains far removed from populated areas. It is a structure made with stone walls and a pitched roof covered with warped tiles or slate. Some of these *ardibordas* or sheepfolds have an upper level for storing hay (fig. 2).

There are also sheepfolds under rock shelters in places where an overhanging cliff extends out far enough to provide a roof. *Olanda'ko arpia*, "the grotto of Olanda," is one of these, located on the northern slope of Urkizelai (fig. 2: 1). Beneath the rock hollow called Atekaleun (on the eastern flank of Larrune) there is another shelter formed by two inclined cliffs joined at the top, which is used as a shelter for *pottokas* (ponies) and sheep. On the western slope of Urkizelai there exists a similar small shelter for the mares put to pasture on that mountain.

Here is a list of the sheepfolds or *ardiborda* of Sara: Maxinakin-borda (in Ortolopitzbeherea), Landaburuko-ardiborda, Iturriagako-

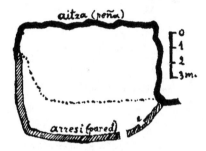

1.—*Grotto or ardiborda to the north of Urkizelaiko-harria, in a rocky overhang or grotto formed by a cave-in, measuring 9 meters in width, 5.5 meters in depth, and 1.5 meters in height. The front part is enclosed by a stone wall and the roof is finished with a slate cover.*

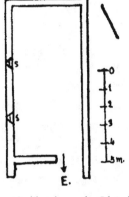

2.—*Ardiborda on the Olain hill. Its name: Mailuenborda-zaharra. Constructed with dry stones and a slate roof.* **s s**: *niches.*

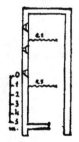

3.—*Floor plan of the ardiborda of the Jomildegikoborda farm on Mount Olain.* **es**: *partition of interwoven sticks.*

4—*Ardiborda of the Altzuortea farm, located on the eastern slope of Baztarreko-harria. To the right of the entrance it has an enclosed corner (Etx.) which is the shelter for the shepherd with an entrance A that can be closed with a stone slab.* **pp**: *poles.* **s**: *niche*

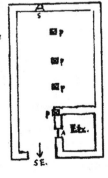

Fig. 2.

ardiborda (in ruins), Yaiberriko-ardiborda, Aniotzko-ardiborda (in ruins), Argaitzeko-ardiborda, Haldunbehereko-ardiborda (in ruins), Kukulluen-ardiborda (in ruins), Larraldeko-ardiborda, Uhaideko-ardiborda, Xantakoneko-ardiborda, Iratzeburuko-ardiborda, Lezabeko-ardiborda, Irlandako-borda (today, ardiborda of Uhaidea), Uhaideko-ardiborda (near Txillardiko-borda), Olalandako-ardiborda, Betrieneko-arpia (grotto of Betrienea), Etxargaraiko-ardiborda, Betrieneko-a., Aldagaraiko-a., Arburuko-a., Aranburuko-ardiborda, Jomildegiko-a., Etxegoyengo-a., Mikeletegiko-bordako-a., Xuitegiko-bordako-a., Kattienbordako-a., Teileriako-a., Ttakoinen-bordako-a. (in Faardiko-harri), Sabateneko-bordako-a. (to the right of Tombako-erreka, or the arroyo of the tomb), Uzkinaineko-a., (to the right of the arroyo Ukumeleko-erreka), Ithurbideko-bordako-a. (on the road to Saiberri), Mutilain-a. (near Munoenborda), Dendaldegiko-bordako-a., Arotzaeneko-bordako-a., Arrosagaraiko-bordako-a., Juanaenbordako-a. (today it is called Iguzkiagerreko-borda), Bordatxarreko-bordako-a., Bordaberriko-bordako-a., Arrosako-bordako-a., Iriburuko-a., Axain-a., Olabideko-a., Zimiztaineko-a., Zulobiako-a., Goxaingo-a., Haristegiko-a., Elhordiko-a., Elhordiko-borda (today converted into an *ardiborda*), Uharteko-a., Hiitiko-a., Leureko-a., Beherekoetxeko-a. (these are two folds in Ortolopitzbehere), Gaineko-etxeko-a. (of Ortolopitzgaine), Uhaldeko-a.

Jeiztei, Deiztei —Beside the shepherd's hut or beside the sheepfold there are often one or two flat rectangular areas enclosed by low stone walls one meter in height, like the ones near the hut of Argaitzea on Mount Altsaan; or by large, upright slabs, placed in a closed row, as in Iturriadarreta and in Debalde. These are milking stalls, called *jeiztei* (from *jeitzi*, "to milk"). When the milking area comprises two sections, like those at Argaitzea and Saiberri, one is used to hold the sheep that are to be milked, the other for milking the ewes one at a time (fig. 3).

Espil, Korralia —Next to these ancient shepherd's huts, in some sites we still find large, circular level areas surrounded by dry walls (in Basque, *arresi*) or stone slabs placed vertically on the ground like cromlechs. These are shelters where the shepherds gathered their flocks, especially at night, to protect them from attacks by wolves. They are called *espil, arrespil, korralia*. One of these corrals still exists beside the ruins of a hut and its *jeiztei* in Iturriadarreta in the town of Ascaín (fig. 3: 1).

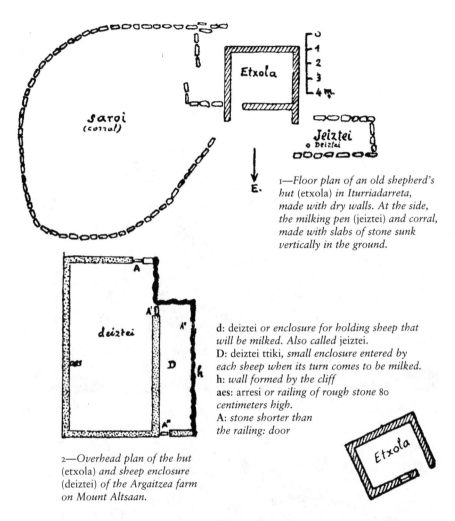

1—*Floor plan of an old shepherd's hut* (etxola) *in Iturriadarreta, made with dry walls. At the side, the milking pen* (jeiztei) *and corral, made with slabs of stone sunk vertically in the ground.*

d: deiztei *or enclosure for holding sheep that will be milked. Also called* jeiztei.
D: deiztei ttiki, *small enclosure entered by each sheep when its turn comes to be milked.*
h: *wall formed by the cliff*
aes: arresi *or railing of rough stone 80 centimeters high.*
A: *stone shorter than the railing: door*

2—*Overhead plan of the hut* (etxola) *and sheep enclosure* (deiztei) *of the Argaitzea farm on Mount Altsaan.*

Fig. 3.

Structures Attached to the House

In the chapter referring to the community and the population system of Sara, we said that the rural house of Sara "is not generally an isolated, separate structure, but rather it includes other structures in addition to the main building, some contiguous or near to it, others scattered throughout the land belonging to it." It is, then, a group or constellation of structures, such as the *aldatei* (granary), *ongarritei* (fertilizer bin), *labetei* (shed for the oven for baking bread), *zerritei*, or *zerrizola* (pig sty), *arditei* (corral), *oilotei, ollotei* (chicken coop), *mastietxola* (shelter for those who work in the vineyard), *kisulabe* (lime pit), *gaztain-espil* (circular area surrounded by a stone wall, used for storing chestnuts), *yarleku* (site in the parish church) and *ehortzeleku* or *tomba* or *ilharri* (family sepulcher inside the church or in the cemetery). See figures 4, 5, 6, 7, and 8, drawings of several types of houses made by don Julio Caro Baroja in 1949.

Fig. 4. Ainesenea (Sara).

Fig. 5. Kapetenea (Sara).

Fig. 6. Kaikuenea (Sara).

Fig. 7. Aldabea (Sara).

Fig. 8. Angonea (Sara).

Yarleku —Each house possesses on the floor of the parish church a reserved space that is an extension of its property. This is called the *yarleku* (seat). This is where a woman from the house sits to attend a ceremony or religious event. The cloth called *sayal* is spread over it, and when it is time for her to sing the response, she lights the torch (in Basque, *xirio*) and the small spiral-shaped candles (*ezko*) following a requiem mass which she requested in honor of her ancestors. If it is not a requiem mass, the ceremony comes first.

The *yarleku* and adjacent areas are in many cases identified by inscriptions overlaid or carved into the sandstone slabs that form the floor of the church. In figure 9 we indicate some of these inscriptions.

Ilharri, Ehortzeleku, Tomba —Each house has its tomb in the cemetery, which, like the *yarleku*, is considered to be an extension of the home to which it is assigned. The names used to refer to these are *ilharri*, "stone for the dead," *ehortzeleku*, "burial ground," *obi*, and *tomba*. The cemetery where the tombs are located is called *ilarguieta* or *ilharrieta*, "place for sepulchers," and surrounds the parish church.

The sepulcher is, then, incorporated into the house. It is a part of it. When the house is sold or bequeathed to heirs, the sepulcher is also assumed to be sold or inherited. This consists of a rectangular parcel of ground, covered by one, two, or three slabs of sandstone. A stone cross or an upright iron cross stands at the head. Only once did we see a disk-shaped stele (fig. 10), which disappeared in the year 1952.

HARRIA
GACOIA
RLEKHU
A

(Asiento de Arriaga)

(Seat of Arriaga)

CVEL
BEHE
RECO
IARLE
CKHVA
1707

(Asiento de Zuel-
behere 1707)

(Seat of Zuelbehere
1707)

MOSCOR
RONDOCO
THOMBA
DAHAU

(Esta es la tumba
de Moscorrondo)

(This is the tomb of
Moscorrondo)

IHALARRE
HAROZARE
NECOIARLE
CHVA1723

(asiento de Haroza-
rene de Ihalarre
1723)

(Seat of Harozarene of
Ihalarre 1723)

BARATCHARTECOI
AR'LECCVA ETA
EMANA' HARRIA
1707

(Asiento de Baracharte y
piedra tombal. 1707)

(Seat of Baracharte and
tombstone, 1707)

ARROSSAGA
RAICO.IAR
LEKHUA
1721

(Asiento de Arrossagarai
1721)

(Seat of Arrosagarai
1721)

CVBIETACO
IARLEKUA

(Asiento de Zubieta)

(Seat of Zubieta)

ETA ICANEN
DIREENEN IAR
LECVA ETA
SEPVLTVRA
HAVTATVA

(... y de los que fueren
asiento y sepultura
adoptada)

(... and of those occupying
a seat and adopted tomb)

LEHEN
BURUC
OIARL
EKHUA

(Asiento de
Lehenburu)

(Seat of Lehenburu)

TEILERI
ACOAIA
RLEKHV
A

(Asiento de Teileria)

(Seat of Teileria)

Fig. 9.

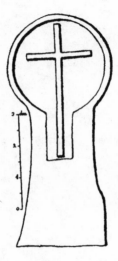

Fig. 10.

Most of the sepulchers, especially the ancient ones, are oriented
from east to west. The cadaver is deposited in the grave that is dug
beneath the slabs—which are removed for this purpose—so that the
head is placed at the west end and the feet to the east.

Today sepulchers are made in the form of vaults.

On the slabs that cover the sepulcher, an inscription indicating
ownership is frequently visible. On ancient sepulchers, the name of the
house to which it belongs is inscribed; on those from this century, the
name of the family. This change corresponds to the change that has
occurred in the conception of the house, its functions and those of the
domestic pantheon. See examples of such inscriptions in figure 11.

Arditei —Many houses have a lean-to abutting one side of the
building. It consists of three stone walls and a straw roof, with a door
connecting to the inside of the house and another to the outside at the
front. This is the shed or stable where the sheep are sheltered, especially
during winter nights when the flock is not pasturing on the high mountains. It is called the *arditei*.

The *zerritei* (pigpen), also called *zerrizola*, is a shed or lean-to made
of dry stones or stone slabs, with a roof of the same material, usually
built against the wall of the house. It has a wooden door to allow clos-
ing off the small enclosure.

Zerrietxola, "pig hut," is the shelter built on the mountain by each
inhabitant who takes his pigs there during acorn and chestnut season.
This is where the animals stay at night. It is a rustic structure built on two
vertical wooden posts that are forked at the top. On these, a thin beam (in

Tombs of the Lezabia house 1838

Tombs of LAHETE, HAROZTEGUI, MUSKETENE, ARROSSAGARAI.

Tomb of Mendiondo

Tombs of Bordakoborda

Tomb of Portu

That of Hindarte

Those of Carricaburu

That of Elizalde-Landagaraya.

SEVERAL OTHER TOMBS WITH BASQUE NAMES INSCRIBED

Fig. II.

Basque, *bizkar*) is laid to form the trestle. Two rows of sticks are placed along the sides of this. A covering of ferns is spread over it and on both sides. Only in the front is there an opening, which is the entrance.

Oilotei —This is the name for the chicken coop that some houses have outside their enclosures. It is a structure of stone walls and a roof covered with curled tiles. On the front wall, facing east, there is a door, and on one side, fairly high up, a small window through which the hens come and go, climbing and descending to the floor by a small stick ladder.

Mastietxola (vineyard hut).—In some vineyards there are small shelters or rectangular huts built like the *oilotei*, but without windows. They do have a round hole above the door for light and air to enter from outside. These serve as shelters for workers in the vineyard as well as storage space for the tools they use.

There are also huts where men who work in the apple orchards take shelter. There is one of these a hundred meters north of the Larraburuko-borda farm, made with four large sandstone slabs: three forming the sides and one for a roof (fig. 12). It resembles the chamber in a dolmen.

Aldatei —This is another rustic structure formed by stone walls and a pitched roof covered with tile. It consists of the ground level section, open on one side, where carts and work tools are kept. Above this, there is another level that serves as a grain loft. It is, then, a structure used as a granary or Bizkaian *garaixe* or Navarrese *gare*. Granaries like these are to be found on a number of farmsteads in Sara, as in Etxegaraia, Dundurienea, and Arantxipiko-borda.

Ongarritei, "fertilizer bin."—This is a shed with a pitched roof, similar to the *aldatei*, but without an upper level, and open on one or two sides. It is used to store manure from the stables. It stands near the main house, or abuts it, in which case it has a roof that is merely slanted.

Labatei, "place for the oven."—A structure like the one just described, though smaller, containing the oven for baking bread. Sometimes it abuts the house, on one side of the *lorio* or open portal; at other

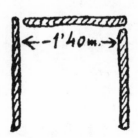

Fig. 12.—Floor plan of the *etxola* of Larraburuko-borda.
Height of the roof: 1.30 meters.

times, it is some distance away from the house, as in the Andoitzen-borda farmstead. More frequently, however, the oven is integrated into the kitchen or has its opening facing into it (fig. 13).

Gaztain Espil —From *gaztain,* "chestnut," and *espil,* "enclosure" or "round preserve." This is a structure found in chestnut orchards, made with a dry wall 80 centimeters high and 50 centimeters thick. It forms a level space that is usually circular, whose diameter ranges from 1.5 to 3.0 meters. On rare occasions it has an opening for an entrance; in such cases, it has a stone slab over a meter and a half high placed side-ways that serves as a door (fig. 13: 3). The workers beat the trees, collect the chestnuts, and place them in these walled enclosures. Afterwards, in winter, when other chores let up, they take them out and transport them to their houses in carts.

Kisulabe (**Lime Pit**) —The lime pit is a structure usually made against an earthen outcrop or dug into it. Its drum or tubular oven, which measures three or four meters in diameter, is formed on one side by the earthen bank lined with a thin wall of stone, and on the outside by a thick wall two meters thick and six meters high.

The base of the lime pit is a cask, smaller in diameter than the cylindrical oven, shaped so that its upper edge forms a rim (in Basque, *xapalda* or *erlaxa*) supporting the limestone vault or first layer of the material to be loaded into the oven. The cask, or firebox, is called *eltze* in Basque: it communicates with the outside by a tunnel that comes from the bottom. The air for fanning the combustion of the wood in the firebox comes through this tunnel. The ash formed there is also removed

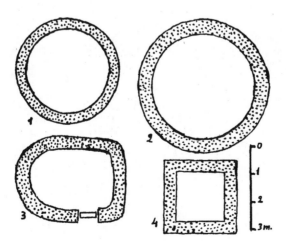

Fig. 13.

through the tunnel. The fuel is introduced through the oven door (in Basque, *ate*, *ao*), the threshold of which is level with the upper rim of the firebox. The lime is taken out through this door when it has cooked (in Basque, *erre*)—see figure 14.

During the cooking, the door is closed with slabs called *kaikuarri*, but a small window (in Basque, *agoxume*), through which fuel is continuously fed into the firebox, is left open.

Once the vault (in Basque, *giltzadura*), or the first layer of limestone, is finished, the oven is heaped with stones until a small mound is formed at the top of the oven. One oven receives a load capable of producing 100 carts each carrying 1,400 pounds of lime.

On the highest part of the limestone heap crowning the oven, a branch of white hawthorn (in Basque, *elorrixuri*) is planted. If this is not done, the key (*giltza* in Basque) to the arch, or first level of material on which the entire load of limestone for the oven rests, breaks; so said the ancients, that is, those who are the elders today (1942).

Furze, or gorse, is the fuel (in Basque, *erraki*) of choice. Since it is necessary to feed the firebox day and night, this job requires the participation of many people. The neighbors are the ones who collaborate in this work. The operation lasts five days and nights. The month of April is the best time for making lime. The burning of the hawthorn branch that crowns the oven is the sign that the lime-making process will be good and have good results.

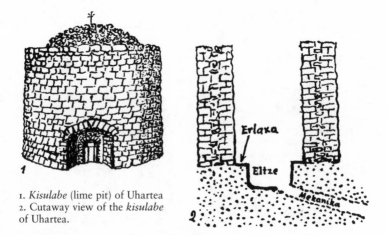

1. *Kisulabe* (lime pit) of Uhartea
2. Cutaway view of the *kisulabe* of Uhartea.

Fig. 14.

Tools and Equipment of the Rural House

In the Kitchen —For banking the fire and keeping the coals burning there are two andirons (in Basque, *suburdin*) and a crossbar (in Basque, *subarra*) made of iron. They call the charred wood *ileti,* the coals *ikatz.* The most commonly used fuels are oak, beech, and furze (fig. 15: 1).

Beside the firebox are iron tongs (*pintzetak*), which in some houses are shaped like pincers, and a bellows (*ausko*). When they used to be made of wood, the tongs were and still are called *sardaka,* or *matxarda* in other communities. (Fig. 15: 2, 3)

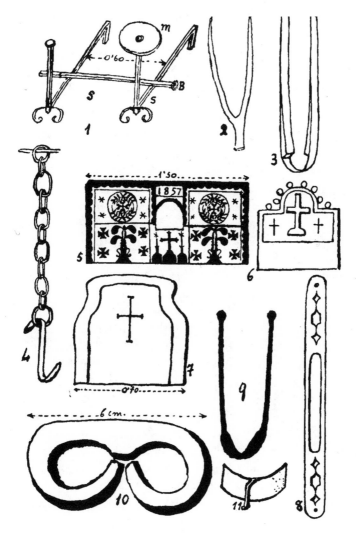

Fig. 15.

The pot hook (in Basque, *laatz*) hangs from a wooden crossbar located in the upper part of the bell of the chimney. This is formed by a thick iron bar bent at both ends into a double hook, and passed through the links of an iron chain from which it hangs. From the lower bend or hook, which is open, they hang the stew pots in which the food is cooked (fig. 15: 4).

The pot hook, like the hearth, is in some cases a symbol representing the house: the coals deposited beneath the boundary stones of a plot of land represent the limit of the property belonging to the house; when a cat is brought to the house as a purchase or gift, they walk it around the pothook in the kitchen three times so it won't run away to look for a different place to live. Servants do this as well when they first come to work in the house, according to a custom in Liguinaga.[1]

Austegui is the name of the ash pit or depository, a hole or entrance in the kitchen wall beneath one of the windows. On top of this depository, it is common to find a pair of small ovens which complement the hearth when the cooks need them. The façade of the ash pit is sometimes formed by a stone slab. In some communities, it has been the custom to decorate these with curious sculptures or bas-reliefs, like the one in Heleta (fig. 15: 5).

Decorative work similar to that on the façade of the ash pit is found on the large stone slab that serves as the back of the firebox in many kitchens in Lower Navarre. In Sara today, such stones are rare and have been replaced by sheets of iron. The few that still exist (in Ortolopitzgainea and in Lezabia) have very simple decorations (fig. 15: 6, 7).

In many houses there is a *zizailu* in front of the fireplace. This is a high-backed wooden bench that can seat five or six persons. It is a useful piece of furniture because of this and because it helps keep the kitchen warm by reflecting the warmth from the fireplace.

Maira is a large wooden trough found in kitchens for kneading dough for loaves of wheat or cornbread. Some of these are called *maira-maina*.

Balutra is the sieve used to sift wheat flour, and one with a larger mesh for sifting corn flour is called *zetabi*. A wooden frame called an *idinpasatzeko,* laid across the trough, serves as a base over which the sieve is drawn when sifting the flour (fig. 15: 8).

Maina is the wooden table where meals are served. It has a drawer (*tireta*) for storing everyday utensils.

Kadira is the chair, with a seat called *kadiraiia*, made of reed (in Basque, *iia*).

Alki is the name used to designate the small wooden benches.

Manka is a cupboard made of wooden planks that abuts one of the kitchen walls. In it are kept pots and pans frequently used for cooking.

Alasi is the sideboard on top of the cupboard or *manka*. It is fitted with latches (in Basque, *maila*) and wooden bars or strips (*alasiko-fara*) where plates are supported at an incline. The two pieces of furniture together are called *mankalasi*.

Tupin is the name of a large stewpot of enameled metal used to cook vegetables; *eltze*, the stewpot of fired clay; *kokela*, a clay pot with a long handle used for frying.

Kaiku is a one-piece wooden vessel in the shape of an oblique cylinder with a protrusion on the back with a groove cut into the upper edge and extending inward to the center. This extension of the *kaiku* serves as a handle, perfectly suited for the principal use of this vessel, which is used in the milking of cows and ewes (fig. 16: 1).

Abatz is another wooden vessel, shaped like a truncated cone, large enough to hold 15 or 20 liters. It is used to curdle milk for cheese-making. It has two handles on opposite sides (fig. 16: 2).

Terrina is a clay vessel similar in form to the *abatz*, which is almost extinct, and used in place of it (fig. 16: 3).

Opor is a wooden glass or cup, cylindrical in form, with a handle on one side (fig. 16: 4).

Gatilu is the name of the clay or porcelain cup most commonly used today.

Asieta is the name of the china plate common in houses today. Wooden plates (*txali*) like those found in other communities are no longer used (fig. 16: 5).

Today they use metal spoons (*kulier*) and forks (*furtxeta*). In former times (about fifty years ago) the use of wooden spoons with an oval cavity and straight handle was frequent. More recently, we have observed the use of wooden spoons in other regions of the Basque Country; but also long, curved spoons without a handle, made of horn or mussel shells (in Bizkaia) have been used (fig. 16: 6, 7).

Burdinarri is the ophite stone used to boil milk for curdling and for boiling whey (fig. 16: 8) [This process is explained on p. 227.]

Ferrería is a frame that hangs on a wall, formed by several bars or strips of wood fitted with pegs from which they hang different metal objects such as a *padera* or iron pan with a long handle and two feet to keep the pan level; *kaxo* or large pot with a handle; *erraki-untzi* or iron pan used to roast or fry different foods; *burruntzali* or a small pan with a long handle used to dip stews, milk, etc.; *zimitz* (strainer); *arrapo-kentzeko* (slotted spoon or skimmer), *esneuntzi* or cooking pot for carrying milk; *xokolatier* (vessel for making chocolate); *imitu* (fun-

Fig. 16.

nel), *artoxiortzeko* (iron apparatus with a handle used for toasting corn cakes); *opilburdin* (long iron paddle for cooking corncakes); *iruxango* (iron trivet), etc. (fig. 16: 9–14). In the *mankalasi*, or built into a wall, you will find a small wooden box, which is the salt bin (in Basque, *gatzontzi*).

Pitxar is what they call the pitcher made of clay.

Pegarra, a large clay jug for carrying and storing drinking water (fig. 17: 2).

Kafe-errota is the coffee grinder.

Xokolat-makila, the wooden whisk for beating chocolate (fig. 16: 15).

Lisa-burdin is the iron for smoothing and polishing clothing.

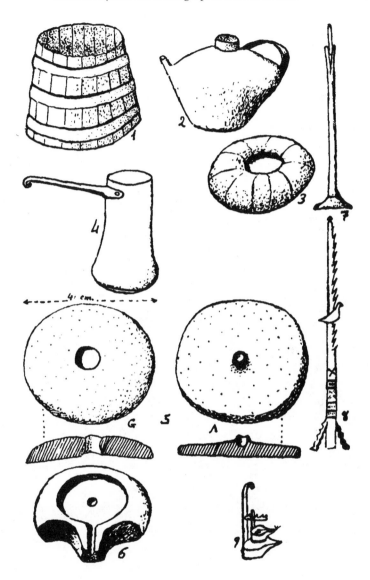

Fig. 17.

Lukainka-aga is a horizontal stick hung from the ceiling of the kitchen by two chains or *zumiak* (willow cords). They use it for hanging sausages made every year when the pig is slaughtered.

In the drawer of the kitchen table or on the ledge at the base (*ximini-uztarri*) of the bell of the chimney, eighty years ago you would find the following objects: a chain link (in Basque, *ferreta*) forged in one of the local forges (fig. 15: 10); a flint stone (in Basque, *suarri*); a half burned or charred piece of rag (*drunda*) or tinder (*kardo*). These were used to light the fire. The *drunda* was kept in a tubular metallic box called a *drundabarril*.

To light the fire (when my informant Piarrezume Camino was young—now in 1944 he is nearly ninety-three years old) they were already using matches like the ones they call *alumetak* today but *sub-rametxa* then; but these were more expensive than the old system for lighting a fire and were not practical when the wind was blowing.

Today they use electricity for lights, except in a few households, where they still use coal lamps (*karburu-lampa*). Before that, they used oil lamps (*petrolampa*).

Previously, there were candles of resin (*arroxina*) and wax (*ezkox-igor*) for lighting the kitchen, placed on vertical wooden holders that ended in a fork. The name of this holder is *argimutil* (fig. 17: 7, 8). A horizontal stick partially embedded in the kitchen wall was also used to support these candles.

It has been almost a century since they last used oil candles called *lampion* or *krisailu* (fig. 17: 9).

They use different types of electric lanterns for walking outdoors at night; but they also still use glass lanterns with a candle, called *lanterna*, and sheaves of wheat straw or a kind of light or torch called *lastoargi*.

In some kitchens that have an oven for baking bread in the same room, two kinds of wooden paddles are generally used for that operation: *abaro* and a paddle called *endai* or *labendai* in other places; the latter for putting loaves into the oven, the former for taking them out.

THE HOUSEHOLD

Consanguineous Relationships

Familial Relationships: Notions and Vocabulary.—Relationships between people and objects are expressed by words that originally stood for commonly used material things. The following are some of the most frequent names and phrases used for such relationships: *Esku, eskubide,* "right" (from *esku,* "hand," and *bide,* " path"); *esku guztiak eman,* "to confer upon him all rights"; *Gizonak badu lur bat, berain bizitzeko eta berain ehortzeko,* "A man has a piece of land (has a right to a piece of land) for himself to live on and to be buried in"; *eginbide,* "obligation" (from *egin,* "to make," and *bide,* "path"); *zuzenbide,* "justice" (from *zuzen,* "straight" and *bide* "path"); *gizabide,* "justice" (from *gizon,* "man," and *bide,* "path"); *ikuskizun,* "responsibility" (from *ikusi,* "to see" and the suffix *kizun,* "material"); *jaun,* "gentleman"; *andre,* "lady"; *nausi,* "master"; *jabe,* "owner"; *etxaldun,* "(male) householder"; *etxekoandre,* "lady of the house"; *etxe,* "house, family"; *ondorio,* "heir, descendant"; *ondoko,* "heir, descendant"; *sehi,* "servant"; *mutil,* "male servant"; *neskato,* "female servant."

The closest familial ties of all are those linking spouses. Then follows the relationship between parents and children, between grandparents and grandchildren, between siblings, between uncles and aunts and their nephews and nieces, between cousins (the children of siblings), between second cousins (the children of cousins), and between third cousins, with whom family relationships are considered to end. One's relatives (*adreria* in Basque) thus include all consanguineous relations in a direct vertical line, consanguineous relations in a lateral line through the fourth generation, and their spouses. Consanguineous relatives to any further degree are termed *aidekutsu,* "vestigial relatives" (literally "relics of family relationships").

The order and degree of relationships is respected, for example, in funeral processions. When accompanying a deceased family member's coffin to the church and cemetery, relatives form a line based on their respective degrees of relationship to the deceased, and this order is maintained on the way back to the house as well. In first place walks the spouse, followed by the father; then the son, the brother, the brother-in-law, the uncle, the nephew, the cousin, etc. If several brothers are present the eldest precedes the rest, and the same order of age is observed when there are several uncles, nephews, and cousins in attendance. The same applies in funeral processions if the deceased is a woman.

Nouns expressing the various degrees of family relationship are: *aideak, jendakiak,* "relatives." If these are paternal relatives they are called *aitain aldekoak,* and when maternal *amain aldekoak.* Others are *jaun-andreak* (Mr. and Mrs.), "spouses," "husband and wife," "married couple;" *nee jauna,* "my husband", *nee andrea,* "my wife"; *aita,* "father"; *ama,* "mother"; *buraso,* "father" or "mother"; *burasoak,* "parents"; *arbasoak,* "great-grandparents" or earlier ancestors; *seme,* "son"; *alaba,* "daughter"; *anaya,* "brother"; *arreba,* "sister" (in relationship to a brother); *aizpa,* "sister" (in relationship to another sister); *aitatxi,* "grandfather," "godfather"; *amatxi,* "grandmother," "godmother"; *osaba,* "uncle"; *matanta,* "aunt"; *iloba,* "grandson," "granddaughter," "nephew," "niece"; *semeautsi,* "godson"; *alautsi,* "goddaughter"; *aitaginarreba,* "father-in-law"; *amaginarreba,* "mother-in-law"; *sui,* "son-in-law"; *errain,* "daughter-in-law"; *koinata,* "brother-in-law," "sister-in-law"; *aurride,* "brother" or "sister"; *aurrideak,* "siblings"; *kusina,* "cousin" (to any degree); *leenkusina,* "first cousin" (the son or daughter of an uncle or aunt); *bigarrenkusina,* "second cousin" (the son or daughter of a first cousin); *irugarren kusina,* "third cousin" (the son or daughter of a second cousin).

House and Family — As *etxe* means "house" and also "family," relatives refer to themselves as *etxekoak* (people of the house), and in many cases their surname or family name is the same as that of the house in which the family originally lived. One hundred and fifty of the surnames inscribed in the *Liber baptismalis* of Axular (for 1609–1624) are names that the same number of Sara households have preserved to the present day. Nowadays only the father's surname is passed on to the children, but in the past it was not unusual for the name of the house to be passed on to children as a surname whether or not it coincided with the father's surname. This occurred in the eighteenth century with the names Olha, Haranburua, and Lahet, and must have been the general rule even before that. It was not unusual, therefore, that the mother's surname, rather than the father's, was passed on to their descendants if it was she who had inherited the house. Thus in the *Liber baptismalis* of Axular, the certificate of baptism dated January 31, 1610 refers to *Joannis de Aldabe filius Joannis de Urdax* (Juan de Aldabe, son of Juan de Urdax).

When used in reference to a person, the actual surname is employed only in letters, in military barracks, and in official functions and ceremonies. It is very rare for an individual to be called or known by his or her official surname. The manner of referring to an individual nowadays is the name of that person's house, probably the same manner used in the time before his or her paternal surname began to be employed as the only valid one. So the head of the family of the Altzuarte house is commonly known as *Altzuarte*, although his official surname might be Etxegoyen, and the rest of his family are called by their given names or by their state or profession, followed by the name of the house: *Altzuarte'ko etxekoandrea* (Altzuarte's wife), *Altzuarte'ko Mariana* (Mariana of Altzuarte), etc.

A wife adopts her husband's surname, but this custom is recent, having originated in the twentieth century. Previously, a married woman would have used her father's surname or the name of her family's house of origin during her entire lifetime, and this would be true for almost all women except among the bourgeoisie, who were always more open to outside influences.

The name of their house of origin serves to refer to the members of a particular family; so *Ibarsoro'koak* refers to the members of a family living in Ibarsoro; *Argaine'koak* names the family inhabiting the house called Argaine, etc. Sometimes this other mode is used: *Ibarsoro'tarrak*, *Argain'darrak*, etc.

Some individuals are addressed by nicknames, but this is rarely the case with entire families.

Given names are chosen from the official list of Roman Catholic saints. The most common are *Ganes* (John); *Ganixon* (John); *Piarres, Pello, Piarrezume* (Peter); *Joset, Kose* (Joseph); *Mizel, Mixel* (Michael); *Xemartin, Mattin* (Martin); *Mayi* (Mary); *Kattalin, Katrin* (Catherine); *Jeane* (Joan); *Mai-Luis, Mariana, Mari-Jeane, Josefina, Ana-Mari*, etc.

In the baptismal certificates found in the Axular *Liber baptismalis* of 1609 and 1610, 593 individuals are named, of whom 302 are males and 291 females. There appear twenty different given names for males and seventeen for females. The male names are: Juanes (130 times), Joangoche (2 times), Jehanmartin (2), Martín (60), Pedro and Pierres (42), Miguel (25), Martisanz (6), Sancho (4), Gabriel (1), Christobal (5), Adrián (3), Sanzin (1), Esteben (8), Antonio (2), Salvat (2), Bernardo (2), Bertrand (2), Lorentz (2), Matías (2), and Joseph (1).

The women's names are: María (147), Joana (58), Joanetta (2), Catalina (23), Sabadina (10), Garagina and Garagena (10), Extebene, Estebaneta (9), Magdalen (6), Laurencina (5), Ana (4), Agnes and Aynes

(4), Graciana (4), Gratena (2), Dominga (2), Domindina (2), Salbata (2), and Marijans (1).

As can be seen from the above, the most common names for men were Juanes, Martín, Pierres, and Miguel; and for women, María, Joana, and Catalina.

Today's given names are not the same as in the seventeenth century, but the differences do not appear to be very great. For the sixty Sara men whose names were inscribed in the town's registry of marriages from 1922–1931, the correlation is as follows: Pedro (10), Juan (9), Juan Bautista (7), Juan-Pedro (4), Miguel (7), Martín (4), Francisco (4), Domingo (3), José (3), St.-Martín (3), Tiburcio (2), Bonifacio (1), Renato (1), Félix (1), Mauricio (1), Gabriel (1), José-Manuel (1), Bernardo (1), Juan-Mauricio (1), Salvador (1), Nicolás (1), Carlos (1), Martí-Jose (1), and Alfonso (1).

For the 126 women who were born in Sara and who married there during the same period, the correlation is as follows: María (31), Juana (9), María-Juana (8), María-Ana (4), María-Luisa (4), Juana-María (2), María-Dominica (2), Catalina (8), Josefina (10), Francisca (8), Engracia (4), Alicia (1), Angeles (1), Antonieta (1), Caticha (1), Cecilia (1), Celestina-Adela (1), Dominica (1), Isabel (1), Estefanía (1), Emilia (1), Enriqueta (1), Fabiana (1), Juanita (1), Josefina-Sabina (1), Laurentina (1), Leonia (1), Luisa (1), Magdalena (1), María-Angeles (1), María-Luisa (1), María-Margarita (1), María-Rosa (1), Nicanora (1), Sabina (1), Silveria (1), Teresa (1), Verónica (1).

The most common names in the seventeenth century are the same as today, but several new ones have appeared. Also, Francisco, Domingo, and José are fairly frequent today but were not common before. Another recent occurrence is that there are now many composite names, which was a rare occurrence in the seventeenth century.

Given names are passed on from godfather to godson and from godmother to goddaughter. This custom, according to Axular's *Liber baptismalis*, was strictly followed in the early seventeenth century.

Reciprocal Relationships — Parents addressing their children generally use the pronoun *zu* (Castilian *usted* or French *vous*) until the children reach the age of reason, after which they are addressed in the familiar mode. Everyone else addresses children this way also.

Siblings and friends address each other in the familiar mode. Spouses address each other as *zu* after their marriage, even when previously they had addressed each other in the informal mode. The more formal *zu* is employed by children addressing their parents, nephews and nieces addressing their aunts and uncles, and, in general, by any individual addressing a superior. Addressing superiors in the familiar mode is considered disrespectful.

Parents address their children by their given (baptismal) names. Children address their fathers as *aita* (father) and their mothers as *ama* (mother). Uncles and aunts call their nieces and nephews by their given names, while nephews and nieces address their uncles and aunts as *osaba* (uncle) or *matanta* (aunt) respectively. Spouses call each other by their given names, as do siblings among themselves.

Except on rare occasions, families are not concerned with genealogy. However, in certain houses a coat-of-arms or an inscription showing the construction or renovation date is prominently displayed, at times with the names of those who built or inhabited the house in times gone by. The house is a symbol of the family, which is why its name figures in the old inscriptions on its tomb and its *yarleku,* the place in the parish church corresponding to that house and where certain religious functions take place for the souls of inhabitants now deceased. The following are examples of such inscriptions:

JOANNES DE ECHEGARAI – MARIA DE HARIZMENDI – 1791 (inscription found on a stone in the wall of the main façade of the Ixpilteguia house.)

LEÇABEKO THOMBAC 1838 (Tombs of Lezabea 1838).

ARROSSAGARAICO IARLEKHUA 1791 (Seat of Arrosagarai 1791).

As a consequence of work carried out on the floor of the parish church half a century ago, and as can be seen from their inscriptions, *yarleku* stones are now to be found outside their original sites.

Furthermore, the name of the family (rather than that of the house, as before) is now being engraved on tombs, but until the present the tomb was considered an extension of the house or an integral part of it, regardless of the family inhabiting it.

A family's ancestors are called *arbasoak.* The household is always considered to have certain obligations toward them, and in some cases arranges for a sung mass to be held for the souls of all those who may have died in the house. A few days before a wedding is to take place, the families of the bride and groom arrange for a mass to be sung in the parish church for the deceased of both their houses. Such a mass is said to be *obligazionentzat,* meaning that it is being celebrated in fulfillment of the obligations of both families toward their respective ancestors.

When a family prays the rosary together, something that is done on a daily basis in many houses, they say a final *Paternoster* dedicated as follows: "*Etxe huntaik atea dien arimentzat*" (for the souls who have departed this house), or *"Etxe huntako arima ganentzat"* (for the souls gone from this house).

Descendants consider themselves to have similar obligations toward their paternal and maternal ancestors, although they feel closer and more duty bound to the ancestors of the house in which they live.

Tradition and legend have in some cases perpetuated certain memories of ancestors or of events that have occurred in a particular house. My informant Ganixon Larzabal of the farmhouse Ibarsoro-beherea tells the story of two enormously strong and robust sisters from this ancient house of the rural aristocracy, who used to pull the wooden *trunku* or roller, drawn today only by cows or bullocks.

Ganixon Larzabal also relates that the Ibarsoro-beherea house was the first to be built in the town of Sara (others say that the first was Haranburua), and that a hunter from Vera (Navarre) who was passing by during its construction told his father upon his return home what he had seen in Xareta (the old name for the valley where Sara, Ainhoa, Urdax, and Zugarramurdi are located). The hunter's father then expressed his dismay at the fact that the new house, which was twenty kilometers away, would be too nearby for there to be any peace between neighbors.

Family honor is shown in different ways, especially when one member of the family has been accused of wrongdoing or a crime. When an individual is accused of breaking his word given in contractual matters, the entire family rushes to a vehement defense of its name. The same occurs with regard to an allegation of insincerity, unethical business practices, the reporting of crimes to the authorities, insolvency, poor judgment, or theft. Expressions such as *"Gure etxean ez da olakoik sekulan izen"* (Such a thing has never occurred in our house); *"Oi in duena ez da gure etxekoa"* (Whoever did this is not a member of our family) are often employed by Sara residents against accusations and insults directed at their relatives. The same collective sentiment is shown on happy occasions with expressions such as *"Ohore da olako gauza gure jendakian gertatzea"* (We are honored that such a thing should happen among our relatives).

Relationships among family members are sometimes very close, especially among relatives who were born and have lived within the same house. Having been born in the same house notably reinforces blood ties and those of origin and lineage. Not only does an individual receive special treatment in life from those born in the same house, but he or she—if single—will also be buried in the tomb of that house and will be remembered in prayers and masses by its inhabitants.

One is on a more intimate footing with relatives than with other people. A relative also enjoys greater authority when giving advice or when a reproach is felt to be in order.

Parents and single children reside in the same house, together with the son or daughter who is heir to the house and that person's spouse and family. *Etxekoak* (household members) are therefore often composed of two married couples and their respective children.

Younger sons and daughters (who are not heirs to the house) form a separate family once they are married, and they live in another house, not with their parents. But while single they may continue to live with the inheriting sibling even after the parents have died. And although life may have caused them to move elsewhere, they always consider themselves members of the *etxe* with the right to live there while unmarried. As mentioned earlier, they also have the right to be buried in the tomb belonging to the house of their birth and to benefit from any masses and prayers that may be said in it and in its *yarleku,* situated in the parish church.

Siblings living away from their parents' house for reasons of employment or marital status gather in the house with the rest of the family for *Omia-Saindu* (All Saints Day). Family gatherings occur mainly for the festivities honoring their town's patron saint, a family christening, a first communion, a wedding, or a death. At christenings the person hosting the festivity is a member of the newborn's family; at first communions the host is the person whose first communion it is; at a wedding either the bride or the groom is the host, and in the case of a death the *leenate* (the first neighbor to the right along the road to the church) is the host. In each case the family members celebrate by dining together.

Relatives are the first to come to a family's aid whether for an illness or if there is work to be done. If any children should be orphaned and members of the household are unable to raise or educate them, other relatives (in most cases an uncle and aunt of the children) will take them in.

The parents have authority over the fulfillment of obligations regarding the raising, instruction, and education of their offspring. But as their children's judgment matures, or they attain a lifestyle that does not require supervision, parents gradually respect their initiatives.

To some degree, children are considered subject to their parents' authority as long as they live in the parental home, even in cases (now rather frequent) in which the children do not participate in the household economy or share the same tasks as their parents.

The heir (or heiress) and his or her spouse who reside with the parents invariably recognize the authority of the latter as regards shared tasks and the administration and use of goods, although when it comes to the use of goods the parents comply with the younger couple's prenuptial agreement. Other children, as mentioned above, live with their parents until they marry, either working alongside their parents (or with the heir if the parents are deceased) or contributing some money to the family budget to compensate for the cost of their stay, if they earn enough at their jobs to do so.

It is often the case that emancipated offspring send their parents substantial amounts of money to help out in unfavorable economic situations. Cases also occur in which a married son, given possession all of his parents' goods, turns his parents out of the house to which they have made him heir. This conduct is considered monstrous in the community.

The elderly and the infirm are generally taken care of at home. There are some very rare cases in which they are admitted on a permanent basis to the town hospital, where services related to nutrition, medication, etc. are in fact very good.

The House and Household — In cases of hereditary succession, it has long been the custom to maintain the integrity of the house. The house is to remain undivided and always in the hands of the same family.

It is not considered a good thing to sell a house that has traditionally been linked to a certain family. I once asked a neighbor of the Xomindinia house, himself the owner of the Aldabea residence, if he would sell his house. His answer was, "I cannot sell the house because it is the family home of my parents."

When the owner of the Kapetenia house was asked if she were willing to sell it she answered that she had inherited it from her father and could not sell it without giving grave offense to his memory.

Dividing or splitting up a house is also ill-considered. In 1933 Mateo de Salaberrieta, a resident of Bidartia, told me about an incident showing what people think about such cases:

"It is not seen as a good thing to divide up a house, even if there are many children."

"In Pikasarria [a Sara farmstead], the late Andrés designated his daughter the owner of the house."

"One son was given Sanxoinia [a house in Sara]; the second, another house; the rest received 200,000 francs each at the expense of the daughter of the house."

"In many other cases, if the parents die without making their wishes clear, two neighbors are usually invited to determine what the sons and daughters of the deceased will inherit. They always decide that the house will go undivided to one of the children; the others are apportioned other goods or money from the estate."

Parents may bequeath their property as they will, choosing one of their children as heir regardless of age or sex. For the most part the one chosen is the eldest. If this is a male he is named *premu*; if a woman, *andregaya*. Unless the parents have determined otherwise, the *premu* or the *andregaya* will inherit the house.

When there are no children, a nephew, niece, or other relative is generally designated heir; only very rarely is he or she not a family member.

An heir is officially designated in the last will and testament of his or her parents or in the stipulations of his or her prenuptial agreement. In this second case, the bride and groom and their parents appear before the notary public of Ezpeleta to write up the legal document transferring to the bride or groom (as the case may be) a quarter of the family estate and the obligations now owing to his or her parents and ancestors. That day the bride and groom and their relatives have a celebratory meal at the heir's house.

Even if the parents are not the owners of the house, they choose as their successor the son or daughter that they consider the most suitable for the position. The owners respect their choice.

If the father dies before choosing an heir, the mother will assume this responsibility. If there are no children, the widow cannot dispose of the assets brought to the marriage by her deceased husband, but she has the right to live in his house. If there are children, the widow has the right to the use of those assets, and also to select an heir from among the children; this heir will inherit both the land and the assets acquired during her marriage.

Should the husband and wife be separated the assets acquired after their marriage are divided equally between them.

The heir is awarded a quarter of the house and its accoutrements. The rest goes to endow his or her siblings equally. The heir undertakes this particular function, endowing his siblings in kind or in money such that the house and its territory are not divided. He is responsible for the upkeep of the parents.

Upon the marriage of an heir while his parents are alive, both married couples commonly reside in the same house, or *bi andanak*, as they say here.

The family estate does not always pass to the heir while the parents are alive, but this does happen on occasion, as was previously mentioned.

A dowry consists of that part of the inheritance determined by the parents to be bequeathed to their children without reduction in landed property, to be taken from the assets earned by them after marriage and other assets to be contributed by the heir to the house. The delivery of the dowry takes place when the prenuptial agreement is drawn up for a son or daughter about to become emancipated through marriage. The dowry consists of money, and, in the case of a daughter, other assets to make up the amount stipulated, such as beds and other furniture, bed linen, etc. A son receives a bed, a cow, corn, work tools, etc.

Some childless couples adopt a nephew, niece, or other relative and designate that person heir to their assets. Sometimes an orphan who is not a relative is adopted.

After the religious wedding ceremony the bride and groom pay a visit to their ancestors' tombs to pray for a few moments; this is a way for the most recent member to become a part of his or her new home, or for the newlyweds to feel linked to each other's families.

If the newlyweds take up residence in the groom's house, the new wife assumes the duty of presiding over the religious functions designated by the family to be performed from time to time at the tomb or *yarleku* corresponding to that family in the parish church. These may include various prayers, masses, the illumination of the *yarleku*, and so on. Here the integrity of the house and its protection from alienation appear in the form of the demand for continuity in its domestic religious practices.

The husband is the head of the household, although the wife exercises a decisive influence in most family matters. The spouses address each other in the formal mode using *zu* (Castilian *usted*) after marriage, as has been mentioned earlier, no longer addressing each other in the familiar mode.

The despotic treatment of a wife by her husband and vice versa is generally frowned upon and harshly censured. Equal treatment and rights are considered to be the most just way to proceed and are in keeping with tradition.

Parents, and particularly the mother, have a powerful influence upon the conduct of the young couple, especially if they all live in the same house.

When a young couple does not live with their parents they participate to a lesser degree in the life of the house. However, they try to keep its memory alive through frequent visits, especially at *Omia-saindu* (All Saints' Day), the festival of the town's patron saint, or at important family occasions.

If a married couple is taking a long time becoming parents they visit Our Lady of Lourdes to pray for children.

Only the men work in the mountains (*larre*) and in the woods (*oyan*), sawing, carrying ferns and brush, chopping and carrying firewood, etc.

Both men and women cultivate plots of land, except for the management of the cow- or ox-driven plow, a task that is undertaken by men.

Within the house the men's duties consist of the care, feeding, and milking of the larger livestock (cows, horses, sheep, and goats), and the cleaning of their stables. They are also in charge of the animals' tack and of leading them to work, of their sale and their blessing with holy water and wax on St. Blaise's Day. The maintenance of the house and tasks generally related to carpentry and stone masonry are also done by men.

Work done by women relates to cooking, house cleaning, the laundry, sewing, shopping for food and clothes, the care of the pigs and chickens, and their purchase and sale. Above all, it is a woman's job to raise and educate her children, and, as was mentioned in Chapter 3 of this *Sketch*, to bless the house and its related buildings at Candlemas (February 2) with holy wax, as well as her husband, her children, and the other family members and animals in their care. It is chiefly the woman who supervises the religious functions, both in the home (blessings, prayers, sacrifices, and offerings) and at the tomb and *yarleku* belonging to her house in the parish church. She represents the house on many occasions when neighbors require aid, such as during an illness, upon a death, when offerings to the dead of the neighborhood or town need to be made, etc.

Men and women generally employ the same kinds of tools for common tasks, although each sex has its own hoes (the women's are lighter), rake, and scythe. When knitting, men use two hooked needles, while women use four straight ones. When spinning yarn from sheep's wool men would use the *xabila*, a small mill with two wooden cones joined at the top, whereas women used a *koka* (distaff) and *ardatz* (spindle).

Sehi means "servant." In the case of a man he is referred to as *mutil*; if a woman, *neskato*. Male servants are more common in rural houses than are female ones.

Servants working in farmhouses and in those associated with sheepherding undertake all the various types of work done in those houses. They eat the same meals and at the same table as the family of the house, they generally sleep in beds and bedrooms of the same quality, and are considered members of the householder's family.

Hired hands are now earning (in 1941) 200 and 300 francs per month; forty years ago they earned 20 francs. They are hired subject to monthly contracts; previously their contracts covered years, although they were paid monthly, as they are today. Contracts were never formally written, a verbal agreement between the two parties being respected and fulfilled.

If work has been contracted at so much per year and the hired hand leaves before the year is up, he is not paid for the period he has been working at the house until the year has transpired. If the head of the house breaks the contract by dismissing the servant before the time stipulated in the contract, he is obligated to pay him the entire salary of that month.

In some houses the custom is to give the hired hands a pair of trousers, rope-soled sandals, shirts, and other clothing as gifts.

There is a common saying to the effect that hired help should not start work at a house on a Wednesday or a Friday, or he will not get used to its ways.

Clothing

Clothing is referred to as *soñeko*. It is worn to protect the body and to hide it from view, but also, according to data provided by my informants, as a sign of gender, age, profession, social status, festivities, certain public functions, travel, work, weather, season, etc.

In Sara it is believed that in ancient times men wore a single, rough, sack-like garment that covered them from the neck to the feet.

When my informants, who are now in their seventies or older, were children, adult males wore an *atorra* (shirt) made of linen, *barneko* (jacket) with blue sleeves, blue *galtzak* (trousers) (or white ones made of fine cloth), a *guerriko* (belt) or cummerbund of any color, a black *gapelu* (beret), woolen *zapinak* (socks) in the winter, and a pair of elongated wooden *eskalapoinak* (clogs) ending in an upturned point. As an overcoat sheepherders wore an *ardillaru*, a garment made of two sheepskins that hung from the neck. For harvesting fern and herding in the mountains, men would wear woolen *galtzoinak* (gaiters) from the knee down over their trousers. Most country people went barefoot around the house and its environs.

Women wore an *atorra* (shirt), *azpiko-soina* (underskirt), *gaineko-soina* (skirt), *bazkina* (bodice), *lepokua* or a large kerchief around the neck (or a lace shawl), *tauliera* (apron), *motto* or a cotton covering for her chignon, *kalotxak* or wooden clogs, and cotton *galtzerdiak* (stockings) to wear to church.

Nowadays (1941) there is more variety in what people wear and, generally speaking, clothes are more expensive. Men's apparel consists of a *larruarraseko* (undershirt, usually made of cotton or flannel), *atorra* (a shirt), *trikota* or sweater (in winter only), *barneko* (a vest), *paltu* (a jacket or raincoat), *galtzak* (trousers), *galtzonak* (underpants), *gapelu* (a black woolen beret); *zeintura* (a rubber belt), *eskalapoinak* (wooden clogs), *espartiñak* (rope-soled sandals covered with thick cloth), *zapata-murritxak* (leather shoes), *zapatabotinak* (boots), *galtzerdiak* (socks, which when made of wool are called *galtzerdi-ilariak*). Items of women's clothing are: *atorra* (a shirt), *barnekotrikota* (an undersweater), trousers, *soinazpiko* or *kotilunazpiko* (an underskirt), *tauliera* (an apron) or housecoat, *trikota* (a sweater), *galtzerdiak* (stockings), *espartiñak* (rope-soled sandals), *kalotxak* (galoshes) or wooden-soled clogs, and *zapatak* (shoes). Boys start to wear trousers at three years of age, and girls wear long skirts at fourteen.

Linen was spun at home at the close of the nineteenth century, and it was woven into cloth on looms that existed in several houses in the area. Each family would spin woolen yarn from which one or more of its members would then crochet socks for themselves and the family. In those days many of the people who lived nearby would make clogs and galoshes out of alder wood for domestic use, as they do to this day. The women made many clothes at home, such as shirts, trousers, housecoats, and aprons, but this is rare today. Women now prefer to buy these items in stores or have them made by professionals. When someone wears a new article of clothing for the first time his friends give him a *zimiko* (pinch) on the arm, saying *zimiko berri*.

Motto is the word for a woman's hair. Half a century ago it was the custom to braid it and wear it in a twist at the back of the head. Young girls would wear their hair in one or two braids that hung down the back. At fifteen years of age they would roll it into a chignon, covering the top part with a piece of colored cotton or silk called *motto*. Married women wore a large headscarf, also called *motto* or *buruko*. This could be of any color the woman wished, but those worn by elderly women and widows were black. Nowadays it is only very elderly women who wear their hair the old way with a black *buruko*. Other women have their hair curled and styled at a hairdresser's.

At the beginning of the twentieth century men wore their hair extremely close-cropped. Nowadays (1941) they allow a little bit of *muniko* (toupé) to grow on their foreheads, and, unless they are farm workers, let a little hair grow on the top of the head. Farm workers wear berets, but all other men go hatless.

The same kind of clothing is worn on working days as on holidays, although on holidays it tends to be newer or in better condition. While working in the countryside in summertime or in good weather, men wear undershirts, shirts, trousers, a cummerbund or belt, rope-soled sandals, and a beret; when it rains they put on a jacket and clogs.

Women—though not all nowadays—wear metal *petentak* (earrings). It is said that gold earrings help to protect the eyesight of the wearer.

Rings were hardly ever worn by country women at the beginning of the twentieth century, but today they are seen more often. Young women wear them on the ring finger of the right hand, married women on the left hand.

Religious medallions are often worn around the neck, and ones representing the Virgin Mary or Saint Benedict were particularly popular. Saint Benedict medallions were believed to protect the wearer against lightning strikes.

Scapulars (*abituak*) representing the Virgin of the Immaculate Conception, the Virgin of Mount Carmel, and the Sacred Heart of Jesus are also commonly worn.

Men carry a *makila* (a walking-stick to help them as they travel through the mountains). Previously it was also used to go to market. They often carry a *paisola* (umbrella) hanging down their backs from their jacket collars; in days gone by they would tuck them under their arms. The walking-sticks are made at home from lengths of holly or some other resistant material. In Larresoro there is a specialist who makes nicely decorated *makilas* fitted with handles and metal points.

Early in the twentieth century, as mentioned above, yarn was made at home.

According to my oldest informant, Piarrezume Camino, around 1880 *euntegiak* (looms) were to be found in several houses in Sara, but they began to disappear as a result of the invasion of new kinds of fabrics favored for their low cost and novelty. Even so, during the early decades of the twentieth century many women continued to make their own linen thread, which they would then take to Saint-Peé Castle where there was still a working loom and where an *eaile* (weaver) would make *oialhari* (cloth), also known as *etxeoial*. This weaver was still working until his death in approximately 1925. In every household, shirts, trousers, and sheets were made of linen cloth. Today these items are made from fabric bought in local stores, in San Juan de Luz, or in Bayonne. Of course the working clothes that country people wear on the job are made at home as was mentioned above, although some of the fabric is store-bought.

In times past women made winter socks and stockings at home with *ilhari* or wool yarn. Today they use store-bought cotton thread or wool yarn to make them.

Old tobacco leaves are placed among clothes to keep moths (*pipi*) away. *Piper-beltz* (powdered mustard) and *piñuburu* (pine cones) are also used for this.

Footwear is not made at home from animal skins: boots, shoes, and sandals are purchased in stores. Only very young children wear rope-soled sandals, which are imported from Navarre.

A bed (*oe*) consisted of the following: *oekuxeta* (the bed frame), generally made of wood; *laistara* (a mattress), a large bag filled with corn husk or wheat straw; a woolen *matalaz* (quilt); *mihixi* (sheet); *koltxoin* or small bedspread with a white lining called *oelarru* which covered the bed as a mattress pad; *buhurdi* (a bolster or pillow); a *lumatxa* (down comforter), and *zaloin* (bedspread). That was what the bed was like at the beginning of the twentieth century. Nowadays the straw mattress is replaced by a *zumierra* (metal bed base), and in place of a *koltxoin* one finds a sheet over which are placed some blankets.

Spinning and other domestic tasks that have now disappeared were an occasion for neighbors (particularly women) to gather during the winter months around one of the neighborhood hearths. There they would discuss all the problems and happenings of the area, relate legends, sing songs, etc., all of which kept alive the connection between the local people and the traditional knowledge of the community.

Food

The general word for food is *otruntza*. There are three main meals of the day. The first is called *gosari* (breakfast) and is taken at eight or nine o'clock in the morning, depending on whether it is summer or winter. The second meal is *bazkari* (lunch), eaten at noon, and the third is *afari* (dinner), taken at nine o'clock at night in the summer and at eight in winter. These were the rural families' only meals at the beginning of the twentieth century.

Nowadays people generally have *gosaritxiki* (a "little breakfast") before starting work in the morning.

When laborers are employed they are given free *amaiketako* ("elevenses," a late morning snack). In summer it is now customary to have a *krakada* (snack) at five o'clock in the evening.

J. M. Hiribarren wrote the following about Sara:

Aza ilharrak dire	Kale and beans are
Saran aiphatuak,	Celebrated in Sara,
Hetan dire egiten	That's why the people
Gorphutz hanpatuak.	Become pleasantly plump.
Dutenean hetarik	When they have
Beretzat sobera,	Enough to spare,
Oihu egiten dute	They loudly and generously
Lainhoki hauzora.[2]	Inform the neighborhood.

Bazkaria (lunch) is the main meal of the day. When one is invited to a meal it is understood that it will be *bazkaria*.

Meals are prepared in the kitchen. When family members and hired help are working at some distance from the house, it is customary for their meals (with the exception of dinner) to be brought to them.

Meals are better than usual during the wheat harvest or in the threshing season, or when other important work is being done. In summer, workers have a mid-afternoon snack and more wine is consumed at mealtimes.

Early in the twentieth century, meals were generally simpler or more frugal than they are today.

Gosaria (breakfast) consisted of *arto t'esne* (cornbread and milk) or *arto-opil t'esne* (corn cakes and milk). Cornbread thicker than a centimeter is referred to as *arto*; thinner cornbread in disc-shaped pancake form is called *arto-opil*. Sometimes breakfast consisted only of *ai* (pap) made from wheat flour and milk. This pap was in some cases replaced by another kind made from corn flour and whey from sheep's milk, or else by *orreboroaska*, made from corn flour and milk.

Bazkaria (lunch) comprises two courses: *eltzekaria* and *jakia*. *Eltzekaria* is a stew made from beans, potatoes, or kale together with stock and leeks, onions, garlic, and sometimes carrots. It is served with oil or lard as condiments.

Jakia consists of *xingar* (bacon), or cheese, or meat.

Afaria (dinner) consisted of *eltzekaria* as at midday, and some milk.

Even today these same meals are commonly eaten in most rural houses. *Gosaritxiki* (the "little breakfast") is also usual, in the form of sweetened coffee. Bread, cheese, and sometimes a little wine make up the *krakada* or early evening snack. The *amaiketako*, which is only eaten when there are hired hands present or when working the wheat harvest, is like the *krakada*.

Nowadays milk is boiled in a metal cauldron set over the flame in the kitchen hearth. This operation is called *esnia egosi* or "boiling the milk." To make *gaztambera* (curds), the milk is not boiled in its cauldron over the fire but by having white-hot stones placed into the cauldron. This operation is called *esnia erre* or "burning the milk." Whey is also boiled through the addition of white-hot stones, a process called *arritan egosi*, "boiling in stones." It is said of whey that "*Erretzen delarik, egosten da, irakiten du*" (When it burns, it boils, it bubbles).

Edan means to drink. All ingestion of liquids is referred to as *edan*, or *irentsi*, which is literally "to swallow." But if milk is consumed with bread sops, this is called *esnia jan* or "eating milk."

Drinks are uncommon except for a variety of light cider known as *pitarra* which frequently accompanies the midday meal. Wine is rarely used.

The household all eats together at the same table, men and women, children and hired help alike. My informant says that, "*Seiak eta nausiak berdinak dire laborari-etxetan, laneko eta jateko: denak main berean*" (Servants and masters are on an equal footing in farm-houses, whether at work or eating: all at the same table).

Each person at the table eats from his own plate, but the family uses a common glass for wine and cider.

Today people use china dishes. Previously, double-handled pots were used, made from somewhat less refined earthenware glazed on the inner surface; these were called *kaxola*. Also employed was a terracotta cup with the edge bent inward; this was called *opor*, and was used for milk with bread sops. The only wooden kitchen vessels used today are *kaiku*, or the bowl used in sheep milking, *abatz*, *opor* (bowls similar to the earthenware version), the *zimitz* (cheese press), and the *suilla* (pail). (See Fig. 16 in the previous segment, page 208.)

A cup is *katillu*, but the large china version is known as a *bola*.

A spoon is referred to as *kullira*. It is used for taking up and eating any liquid or semi-liquid food.

Bacon is eaten entirely with the fingers. In the nineteenth century and even a little beyond, everything referred to as *jaki* (bacon, meat, cheese, tomato) was eaten in this manner. Fruit is also eaten with one's fingers. Older people today have heard their parents comment that stew used to be eaten with the hands: *ahurka* (from *agur*, the cupped hand).

People use spoons made of metal rather than wood. My informants have seen wooden spoons in Zugarramurdi. One of my informants, who lived there for a time, carves them out of boxwood.

A knife is *kanieta*; a pocket-knife, *naala*. These are not used during family meals except for slicing bread. Knives are used for cutting meat and fruit only when visitors are present.

Making the sign of the cross before meals is customary. In some households a grace is also offered, such as the following: *"Jauna, benedika gaitzazu gu eta artzera goazin janaria eta edaria"* (Lord, bless us and the food and drink that we are about to receive). Few people pray after a meal. The sign of the cross is also made when eating the first fruit of the year.

Me egin (fasting) is observed on days indicated by ecclesiastical law. On such days the traditional foods are potatoes, beans, cheese, tomatoes, and milk.

Special and more costly meals are only served on those days honoring the patron saint of the town. On Easter Sunday lamb is a fairly common meal, and at Carnival people make *kruxpeta* (beignets) from wheat flour and egg boiled in water.

Home-baked bread is made either from wheat or corn flour. If wheat flour is used the bread is called *etxeogi*; if corn flour, *arto*. Each house was equipped with its own oven for this purpose, but nowadays (1941) not every household bakes bread.

Generally, leavening made with corn flour is used in bread-making. It is said that the dough ferments better with this leavening than with one made from wheat flour. The Basque name for this leavening agent is *orrantz* (or *artozezen* in the Itxasu region).

Bread dough is called *orre*. Kneading is referred to as *orratu*.

Flour is kneaded by hand once warm water is poured into a well made in the center of the pile of flour in the wooden *maira* (kneading trough). At the same time, the leavening is gradually added to the dough.

Home-baked wheat bread is given a rounded, rather flat shape and weighs around nine pounds (four kilograms); cornbread is less flat and weighs about eleven to thirteen pounds, or five or six kilograms.

Corn cakes (*arto-opil*) are made from corn flour, and also wheat flour in some cases. When the *arto-opil* have been half-toasted on a long iron paddle (*opil-burdin*) placed over the fire, they are set in front of the embers in the hearth, supported by a kind of iron easel called *opil-mantenu*. There they are left to rise, and the process comes to an end. Cornbread is generally eaten in slices toasted before the embers on a device called an *artoxigortzeko*. (See Fig. 16, no. 14 in the previous segment, on page 208.)

In almost all rural households it is customary to kill a pig every year for family consumption.

When the pig is killed—sometime between December and the end of March is the appropriate period for this—slender *odolkiak* (blood sausages), *andoilak* (thick blood sausages), and *lukainkak* (in Castilian *chorizos*, or garlic-and-paprika-flavored pork sausages) are made. The first kind of blood sausages are made from a mixture of blood, onion, meat from the pig's head, pepper, and parsley, placed in casings made from the small intestine. Once the basic sausage is made and its ends tied with string, it is rolled into twists which are tied off with wicker. The sausage is then put into a cauldron of water over the fire and boiled for ten minutes, after which it is taken out of the pot and placed by the fire to darken. It is then boiled for another ten minutes. Each twist makes one blood sausage.

Andoila is made in the pig's large intestine from *trinpoila* (stomach), lung, garlic, and bell pepper finely chopped with an ax or some other instrument. It is boiled in a cauldron and dried by the fire.

Lukainka is a sausage with a casing of large intestine; it is made from *giñarra* (lean pork), garlic, salt, and sometimes mustard. It is boiled in the same way as blood sausages. It is hung over a horizontal paddle, which in turn is suspended from the kitchen ceiling, where it is smoked and dried for some days; it is then put into a jar containing melted lard, after which a little oil is added.

It is customary to give blood sausages (a couple of twists) as gifts to each of the families in the neighborhood and to friends and relatives. Generally the children are given the task of distributing these sausages, receiving a prize of two or three francs in return.

The man responsible for the pig's slaughter is given his daily wage plus the pig's tail.

Like *chorizos*, pork steaks are preserved in a jar with lard and oil.

In many households a sheep is generally slaughtered for the celebrations in honor of Sara's patron saint (August 15) and during the threshing period or that of another important task. This is when sausages called *arditripak* are made from chopped tripe, lung, onion, and bell pepper and stuffed into the *gatxagi* (maw) and into the small intestines. They are cooked in the same way as blood sausage, but for longer. Then they are eaten.

During Fat Thursday and Carnival a gift of pork (bacon, blood sausage, *chorizo*) is traditionally given to children and adults who come asking for treats. When they arrive at a house they shout *"Iaute, iaute, zingar t'arrautze"* (Carnival, carnival, bacon and egg). And they skewer the pieces of bacon, *chorizo*, and blood sausage on a wooden lance called a *gerren*.

The fruits and nuts consumed by each household have mainly been grown on the land belonging to it. These foods are chestnuts (nowadays rather scarce); apples and pears picked before they are completely ripe and spread out on straw where they mature and take on a yellowish color (*goritu*); cherries, figs, and (rarely) grapes, harvested after a fall frost and placed on hay to ripen (*usteldu*, to rot); also hazelnuts and walnuts left on the tree until they are ripe and about to fall. Quinces are used to make a sweet concoction.

There is a great deal of coffee consumed nowadays, mainly with breakfast. At the beginning of the twentieth century it was only served during the festivities in honor of the town's patron saint or on an important family occasion.

A complementary food that sometimes puts in an appearance in the kitchen is fish from local rivers: *amorrain* (trout), *aingira* (eel), *xipa* (bitterling), and *zarbo* (barbel).

As a rule, the native population does not eat snails, although some people may eat them on rare occasions. This is a custom brought in from abroad by guards and other individuals.

At the beginning of the twentieth century no mushrooms or fungi of any kind were consumed. Even now, spring mushrooms or *Agaricus tricolom* are not eaten, but other mushrooms and certain other species of fungi such as *gibelurdin* (*Russula virescens*) are consumed.

In many households cheese (*gasna*) was made from sheep's or cow's milk, and sometimes from a mixture of goat's and cow's milk. During milking the milk was collected in a wooden container (today zinc ones are also available) called a *kaiku*.

A small piece of lamb's rennet, wrapped in a rag, is left in a little milk until it is soaked through. Then it is taken out and squeezed inside its rag until the milk—now infused with rennet—is strained into the terrine containing the warm milk that is to be turned into curds. These days artificial rennet is also used, such as the La Presure Fabre brand, which is called *gatzagi-ezpiritu* (spirit of rennet). The milk turns to curds in a few minutes. *Hartzen du* ("it takes it") is the expression used to signify that this process has taken place. *Matoin* is the term for milk curds.

The cheese-maker then stirs the mass of milk curds with his hands, gathering it together and squeezing it against the sides and bottom of the terrine. He then places a wooden frame called *kartola* across the top of the terrine. On top of this he places a cheese press (*zimitz*), into which he inserts part of the *matoin*, squeezing it with his hands until all the whey has been wrung out. He sprinkles a little salt onto it and leaves it for a few hours. Then he takes it out of the press and adds salt to the other side. The cheese thus formed is placed on a square presser frame called a *xareta*, which is made of hazel sticks and is suspended from the ceiling in one of the rooms in the house.

The cheeses are rounded, often slightly cylindrical, and frequently somewhat flat.

Dry cheese is called *gasna-zahar* (old cheese). Sometimes it becomes wormy, and is then referred to as *gasna-galdua* and considered to be of the highest quality.

Junket (*gaztambera*) is made from milk, generally sheep's milk. It is boiled using white-hot stones. This process is called *esnea erre* (burning the milk). A rounded ophite pebble no bigger than eight centimeters in diameter is placed in the hearth until it is incandescent. Then it is inserted into the pot of milk and in a few seconds will cause a liter of milk to boil. When the milk cools down a little rennet is added, and in a while the junket is ready.

Whey (*gazur*) is consumed in some families. In some cases it is sold in bottles as a laxative, and some people give it to the pigs to drink. Others heat it up to make cottage cheese (*zenberen*). This was previously done with white-hot stones. As the whey heats up it gradually causes a white substance to rise to the surface, where it is skimmed off using an *iazki* (strainer) and deposited into a bowl. Cottage cheese is eaten as a dessert at mealtimes. The leftover whey is given to the pigs.

Soured milk is called *esnemindua*; if it is extremely rancid it is known as *esne-galdua*.

Burra, or in other places *gurin*, is the term for butter. It is made from *esnegaina*, the cream taken from unboiled milk. The cream is scooped out in a strainer and placed into an earthenware pot or bowl, where it is stirred with the hands or a spoon until it solidifies into butter. It is then taken from the pot and placed into a bath of cool, frequently-changed water, and the butter is squeezed by hand until no more whey remains and the water no longer turns white. The whey left over from butter-making is either boiled and drunk, or given to the pigs.

On some farms with vineyards, wine is made for household use. The following are some common terms relating to this process: *maats* (grape, vine); *maats-bihi* (grape seed); *murko, maats-murko* (bunch); *maasti* (vineyard); *arno* (wine).

Wine-making includes the following operations: the bunches of grapes are placed into a large barrel called *kuela*, which is stood on end and open at the top; the bunches of grapes are then stripped by several people stamping on them in their bare feet. The stems (*zurtoin, txurtoin,* or *girtoin*) are separated from the grapes, although sometimes this process is omitted. The solid part that lies at the bottom of the barrel is thrown into the wine press, where it is pressed. The resulting liquid passes into a recipient (*tina*). From there it is placed into several medium-sized or one large barrel called *gupela* or *pipa*, where it is left to ferment. Water is poured onto the grape residue remaining in the press, from which, after a few days, a drink called *minatxa* is obtained.

Tobacco is called *belar* or *pipa-belar*. Nowadays it is smoked in cigarette form, but in the past, pipes made of wood or plaster were used. Some people use *arraspa* (snuff, powdered tobacco), especially women. Women from rural farms do not smoke tobacco.

Instead of tobacco, some people at the beginning of the twentieth century smoked the dried leaves of a plant called *kukubelar* (digitalis).

Boys are generally allowed to start smoking at about eighteen years of age.

The following item regarding food is taken from my notes written on November 24, 1942, during the German occupation:

> Food supplies are extremely difficult to come by for those who do not own land or livestock. Milk is scarce, and costs 3.20 francs a liter if available at all; bread (200 grams a day per person) costs 3.80 francs per kilogram; beans (when available, as they are very scarce) cost 30 francs per kilogram; corn, 20 francs; potatoes, 10 francs; a kilogram of cheese costs 35, 55, or 60 francs; a dozen eggs, 80 francs; frying beef, 50 francs per kilogram; chicken, 100 francs per kilogram. Feed for livestock is very costly: 100 kilograms of hay costs 400 francs. Because of this the Argainborda farmers have been forced to sell their cows, and their employer has become a journeyman. The Germans pay the young men they transport to Socoa to dig trenches 7 francs per hour per person, although the workers have to pay their own fares (20 francs). Owing to this general rise in prices, all sense of fairness in the measurement and worth of foodstuffs has been lost. For example, two days ago I sent 7 kilograms of corn to be ground at one of the mills in Sara, and I was given back only 3.700 kilograms of flour; that is to say, the miller's fee consisted of almost half the corn delivered to be milled. The town's other millers are proceeding in the same fashion.

Rites of Passage

Birth and Christening — Children believe that newborn babies are brought from Paris by the *emain* (midwife). These are women of the neighborhood who are practiced in the delivery of babies. If a baby is born with an elongated head, they press it between their hands to make it round. They also stretch the nose a little bit so the baby will not be snub-nosed. They swaddle the baby's legs with white *troxa* (bandages) to keep them straight. These bandages are kept on until the child is two or three months old.

A baby's birth is not celebrated with a special festivity. A member of the family or a neighbor announces the birth to those going to be godparents at the christening. As established by custom, these individuals have usually been invited beforehand to render this service. *Altxatu* (lifting up) means to stand as godparents at a christening.

If the child to be christened is a couple's firstborn, the mother of the spouse who is heir to the house will be its godmother; its godfather will be the father of the spouse that has married into that household. For the second child, the godfather is the heir's father, and the godmother is the mother of the spouse that has married in. For the christenings of any subsequent children the godparents are siblings of both spouses, beginning with the eldest; the godfather comes from one side of the family and the godmother from the other, and so on in descending order of age.

It is commonly said that if someone who has been invited to stand as a godparent declines the invitation, he must perform this function for seven children without being invited to do so. "*Zor izain du zazpi haur altxatzea berak galdatuz*" (One should act as a godparent for seven children at one's own behest).

The Basque term for godfather is *aitatxi*; for godmother, *amatxi*; for godson, *semeautxi*, and for goddaughter, *alautxi*.

The christening takes place in the Sara parish church, generally two or three days after the baby is born. The *emain* carries the baby to the church; custom dictates that she be the *eremaile* or "bearer." She is accompanied by the child's godparents.

During the christening the child is held in the *eremaile*'s arms with the godfather holding its legs and the godmother its head. In this ceremony the child is given its name. If the child being christened is a boy, the godfather proposes the name, which is generally his own; in the case of a girl the name is proposed by her godmother.

In Sara it is very common for children to be named *Kose, Joset* (Joseph); *Ganes, Ganixon, Jean* (John); *Ganaurra, Ganttipi* (Joan); *Pedro, Pello, Piarrezume, Piarres, Pier* (Peter); *Pol* (Paul); *Frantxisko, Franzua, Patxiko* (Francis); *Inazio* (Ignatius); *Mizel, Mitxu* (Michael); *Anton* (Anthony); *Luis* (Louis); *Janmattitt* (Jean Batiste); and *Mari* (Mary).

After the ceremony the godparents and the *eremaile* host a meal or other refreshments—depending on whether the christening takes place in the morning or the afternoon—in one of the town's inns. Chicken is the traditional food for this celebration. The godparents pay the bill.

It is the custom for *aideak* (relatives) and *auzokoak* (female neighbors) to visit the mother of the newborn shortly after the birth and to take her presents. These gifts (*bixita*) consist of a pound of chocolate and a dozen cakes or a kilogram of sugar. The visitors are treated to refreshments consisting of hot chocolate and bread with jam or cheese.

After giving birth a woman must not leave the house until, duly healed, she goes to church to fulfill the rite known as *elizan-sartze* (entry into the church, or "churching"), which consists of attending church with her newborn child to receive the postpartum blessing from the priest. She then leaves a candle in the church and gives the priest two and a half francs. If at any point between the birth and the churching ceremony the woman should need to leave the house, she must do so with a shingle on her head. "*Ama Berjinak berrogei egunez ebili zuela teila buruan errateute elizan sartu artean*" (They say that the Virgin Mary carried a shingle on her head for forty days before she set foot in the church).

The mother's healing is not celebrated with a festival or banquet in Sara; in Zugarramurdi, however, female relatives and neighbors are usually invited to a banquet.

Stillborn children and those who die unbaptized are buried in an orchard beside the house.

From time to time before children reach the age when they make their first communion, their godparents present them with a gift of clothing. They are also given the large candle used in the first communion ceremony, a prayer-book, or another appropriate gift. On the day of the ceremony the children making their first communion visit their godparents and invite them to a celebratory meal at their home. Presents given on this and other occasions are known as *ikustate*. *Ikustategabea* (one who has no gifts) is an expression used to signify an ungrateful person.

A newborn child remains in its *seaska* (cradle) for two or three months, although it is taken out to be breastfed, washed, and to have its bedding changed. Later on the child is taken out for a daily walk in a relative's arms. The cradle is a kind of rectangular wooden box on two transversal beams forming inverted arcs which rest on the floor and allow the cradle to be rocked.

At three months of age they begin to give the child pap made of sweetened milk and wheat flour.

Newborns have a little bag tied around their necks by way of an amulet; this contains the first words of the Gospels written on a piece of paper. This amulet is said to protect them against *xarmazionea*, that is, any kind of illness supposedly brought about by the *begizko* or evil eye. Such an illness is cured by having the child blessed by a priest within nine days of falling ill. These and other amulets are sometimes also used by adults suffering from an illness. The son of my Ibarsoro-berria informant wears a stone brought from Santa Lucía.

First Communion — A child's first communion (at ten or eleven years of age) marks another stage in his or her life and is accompanied by a great deal of ceremony. Children making their first communion are dressed in white and are presented with numerous treats and gifts by their parents and godparents. The religious ceremony takes place in the church with much singing and a large attendance of the congregation. The child renews aloud the promises that were made in his name by his godparents at his christening, and he leaves a candle in the church as an offering. At home a banquet, attended by relatives and family friends, is given in his honor.

Youth — There exists no permanent, official association of unmarried people in the town other than the congregation of the Daughters of Mary. The *gazteri* (youth) lack any particular social organization but are nevertheless subject to various vague trends that influence the behavior of each particular young person and induce him or her to adopt attitudes or follow paths that are sometimes in conflict with family tradition. This behavior translates into frequent battles between young people and their parents.

Single people in the Elbarrun neighborhood belong to a kind of brotherhood and sponsor a mass every New Year's Day. They also sponsor masses for the souls of any comrades who have passed away.

Young people get together before the festivities of the town's patron saint (the Nativity of Our Lady, September 8) to organize a collection to pay the musicians who will be playing dance tunes for the three days of the festivities. These dances are *lotuak* (modern slow dances), since the traditional individual dances are hardly ever done these days.

The young people of Sara hold a public dance every Sunday. However, many go to the tavern at Lizuniaga (south of Mainharria), where they dance every Sunday to the sound of the accordion. Before this current war people were also beginning to organize Sunday dances at the taverns at San Ignacio and Aimainea, but these were later abandoned.

Older single people are not unusual in Sara. An older unmarried man is called a *donadu*, and an older unmarried woman a *mutxurdin*.

Both groups are considered to be missing something and to be ill-tempered and unpleasant to deal with.

Courtship and Marriage — In the nineteenth century it was still common for parents to play a part in the marriage of their children, even when it came to their choice of a spouse. Today young people may marry whomever they please.

It is usually the man who takes the initiative at the beginning of a courtship, although there are some cases in which the first indication of interest comes from the woman.

Once the young couple has agreed to marry, the girl begins to prepare her trousseau, which consists mainly of clothing and household linens such as bedclothes and kitchen towels, etc. The pair meets frequently, especially on holidays, and go about together. Sometimes a couple has a child before the wedding, or the wedding is brought forward because of an imminent birth. This is not well looked upon, but it is becoming more and more tolerated.

Yoaiketa is the term given to the trip the engaged couple makes (sometimes accompanied by close relatives or friends) to a commercial town to purchase certain clothing for the wedding. This clothing is called *yoiak*. Some brides buy small items that they present as *oroitzapen* (souvenirs) to their parents and siblings.

A *kontratua* (marriage settlement) is formally drawn up before the Ezpeleta notary. As was noted above, this is the moment when the heir to a household is chosen and his or her duties and rights are stipulated, as well as the conditions regulating that individual's relationship with parents, siblings, etc. On this occasion the spouse who is marrying the heir presents his or her cash dowry. Later there is a banquet at the heir's house for the engaged couple and their relatives.

Once the wedding date is set the parish priest is informed and he announces the *kridak* (banns of marriage) one, two, or three Sundays before the wedding. When the last banns have been announced the couple and their relatives have a celebratory meal at the heir's house or at an inn.

Aitatxi (the godfather, "best man") and *amatxi* (the godmother, "matron of honor") are present at the wedding ceremony. The groom arrives at the church on the arm of his *amatxi*, who is usually his mother, or—in her absence—his grandmother or an aunt (preferably his baptismal godmother), or else another elderly female relative. The bride arrives on the arm of her *aitaxi*, generally her father, grandfather, or an uncle (her baptismal godfather). Previously it was not customary for the bride and groom to arrive at the church on their sponsors' arms.

The bride and groom are each accompanied by two witnesses called *esposlagun* (wedding companions). The groom's are two unmarried young men, one from the *leenate*, the "first door" or first house on the right on the way to the parish church from the groom's house, and the other is a person of the groom's choice. The bride's witnesses are two single women, one of whom is from her *leenate* and the other a woman of her choice.

In years past the best man would present the bride with a *zikiru* (ram); today he gives a monetary gift. The matron of honor would give the groom an article of clothing and a pair of hens; nowadays she gives him money. On the eve of the wedding these presents were taken to the house where the couple would establish their home.

Each of the groom's witnesses gave him half a dozen bottles of *etxearno*, "homemade wine." Two days before the wedding, a young woman would carry the bottles to the house where the wedding was being celebrated in a *saski* (basket) on her head. The basket was covered in a *londdera*, a white cloth tied to the basket with colored ribbons that hung behind and around the sides of the girl carrying it.

The bride's witnesses presented her with two *kolineta* or bars of marzipan, which would be taken to the bridal house in decorated baskets like those used for the bottles of wine.

Some of the groom's *gaztelagunak* (childhood friends) also gave him a cash gift or a gift in kind; others paid for the music at the wedding.

The bride's *gaztelagunak* also presented her with gifts in round, handleless wicker baskets made to be carried on the head.

The *saskigaileak* (basket bearers), laden with gifts, gathered at a specified location and set out all together for the house, where they had to unpack their baskets. Along the route one or two young men would fire off guns, as if trying to prevent the group from advancing. When they arrived at their destination the gift bearers were immediately treated to a snack.

Nowadays wedding presents consist of cash gifts, coffee sets, flatware, mirrors, or other objects.

A few days before the wedding, the bride or groom visits the place where the couple will live. This visit is called the *etxesartzea*.

If the wedding is to be celebrated with a banquet and other festivities, the engaged couple invite the following people to the church ceremony: their respective families, their *leenateak* (the adult neighbors who live in the first house on the right on the way to the parish church), the young people from that house who are over fifteen years of age, the couple's aunts, uncles, and cousins. All these guests then go on to attend the wedding banquet. If there is to be just the wedding ceremony, only the relatives, the godparents, and the witnesses will attend. The groom presents the bride with an *erreztun* (ring).

The day before the wedding the families of the bride and groom have a mass said in the parish church for the souls of both families' ancestors.

It was previously the custom to marry on a Wednesday or a Saturday; nowadays a Thursday is generally chosen for weddings. The wedding day is called *esposegun*.

Just before the wedding the bride and groom and all the guests form two retinues, one composed of people from the bride's side and one from the groom's. These groups then meet on the way to the church, or the groom and his group will set out to meet the bride's party and everyone, with the bride and groom at the head, will proceed to the Town Hall (where the civil part of the wedding takes place) and then to the parish church.

The bride and groom are dressed in black, though it is becoming customary for a bride to wear a white cloak over a black dress. She also wears an *urrexena* (necklace) of the same material as her earrings and wedding ring, and a pair of *eskularruak* (gloves).

After the wedding party enters the church, the bride, the groom, and their witnesses sit on the six chairs placed especially for them next to the presbytery. The other members of the wedding party stand behind the bride and groom, and the wedding and the nuptial mass are held at that spot. When the ceremony is over the newlyweds and their entire retinue go to the sepulcher belonging to the family of the inheriting spouse and pray there for the souls of his or her ancestors. If it is located in the same cemetery, they also go to the sepulcher of the family of the other spouse, and offer prayers there too.

From their wedding onward, spouses will no longer use the familiar pronoun when they address each other, as that would now be considered undignified. They will instead address each other using the formal pronoun *zu*.

A wedding carriage is not customary, but at some point before the wedding the household goods will be moved by cart to the house where the newlyweds will take up residence.

The main door to the newlyweds' house, where the banquet and other festivities are to take place, is decorated with flowers and green branches before the couple gets back from the wedding ceremony.

When she gets home, the bride shows the female guests the furniture, household linen, etc. that have been acquired for the occasion and takes them to the *esposgambara* or "wedding chamber."

After the wedding feast the young people and the newlyweds dance to accordion music throughout the evening and into the night. An accordion player from the town is hired for this purpose by the young people attending the wedding.

It used to be the custom for newlyweds to invite their closest relatives to a special lunch on the Sunday after the wedding.

In order to avoid being seen and subjected to ridicule and the mocking blasts of the *tuta* (horn cornet), widows and widowers get married in the pre-dawn hours. This blowing of the *tuta* is known as *turrutak jo* (making chaotic noises) or *toberak jo* (giving a serenade). For one night or more before the wedding of a widowed person, young people take up positions near the couple's homes and stage these noisy sessions. Sometimes they set up pairs of dolls representing a man and a woman near their houses. When the widow's or widower's wedding date and planned route to the church become known, trees, branches, and other obstacles are placed along the way to block their path. But the bride and groom sometimes manage to avoid this by treating the young people in their neighborhood to some wine.

Old people attempting to get married are subjected to the same pranks as the widowed.

The wedding of Ignacio Perugorria and Marta Arburua that I am about to describe illustrates what happens nowadays.

This is how, on the 10th of January of 1943, the parish priest of Sara announced the banns of marriage for this young pair:

"*Ezkontzako Sakramenduaren errezibitzeko xedetan dire.*" (The following persons intend to enter into the Sacrament of Marriage):

"*Inazio Perugorria, Sara-Aimaenean sortua eta dagona. Xanpier Perugorria zenaren eta Bernardina Lamothe'n seme lejitimoa, alde batetik.*" (Inazio Perugorria, a native and resident of the Aiemaenea farm in Sara, legitimate son of the deceased Xanpier Perugorria and of Bernardina Lamothe, on the one hand)

"*Eta bertzetik Marta Arburua, Sara-Ibarsorogainean sortua eta dagona, Antonio Arburua eta Teresa Anzizar'en alaba lejitimoa.*" (And on the other hand Marta Arburua, native and resident of the Ibarsorogaina farm in Sara, legitimate daughter of Antonio Arburua and Teresa Anzizar.)

"*Lenengo eta azken agertzea.*" (First and last announcement.)

The day before the wedding the *ezkongai* (engaged couple) sponsor a mass for the souls of the deceased members of both their families. This is attended by the couple themselves and some of their relatives, and as is the custom, they receive Holy Communion.

This mass and communion are considered ceremonies through which the spouses become part of each other's family.

A month before the wedding the bride and groom invite their respective uncles and aunts to the ceremony and to the luncheon and dinner that will be held on that day. One member of the offspring of each uncle or aunt will also be invited. Also invited are a young bachelor from the groom's *leenate* (first neighbor), that is, from the first house to the right along the road to the parish church, and a single girl from the bride's *leenate*.

The bride and groom invite their closest friends as well.

Since the bride's family from the Ibarsorogaina farm are tenants, the *etxekoandre* (lady of the house) or owner and her son have also been invited.

Very early on the 16th of January—the wedding day—a bus leaves for the Etxegaraia farm to pick up the bride's uncle, aunt, and a female cousin. It then goes to the Arrosa farm to pick up one of the groom's male cousins. From there it makes its way to Ihartzebeherea to take on board an uncle and a female cousin of the bride, then on to Aiemaenea for the groom, his mother (his father is deceased), his two sisters, an uncle, and two friends. It drives all of the above to Ibarsorogaina, the bride's farmhouse. Here the groom, one of his sisters and one of the bride's cousins alight from the bus and go into the bride's house. Inside the house, ready to go, are the bride's family and three of her female cousins, the young woman from her *leenate,* and the family from Xantakonea—the farm where the groom was raised. Everybody gets into the bus, which then sets off for the town square. The unmarried girls wear flowers, as does the groom, who has had them pinned on by one of his sisters.

In the bus the groom sits in one of the front seats, the bride in the back. During the ride everyone is told who their appointed partner will be during the ceremony.

When the bus arrives at the town square, everyone gets out and the single girls pin flowers on the lapels of their respective bachelor escorts.

The bride's sister lines up the wedding party in the usual order for weddings: (1) the bride and her father; (2) the groom and his mother; (3) the *esposlagun* or bride's witness with the young man from Arrosa (the groom's second witness); (4) the man who shared the same wet-nurse as the groom and who is the groom's witness, with the young woman from Etxegaraia, who in turn is the bride's second witness; (5) a female cousin of the bride (from Oleta) and one of the groom's friends; (6) one of the groom's sisters and one of the bride's male cousins; (7) a female cousin of the bride (from Ihatzebeherea) and one of the bride's brothers; (8) a female cousin of the bride (from Zugarramurdi) and one of the groom's friends; (9) the girl from the bride's *leenate* with one of the brothers from Xantakonea; (10) the girl from Xantakonea with one of the groom's friends; (11) one of the bride's friends with the son of the owner of Ibarsorogaina; (12) one of the groom's sisters with one of his friends; (13) one of the bride's sisters was unaccompanied because her fiancé was unexpectedly called away; (14) the married women in a group, and (15) the married men, also in a group.

In this order everyone enters the *Erriko-etxea* or Town Hall where the legal ceremony of civil marriage is carried out before the judge. The party is then transported in the same order to the parish church, where six chairs have been set out near the presbytery. In the first two sit the bride and groom (the groom on the right and the bride on the left); the other chairs are occupied by the witnesses. The father of the bride and the mother of the groom, who came in on the arms of their respective offspring, have now taken seats further back. All the other guests occupy the chairs designated for the public, with the men seated on the right and the women on the left.

The priest immediately presents himself and asks the questions dictated by the ritual. The marriage takes place, followed by *esposmeza* (the nuptial mass). Then the newlyweds, with the members of the wedding party and guests closest to them, enter the vestry through the right-hand door and there they sign their marriage certificate, followed by their witnesses. The bride presents the priest with a bouquet of flowers to place before the statue of the Virgin Mary.

The newlyweds take each other's arm and leave through the other door of the vestry. They are followed by the rest of the party, paired off in the same order in which they entered the church. They then exit the church through the main door. A woman offers them holy water, and everyone makes the sign of the cross with it. They proceed to the *ilarrieta* (cemetery) and to the sepulcher belonging to the Ibarsorogaina farm, where the bride leaves a bouquet and everyone recites a short prayer (a Paternoster or two). Afterwards they proceed to the Aiemaenea sepulcher, where they also stop to pray. This is one more act through which bride and groom each affirm having joined the family of their spouse.

Following this everyone goes to the Munddurienea house, where the new husband and wife will take up residence. They all get out of the bus, and paired in the same order in which they left the church, they walk toward the house. The women who are going to be the couple's new neighbors have set up two archways made of yew branches and flowers, one between the road and the house, the other at the front door. Two mandarin oranges hang from each arch, one for each of the newlyweds. As they pass under the arches they pick off the mandarins. The entire wedding party then goes up to the attic, which has been tidied up and converted into a dining-room for the occasion. Two long tables have been set up. The newlyweds are seated at one table with the other unmarried couples and with their witnesses seated on either side; the married people are seated at the other table.

When the wedding party arrives they are served specially aged wine and cookies by young women who have been placed in charge of the menu. Then comes the luncheon: chicken noodle soup; boiled beef with carrots and leeks; chicken and minced beef with rice and red peppers; lamb and gravy; roast chicken and salad; flan and cake with champagne; ordinary wine (served throughout the meal), and, finally, coffee with liqueurs and cigars. Between courses the guests sing with great gusto songs such as "Maritxu nora zoaz," "Gazte-gaztetandikan," the Saint Ignatius March, etc. When the lamb is about to be served the bride and groom kiss, the groom then turning to kiss the female witness to his right; she in turn kisses the young man to her right and the kiss then goes around the table.

After the roast chicken is served, one of the girls in charge of the table presents the female witness on the right with a dish containing a doll covered by another, inverted dish, all wrapped up and tied with red ribbon. The witness then hands it with a kiss to the young man on her right; he then passes it to the young woman on his right, also with a kiss. The plates are then passed around the singles table in this way until they reach the bride, who finally passes it to her husband with a kiss. While he holds the plates, the bride unties the red ribbon and uncovers the doll, which she holds up for everyone to see.

The feast lasts from one o'clock in the afternoon to six in the evening. Several young couples dance (traditional dances) to the music of the *txistu*. Later on they all—both single and married people—have a good time dancing intermittently throughout the night. They have a late supper there. At daybreak they have coffee and go to church to hear Sunday mass. Later on the young people have breakfast at the Hôtel de la Poste. And this brings the wedding festivities to a close.

Death — M. A. Arçuby published an article on the funeral rites of Sara in the *Bulletin du Musée Basque* (Bayonne, 1927, nos. 3–4). There have been very few changes in funeral customs since then, and any variations from Arçuby's observations will be noted as they arise.

When speaking of beliefs associated with death it is worth mentioning the signs that announce it. Thus, when a dog howls people say "*Erio urbil da"* (the *erio*, or spirit of death, is nearby). It is believed that at that moment the dog can see the spirit of death.

People often say *"Erioa, animaen bilaria"* (the *erio*, seeker of souls).

It is also a commonly stated belief that if the ringing of the bell announcing the raising of the host at Sunday mass coincides with the church bell chiming eleven o'clock (or, according to Arçuby, with any hour at all), someone in the town will die the following week.

If an ailing old man shows a desire to leave the house and spend a few days in someone else's it is said that he is looking for *Erio*, or is in danger of dying.

When someone falls gravely ill, the *leenate* or *auzo* (the neighbor living in the first house to the right on the way to the parish church) has the responsibility of calling for the doctor and the priest. It is also this *leenate* who accompanies the *Sakramendu* (Viaticum; eucharist for a dying person) by walking behind the priest who is carrying it. Today it is frequently a young female first neighbor who performs this service, or else a female from another neighboring house if there is no female first neighbor.

When the Viaticum approaches the sick person's house, the *buru* (head of the family) (man or woman), equipped with two lighted candles, goes out to meet it and accompanies the Viaticum by preceding the priest into the sickroom; there he or she places both the candles on the table or *aldare* (altar) prepared for this purpose. The priest sets the Viaticum on this table, which is covered with a white cloth and upon which a cross and an image of the Virgin Mary have been placed. After the sick person has made his confession and the ritual prayers have been offered, the Viaticum is administered to him. If the patient is near death, the priest will also administer *Anonzio* (Extreme Unction).

A woman from the first neighbor household and some family members are present during these rites. According to Arçuby, one of these relatives repeatedly makes the sign of the cross over the patient, each time circling the patient's head with a lighted candle.

From that night onward—if they have not begun already—people from the neighborhood (usually two) begin the *gaubeila* (night vigil) for the sick person.

As a person is dying, those present recite the litanies of the Virgin Mary and the prayers specified by the Roman Catholic Church for these occasions. A candle is lit (the one blessed in the church at Candlemas) and placed beside the dying person. Using that candle, one of those attending the deathbed makes the sign of the cross on the dying person and sprinkles him with holy water. The room is also sprinkled to keep evil spirits away.

The *leenate* announces the impending death to the *ezkilayoile* (bell-ringer), so that the bell-ringer may toll the bell in the usual manner for these occasions, although this custom has now been abandoned.

In the past, according to Arçuby, nuns whose vocation it is to care for the sick, together with a group of children, would recite the prayers with the priest at the head of the dying man's bed. This is also no longer done.

It is said that those who have the habit of cursing people usually have a long, difficult death, especially if they have not first been forgiven by the people they have injured with their curses. *Madarizione* (a curse) is effective, according to popular belief. If someone wishes another person dead and expresses that wish, especially at a certain time of day known as *oren gaixto* (the evil hour), the wish will come true.

If the dying person has been cursed, one must cut off the *kukurusta* (comb) of the household rooster in order to shorten the death throes.

Those who are thought to be witches take much longer to die, according to a generalized belief, because they first have to bequeath their inheritance—that is, their mysterious powers—to anyone who is willing to receive it. They say that a witch who was dying repeatedly asked *"Ekatzu esku"* (Give me your hand), but nobody would oblige her. Finally someone held out an *itsas-gider* (broom handle), and the witch transferred her powers to the broom and was able to die.

According to Arçuby, the lady of the Goyetchea house was taking a long time to die, having been in the throes of death for eight days. While her attendants had gone to the kitchen for a few moments, she got out of bed and appeared in the kitchen where they were. Then her husband, realizing what was happening, helped his wife back to bed and went up to the attic and took a shingle off the roof. By the time he had returned to his wife's bedside she was dead.

If an adult in the town dies and his death is followed by that of a child, people say, *"Aingerua ereman du beraiki"* (He has taken the angel with him). And if after the death of a child an old person in the town suddenly dies, it is said that the angel took him away.

Certain unknown, incurable illnesses are attributed to Aideko or Aireko. The following is said of those who suffer from them: *"Aire-tikako zerbeit izain du"* (He must be suffering from something that came from Aireko). The cure is usually a blessing from the priest; if this is not given, the patient—whether a person or an animal—will certainly die.

Death is called *eriotze*.

It is said that it is a sign of salvation to die during Easter Week, on Ascension Day, or on a rainy day.

When a person dies the windows and doors of the house are closed or left only partially ajar. This is a sign of mourning that continues until the deceased has been buried. Mirrors are covered with cloths. According to Arçuby (cited above), the windows of the room in which the person has died are opened and, shortly afterwards, closed; any pictures and, especially, mirrors are covered with cloth, as visitors should not see their own reflections or those of anyone else at this time.

The deceased's family do not leave the house until after the burial. The *leenate* and other people in the neighborhood take care of the livestock and other chores.

It is the *leenate* who announces the death to the priest, the bell-ringer, the relatives, and the other neighbors. He is also the person who, together with another neighbor, goes to the church to bring the parish cross and place it in the room where the dead person lies.

In the past, according to Arçuby, a female neighbor would undertake this task.

The bell is tolled in accordance with whether the deceased is a man or a woman. For a man the notes are farther apart than for a woman.

A blessed candle is lit next to the deceased. Some people burn bay leaves and sprinkle drops of cologne in the room.

The body is then laid out in the deceased's best clothes or, if the person was married, in his or her wedding outfit. A neighbor, accompanied by a family member, carries out this operation. An *abitu* (a scapular of the Virgin of Mount Carmel) is placed on the shroud, and a rosary in the deceased's hands.

It used to be customary to sprinkle a little salt and a few drops of blessed wax over the cadaver. Someone closes its eyes.

According to Arçuby, a cloth decorated with bay leaves covers the body of the deceased. In days gone by a special cloth called *hilmihisia* served this purpose. Wealthy families would cover the walls of the room where the deceased was laid out with cloth of this sort. Two neighbors watch over the body until it is carried to the church on the second day after the death. The neighbors gather in the room during the night to pray the rosary.

A close relative of the deceased announces the death to the latter's stabled livestock (cows, sheep, etc.), making them stand if they are lying down. The bees in the hive are also informed by knocking on the hive with one's hand and saying, *"Nagusia hil da"* (The master has died), *"Etxekoandria hil da"* (The mistress of the house has died), *"Etxeko semia hil da"* (The son of the house has died), etc. It is said that tragedies will befall the livestock if this is not done. As regards the bees, people say, "*Damutzen omen zaio ez erratia*" (They were grieved at not being informed), and the hive later dies.

All bells are removed from the cattle. They will not be replaced until the period of mourning is over—that is, for two years if the deceased or his wife was the owner, for one year if the deceased was a son or daughter of the owners. Only the odd sheep grazing on the hillside still wears a little bell. The owner of the Olha house, according to Arçuby, died suddenly while away from home. The cows in his stable began to low, but nobody knew why until the news arrived that their master had died. Then they were informed of the death and they stopped lowing. Something similar happened on the Anihotzea farm: the lowing of the cows in the stable let the lady of the house know that her daughter had died, a fact that was later confirmed. She announced this to the cows and they calmed down.

The deceased's tenants and sharecroppers also announce the master's death to their animals in the same way. But this custom is now falling into disuse.

The cadaver is placed in a varnished wooden coffin equipped with four handles, made by local carpenters. A metal cross is placed on the top. Previously, according to my informant Piarrezume Camino, who is ninety-two years old, the dead were carried to the church on a *gatabotta* (stretcher).

The *gorputzgaileak* (pallbearers) are four or six young, single men. If the deceased is a child who has not yet made its first communion, its coffin is carried by boys or girls, according to its gender. Previously a child's coffin was carried by its godfather. The adult pallbearers are paid ten francs each (at the beginning of the twentieth century the amount was four francs), and after the burial a meal is eaten at one of the town's restaurants.

The coffin of a member of the Daughters of Mary who dies in the town is carried by other members of the organization, unless the church is too far away. In this case it is carried by young men.

If the deceased belonged to a family that has tenants, it is they—whether single or married—who carry the coffin to the church and cemetery.

At the appointed time for the burial the neighbors and relatives of the deceased, the pallbearers, and the parish priest with an altar boy go to the house of mourning. The casket now lies on a table in the foyer of the house. Beside it, on a chair, is a dish of holy water and a sprig of laurel. The priest recites the ritual prayers and the cortège leaves for the church. Meanwhile, the bell-ringer tolls the bells in the church tower, spacing the notes according to whether the deceased is a man or a woman. The coffin is carried along the route known as *elizbide* (the path to the church). Each house has its own. The funeral procession also takes this route.

If the deceased is a male, the funeral procession is organized in the following fashion: the *beetterra* (altar boy) holding up the cross; behind him, if the deceased belonged to a brotherhood within the parish, four brother members bearing the organization's identifying banner by its corners; immediately after them the priest, attired in rochet [an embroidered over-tunic] and stole; then comes the coffin, borne on the shoulders of the *gorputzgaileak*; then the *ahuko* or chief mourners, headed by the *gizon-ahuko* (men's cortège) in the following order: the *leenate* or first neighbor; *aideak* or *jendakiak* (the relatives, including the father of the deceased, his sons, brothers, uncles, nephews, cousins, etc.), in order of their degree of relationship and age; then friends and neighbors; then the women's cortège, beginning with the *leenate* who is followed by friends and neighbors, cousins, nieces, aunts, sisters, mother, and wife. The last woman in the procession is called the *minyuri*, a term also given to the first male relative to follow the *leenate* of the men's cortège.

When the coffin of a woman is being carried to the church, the cortège or *ahuko* walking behind it is formed by female mourners in the following order: the *leenate*, friends and neighbors, *aideak* or relatives (cousins, nieces, aunts, sisters, daughters, mother), and the men's cortège (the *leenate*, the husband, father, sons, brothers, uncles, nephews, cousins, friends, and neighbors).

There is no male cortège if there are no men in the household of the deceased woman, nor at the burial of a very young child.

Nowadays some families try to have the funeral procession preceded by a group of boys or girls (according to the gender of the deceased), each carrying a lighted candle. During the funeral rites these children stand on opposite sides of the coffin in two lines. They are paid for this service.

Arçuby recorded the following in his work:

> The chief mourner, or *minyuri*, follows the next-door neighbor; the woman in charge of the female mourners walks at the end of the funeral procession. Close relatives and the pallbearers (typically, share-croppers on the property of the deceased) are dressed as follows: a large hooded cape for the men, and a cape reaching down to the feet, called "caputcha," for the women.

> Formerly, it was obligatory for all the male mourners to wear the large hooded cape. Later on, it was worn only by relatives, and

at a later period, only by close relatives, as is the custom today. The vestry of the church now provides ceremonial mantles for mourners to wear in processions. The large top-hat was required for all the male mourners. Subsequently, it was worn only by the cross-bearers who marched all the way to the church. Today, it has completely disappeared (making its reappearance . . . in Carnival processions). In Urrugne, until just a few years ago, it was still worn.

Formerly, all those attending the funeral had to wear black. Today, except for those in mourning, many come in colored clothing (the cost of dressing in style makes it impossible to purchase an additional black outfit).[3]

Men attending the funeral generally wear a dark suit and a white shirt with black buttons. The *leenate* and the closest relatives wear black capes over their suits.

Women are also dressed in black, although nowadays they are beginning to wear light colors. Relatives also wear black capes with hoods (*kaputxak*) that cover them from head to ankle. The *minyuri* and other family members of the deceased cover their faces with a *blunda*, a black veil that falls from edge of the hood.

When the deceased is from a distant farm it is customary for the clergy to start the procession at a house that is closer to the church, and the coffin is carried there at the appointed time. Such a house is called an *altxatoki* (lifting place). Thus the deceased from *bordas* (the outlying farms to the south and southeast of the Istilarte neighborhood) are received by the priest at the Espilteguia house (previously Dendaldeguia). From the house of mourning to Espilteguia it is the *leenate* who carries the church cross; afterwards it is carried by the altar-boy accompanying the priest.

The bodies of people who die on farms toward Vera (Bera) are brought to Etxetxarria; those of the farms near Hauziartzia are taken to that house; the Mendiondoa house receives those from the Mendiondokoborda farms and others in that area; the deceased from the Goiburu area are taken to Idatzia; those from the San Ignacio area go to the Aniotzea farmhouse, and those from the Auntzkarrika area are received at Ibarsorogaina. Arçuby states in this regard that,

> The initiation of the funeral procession by the priest takes place at the house of the deceased, assuming he is the owner. If the deceased is a share-cropper or renter, it is done at a house specified for each neighborhood, and closest to the church, to which the pallbearers preceding the cross and followed by the funeral procession carry

the body prior to the arrival of the clergy. No matter how far the owner's house was from the church, this custom was observed without exception until very recently, when the route of the procession was uniformly reduced out of regard for the penury of the priests and the additional charge for the ceremony, despite the loss of dignity suffered by the families.[4]

When the funeral procession arrives at the church the coffin is placed on a simple bier in the center of the church, where it will remain during the funeral rites. The persons forming the funeral procession take their places in an orderly fashion: the women below and the men in the galleries, so that the women wearing hooded capes (the *leenate* and the relatives) occupy the *yarleku* of the deceased's house and the men in capes take up the central part of the first row of the galleries.

The religious aspect of the funeral consists chiefly of a mass—which may be celebrated with a deacon in attendance or not, according to the wishes of the deceased's family—and the prayers reserved for these occasions. The number of flower arrangements and wreaths marks the difference between the funerals of the rich and the poor.

The prayers recited on these occasions are mainly the *Paternoster*, the *Ave Maria*, and *De profundis*.

During the funeral the *yarleku* is covered in sackcloth and black fabric. Two *tortxak* (candles), provided by the church, burn above the cloth; between them is a slender rolled wax taper called *ezko* or *ezkox-igor*, brought expressly by the family of the deceased; next to this one are other rolled candles brought by the female neighbors. Behind the burning candles and wax, the hooded women with their veils down sit on chairs or in *prezdieux*. It has recently become customary for these women to form two or more rows in the center of the church, behind the coffin.

There are no professional mourners at funerals, but the female *minyuri*, even if she is a distant relative of the deceased, frequently dabs at her eyes with a handkerchief, letting it be seen that she is shedding tears.

Members of the *ahuko* remain kneeling during the ceremony.

At a certain point in the Offertory, those attending who do not contribute with an offering (*serbitzu*) taken up during mass approach the entrance to the presbytery, where the priest awaits them with a *pax* (metal plaque with a cross); they kiss this and make their offering by depositing a franc in a bag or on a collection plate held by an altar-boy. This money pays for the services of the priest celebrating the novena mass that will begin that day.

Arçuby reports that, "Until recent years a novena mass took place the week after the death. The offering, the prayer presided over by the priest, and the funeral meal took place on the day following the death; those attending who had made offerings returned for the novena."[5]

After the funeral mass the prayer for the dead is sung. This is also done after other requiem masses are sung or before masses of other kinds that, at any time of year, are celebrated for the souls of the deceased. These prayers are sung by the priest and the *xantre* in the *yarleku* of the household that has requested the mass, with a woman from that house in attendance, wearing a hooded cape and veil.

During the funeral service the close relatives of the deceased remove the *lastaira* (straw mattress) from the deathbed and take it to a crossroads on the *elizbide,* where it is burned. Only a straw *lastaira* is removed; otherwise a little bit of corn husk is taken to the crossroads and burned. This fire and its residual material remind passers-by of the death that has occurred in the house nearby and invite them to say a prayer for the deceased.

After the mass and the absolution or prayer for the dead at the church, the burial takes place. All those attending leave in the same order in which they arrived at the church, preceded by the church cross, the priest, and the coffin. The procession stops when the coffin arrives at the tomb. After the priest has offered the ritual prayers everyone files past the tomb and goes out in the same order, stopping to form a single file on the road to the house of mourning. All present murmur a prayer, such as the *Paternoster, Requiem,* or *De profundis*, and the cortège breaks up. Only those from out of town and the deceased's relatives, invited by the male *leenate*, return to the house of mourning. As they pass the place where the mattress has been burned they stop before the ashes and other burned material, make the sign of the cross, and say a prayer for the deceased. Together with the *leenate* and his wife they enter the house and partake in the *mezatako-bazkaria* (luncheon for a mass), which consists of beef broth, stewed beef, and coffee. Afterwards they say a *De profundis* and then disperse.

During the first few days after the funeral until the following Sunday some of the women relatives of the deceased dressed in hooded capes, together with the female *leenate*, attend the mass for the soul of the recently deceased. They place themselves in one or two rows behind the torches and the rolled taper burning in the deceased's *yarleku*, which has been veiled in black. There they remain throughout the mass and the prayer for the dead sung by the priest and the *xantre*. The masses held in the parish church during these first days are paid for by the donations made during the Offertory at the funeral mass.

The singing of the prayer for the dead takes place at the *yarleku*. An altar-boy holds up the cross behind the hooded women, with the priest and the *xantre* standing in front of the women and the lights. The faces of the hooded women are veiled during the entire ceremony.

In the first few days following the funeral, the deceased's family makes confession and takes communion (the men do so on the first Sunday following). The Sunday after the funeral the priest announces in church the names of the individuals or households who have donated money for the masses, known as *serbitzu*. At the end of the announcement he mentions the amount of money that has been given as *laxada* by the deceased's family. The *laxada* seems to be a vestige of an ancient contribution that households would pay to the church for the tomb. Six *suses* from the *laxada* go to the Santa Catalina hermitage, and the rest is divided equally between the upkeep of the church and fees for masses for souls in purgatory.

The following is an example of the recognition of donors of *serbitzuak* corresponding to April 8, 1945:

> *Jomildegiko-borda'ko etchekoandre zenarentzat eman dute*:
> *Alaba Mari semearekin,*
> *Seme Jean-Batistek andrearekin.*

> (Offerings have been given for the housewife of Jomildegi farm who passed away, by:
> Her daughter Mari with her son,
> Her son Jean-Batiste with his wife.)

> *Alautchi Jeannek,*
> *Semeatchi Sebastianek,*
> *Iloba Frantchak.*

> (Granddaughter Jeanne,
> Grandson Sebastian,
> Niece Frantcha.)

> *Chilardi'ko familiak,*
> *Landagarai'ko aita-alabak,*
> *Adishkide batek,*
> *Askain.*

> (The Chilardi family,
> The father and daughter of Landagarai [house],
> A friend,
> Askain.)

Familiak obligazionentzat,
Lachada 50 libera emanak.

(As the family obligation,
a *laxada* of fifty *libera* [pounds] was given.)

In 1942 the *serbitzu* was 8 francs; three *serbitzu* made up the fee for a mass. In 1945 six *serbitzu* at 10 francs each covered the fee for a mass, 10 francs of this going to the *xantre.*

In 1968 the fee for a mass was 750 francs (7.5 new francs).

Serbitzu masses are celebrated on days assigned by the priest. These are sung masses and include the prayer for the dead, which is also sung. They are attended by one or more close female family members of the deceased and some more distant female relatives, all dressed in capes and veils. They preside over the prayer for the dead in the *yarleku* and light and maintain the candles there. This ceremony is known as *elizatei.*

On the anniversary of the death, or its *urtebetetze,* a mass is sung, attended by one or more women from the deceased's household and other female relatives. After the anniversary the family arranges for yet another mass to be held *etxeko obligazionentzat* (for the obligations of the household), that is, for the souls of all the household members who have passed away.

The rolled taper burning in the *yarleku* during the funeral continues there throughout the year and is lit every day during one of the masses being celebrated in the church. This function is performed by the women of the deceased's household or, in their absence, by the *andreserora.* The position of *andreserora* no longer exists. These were women who took a vow to devote themselves to the service of the church (taking care of the cleaning, the altar-cloths and robes, the candles on the altar and the tombs, etc.). The last of these women was María Dithurbide who died in 1902. After her death several of her functions were taken over by two women, the first of whom died in 1948. The second retired to the town hospital, and never again took care of the candles in the *yarlekuak* or represented there the women of their respective houses. As a result, prayers for the dead are no longer sung in the *yarlekuak* except in a very few cases, because there are no women to preside over them. Since 1953 not a single priest has sung masses for the souls of the dead, nor have any prayers for the dead been sung in the *yarlekuak.*

Dolu is the term for mourning. The family members of a deceased individual employ a variety of signs of mourning. During religious holidays men wear a band of black cloth on their jackets, either on a sleeve or a lapel, in addition to black buttons on their shirts. Women wear dull black clothing when the occasion calls for *dolumina* (full mourning), black and white for *doluerdi* (half mourning). *Dolumina* is worn by the family of the deceased. Widows and mothers wear it for the rest of their lives; daughters for two years (previously for three years); sisters for one year; nieces for six months. *Doluerdi* is worn by female cousins for three months. Widows wear capes to church during major religious holidays, but do not observe mourning if they remarry.

Ilargiak (moons), *ilargieta* (place of moons), *ilarriak* (stones of the dead), and *ilarrieta* (place of the stones of the dead) are different names for a cemetery. The grave is called *obi* or *tomba*. If it is constructed from stone slabs it is referred to as an *ehortze-toki* (burial place). Most of the graves, especially the old ones, are placed east to west, with the head facing the west and the feet to the east

Almost all the houses in Sara have their tomb clearly marked by gravestones and stone plaques in the cemetery surrounding the parish church. The tomb follows the house in any transactions and in the passing of the house to the heir. The tomb therefore belongs more to the house than to the family. Thus on ancient tombs there are inscriptions referring to the houses to which they belong: *Mendiondoko tomba* (tomb of Mendiondo); *Arrossagaraiko thhombac* 1791 (tombs of Arrossagarai 1791); *Harozteguico thombac*; *Sabateneco borda* (Sabatene farm); *Kollaren borda*; *Etchoina*; *Mikelteiko borda*; *Hindartekoa*; *Leçabeco thonbac* 1838; *Bordaco-bordako tombac* (tombs of Bordaco-borda); *Çulubia*; *Laheteco tombac*; *Baratceartea*; *Plaça-etcheberrico thombac* 1884; *Haranberria*; *Tcholdorichco-borda*; *Mailuen-borda*; *Perutegui*; *Karrikaburucoac*; *Larraldia: Agustinen-borda*; *Portuco hobia*; *Mestruainia*; *Ithurbideco hobia*; *Ortolopitz*; *Aniotz-beherea*; *Indianoen borda*, etc. Tombs attached to families rather than to a house are recent ones; *Famille Etcheberry Ortholopitz-beherea*; *Famille Doyarçabal*; *Famille Lastiry*. There are also tombstones showing only the names of the individuals buried in them, like the one in front of the door on the right side of the church, which bears the following inscription: CHRISTOAL DE ITHVRBIDE.

It is believed that on certain occasions the souls of the dead appear to the living. Generally they appear at night in the form of a faint light near houses and not too far from human beings. According to one of my informants, shortly after the death of the man from Zulobia (about fifty years before this writing), a small light appeared one night on the roof of the house, and another appeared at the Mendiondo spring. It was said then that it was the soul of the man from Zulobia. His soul was unable to rest because he wanted to assign a task to the living.

According to my informants, souls that appear like this come to request that masses be celebrated on their behalf.

Sometimes souls appear in their own homes, making themselves known through strange noises. In such cases the person present should ask: *"Zer nai duk?"* (What do you want?).

One of my informants told me the following story about a case that occurred on the Burkia farm, located in the Elbarrun neighborhood:

The Events at Burkia

"My father used to say that when my grandfather died in Burkia a light would appear every evening at dusk and would get in through the framework of the roof. They did not see anything else. But they did hear loud noises—the ringing of cowbells, then the noise of dishes on the kitchen sideboard sounding as if they had fallen onto the floor.

"My grandmother would go with a candle to see what it was. But there was nothing to be seen.

"Because my grandmother slept with her daughter, one night somebody began to take the daughter from the bed to the kitchen, and tried to pull her down the drain in the sink. This scared them and the following day they spoke with the town priest. He asked my grandmother if she would be brave enough to talk to the light. Yes, answered my grandmother, she was brave enough already.

"The priest told her to address it using the familiar personal pronoun.

"That same night, when the light came in through the frame of the roof, my grandmother asked it what it wanted.

"The light answered by asking if she remembered that they had offered to arrange a mass in Lezo. In their youth my grandfather and grandmother had offered to have a mass said in Lezo.

"My grandmother answered that she did remember.

"Then the light told her, 'If you have that mass said, I will go to heaven like a dove.'

"Grandmother said 'Yes, I'll arrange for it to be said.'

"The next day my grandmother set out for Lezo. And between Sara and Ascain she found herself fighting hard to go on, because something was holding her back. Finally, because she wasn't able to walk across, she crawled her way to Ascain.

"After that she had no more problems along the way, and arranged for the mass to be said in Lezo.

"From that time on they never saw or heard anything in the house."

(Related by Ganixon Larzabal of Sara, January 10, 1941, next to the hearth of the Ibarsoro-beherea farmhouse.)

According to my informant from Ibarsoro-beherea, when Goyetxe the butcher died, for a long time loud noises of chairs and scales and weights were heard in the Arrosa house—which he had once owned—located in the Ialarre neighborhood. It was said that the noises were produced by the soul of the butcher who, in life, had misused the scale when selling meat.

Another of my informants—Piarrezume Camino—told me that, when he was a child, an elderly priest whom people called Bikario-xarra (old Vicar) died in the town of Sara. He was buried in the cemetery, next to the church, although until that time priests had usually been entombed inside. Later, when the man in charge of ringing the dawn bell went into the church, he noticed that all the pews and chairs in the church were being violently shaken, causing a terrible noise, and so he refused to continue with his job. Then a priest was brought in from Zugarramurdi to bless the church. He did so, and even spent a night inside it. After this the noises stopped.

HUNTING

None of the residents of Sara practices hunting exclusively. But there are hunters who devote a couple of months each year to dove hunting, obtaining considerable income from it.

Iiztari means hunter. Although *iizi* is the generic name for wild birds, one says *iizian ibili* (to go hunting) not only when the hunter pursues birds but also when he hunts hare, wild boar, or other wild animals.

The object of the hunt includes not only animals whose flesh serves as food for man, such as the dove (in Basque, *uso*), woodcock (*pekada*), turtledove (*torttoila*), thrush (*xoxo*), mavis (*billigarro*), lapwing (*itsas-xori*), hare (*erbi*), rabbit (*lapin*), and wild boar (*basurde*), but also certain harmful animals, such as the badger (*azkenarro*), fox (*azeri*), marmot (*hudu*), civet (*gatu-potots*), and the weasel (*andde-ederra*).

For hunting fox and badger they use poisons and traps (*arte*). To frighten the badger out of the cornfields it is customary to light huge bonfires in them during the night: the sight of the fire and the smell of smoke frighten it. Another method for flushing out the badger is to make noise with scythes and other iron instruments, or make a roaring sound with the *turruta* (a cow's horn with a narrow hole in the tip) or the rustic instrument called *eltzaorr*.

The standard trap is a simple noose of twine or wire placed in narrow paths and openings in hedges frequented by wild animals; this is commonly used for hunting foxes, hares, and rabbits, especially in periods when the use of firearms is prohibited.

Eltzaorr is a drum or cylinder made of a hollow tree trunk open on one side and closed on the other with a piece of cowhide or, better, a piece of badger skin, drawn taut. A string smeared with wax, one end fastened to the center of the cover, is stretched past the open end of the drum. To make it produce a sound, one holds it between the knees so that the cover faces down, and while one hand holds on to the cord, the other rubs it up and down roughly. This rubbing of the hand on the cord produces a loud reverberation through the drum which can be heard from afar.

At the beginning of this century there was an abundance of wild boars, especially in Lizuniaga ravine, where they would go to eat tubers of the plant called *errebelarr* (arum, araceae), chestnuts, etc. To hunt them, the hunters would form parties of up to twenty men armed, with *zizpak* (shotguns) who would go with their dogs into the woods where it was thought they would be found. The hunters would spread out around the area where the dogs had announced the presence of a wild boar; then they would wait until the dogs flushed it out and then give chase, firing with their shotguns. There were years when ten or more wild boars were killed in the territory of Sara. The last year a wild boar was killed in this region was 1939.

Around 1896, a roebuck (*basahuntz*) was killed in Sara. It was Don Cristóbal Lerembure who killed it with a shotgun, on the boundary between Nabarlatz and Arrotola, where his dogs had flushed it out.

There have been no sightings of wolves in Sara in recent times, but the elders remember having heard that in an earlier time there were some, and that in order to guard the sheep against their attacks, they would bring them at night into *korraliak* (enclosures surrounded by large stones). If a wolf came near, the shepherd would come out of his hut carrying a lighted torch (*ileti*) in his hand and the wolf would run away, frightened by the fire. My informant Bernardo Ayetze told me that he heard one of his grandfather's brothers say that when he was young the last wolf ever seen in the mountains of Sara was shot by a hunter in the community called Potzuko-zelai and died in Otsopotzuak (on the slopes of Mount Ibanteli). This happened a mere hundred years ago.

My informant Domingo de Ursuegi says he heard his father, a charcoal maker, say that when he was working in the mountains of Elizondo with some other men, he frequently saw wolves pass through his district. But as soon as the charcoal makers lit their pyres or woodpiles, the animals would disappear. He also refers to his grandfather who used to herd his flock of sheep on Mount Sayoa (Saioa) (Baztán), and who frequently had to use fire to drive the wolves away when they came at night to prey on the sheep.

This grandfather of Domingo de Ursuegi, mentioned above, also told how on a certain occasion a man from Baztán set out on his horse for Mount Sayoa (Saioa), heavily armed and intending to hunt wild animals. When after several days the hunter had not returned, his neighbors went out to look for him; they found him dead beside his horse. There were seven wolves around him, also dead. The flesh of the hunter and his horse and been devoured, except for the man's legs, which were protected by the leather chaps he was wearing.

When a fox, badger, civet (*gatu-potots*), marmot (*bidu*), or weasel (*andde-ederra*) is killed, the hunter himself or someone he trusts carries it around to all the houses in the town. This practice is called *azeri-eske* (collection for the fox), *askenarro-eske* (collection for the badger), etc. It is the custom that in each house the carrier is given a few francs (in earlier days, two or three *sous*) in payment for the service the hunter has provided to the neighborhood by killing a harmful animal.

The shotgun is generally used to hunt birds, except in periods like the present when firearms have been confiscated. Huge nets are also used for hunting by beating the woods in autumn during the period when migrating doves stop to rest. Another procedure for hunting birds that dates back to ancient times is the *segada*. The *segada* is a device consisting of a curved willow branch with another stick or straight wire attached to the ends like the string of a bow. From the curved branch several bristles or horsehairs hang down, their free ends each forming nooses two or three centimeters above the string. The bird that tries to alight on the stick or wire forming the bowstring puts his head in one of the nooses, becoming trapped. The *segada,* then, is a kind of trap (*arte*) like those mentioned above.

Dove Hunting —The region of Sara is one of the Pyrenean passes most frequented by doves during their autumnal migrations. The hills between Ibantelly (Ibanteli) and Atxuri offer adequately low and wide passages through that part of the mountain range. There are two sites where dove hunting is practiced: *Sarako-usategieta* (the dove pass of Sara), located on Mount Nabarlatz, and *Etxelarko-usategieta* (the dove pass of Echalar (Etxalar)), on Mount Jauzmendi. The hunting season runs from September 24 to November 15.

The dove pass of Sara forms a horn-shaped territory, wide on the side where the doves enter and narrow like a canal or river mouth on the other side. The sides are marked by Mounts Saiberri, Debalde, Larria, Usategi, and Faardiko-harria, with a depression or canyon between them called Tombako-erreka. The terrain, then, lends itself to the practice of hunting by herding. The flocks of doves enter the fan of hills and mountains forming the dove pass, driven by the shaking of flags, the throwing of wooden disks, the blowing of trumpets, and the combined shouting of the hunters. They hurl themselves toward the only apparent exit—the mouth—where they are trapped in the invisible nets awaiting them.

The last section of the channel or mouth is a flat area between forests of large oak trees that function as two hedges that converge toward the southwest as far as the top of a hill where an exit sixty meters wide and twelve meters high is left open. Across this mouth or corridor formed between the oak groves on either side through which the doves have to pass, the hunters stretch their nets (in Basque, *sareak*). This gives the place its name: *Sarelekua* (the place for the nets).

Six nets made of wire close the exit from the pass. Each one is ten meters wide and twelve meters high, and is stretched between two oak trees or between a post and an oak tree serving as supports. Each net is held in place by two cords—one on each side—tied to the upper corners. These cords, each one running through a pulley fastened to the top of the supports, go all the way to the ground where they hold the net in place, anchored at the bottom by a release lever or trigger.

The trigger is an iron lever placed vertically on a wooden structure that anchors it to the ground. Its upper arm, which is bent, serves as a hook for the tightrope that holds the net up, while its lower arm is connected by a thick wire to another lever (*giderr*) made of wood. These triggers—one for each tightrope—hold each net down. Both are operated by a *sarezain* (net guard) by means of a single *giderr* used to instantaneously release the tightropes at the opportune moment, causing the net to fall suddenly to the ground.

The net is stretched at an incline so that it opens toward the southwest, offering its inner face as an attack surface to the flock of doves that come from the northeast. Its lower edge is held to the ground by several stones laid on top of it.

At the moment the doves enter the net, the *sarezain*, pushing the *giderr* of both triggers, releases the tightropes. Instantaneously, the net falls, pulled down by two ring-shaped iron weights (*erraztum*) hanging from the corners where the tightropes and net are joined. The doves are trapped between the net and the ground.

Six nets close the corridor or mouth of the dove pass. The names of these nets, starting from the southern side, are: *Gainekoa, Xiztakoa, Pagokoa, Harrikoa, Orrazekoa,* and *Beerekoa.* They are lined up in a slightly curved arc sixty meters long, its concave surface facing northeast. Each net is operated by one man (who, because of his function, is called *tiralla* (puller) or *sarezain* (netkeeper)) except for the last two, which are operated by a single man. The *sarezain* is assisted in his work by a man they call *karrotabiltzailea* (the disk-gatherer), a name denoting one of his functions, which is to gather up the disks or *karrota* thrown by the *trapari* or leader of the hunting party.

There are shelters (one between each two nets) that serve as screens made of boughs, behind which the *sarezain* hide when a flock of doves approaches the nets. *Estalaria* is the name for these shelters.

The hunters who flush out the doves and herd them toward *Sarelekua* are fourteen in number: nine *xatarlari*, each holding a white flag, *xatarr* (also called *abatari*, from the word *abata*, which designates the place where they stand); three *butatzaille* or throwers of disks (*karrota*)[6]; one *traparia* or *nausia*, the leader, called this because of the place where

he stands, which is *Trapa*[7]; and one *trapagibeleko,* the man who occupies the *Trapagibela* (the spot behind the *Trapa*).

The hunters are distributed in different places around the perimeter
of *Usategieta* or dove pass. Starting from the *Sarelekua,* or the exit from
the pass, five *xatarlari,* called *Orrazekoa, Aitzekoa, Harrikoartekoa,
Harrikoa,* and *Beerekoa,* form the left wing. *Orrazekoa* occupies a
small cage made of sticks at the top of a tree, a few meters from *Sarelekua.* To the north, on the same side of the mountain, is *Aitzekoa,* also
in a cage supported by branches at the very top of an oak tree. Farther
north, *Harrikartekoa* sits atop another oak tree. *Harrikoa* has his cage
on top of a tower made with sheets of iron at the top of the cliff called
Faardiko-harria. Even farther north, in a shelter made of sticks and
ferns located on a hill at the foot of Faardiko-harria, *Beerekoa* hides.
He is the hunter who occupies the most advanced site on the left wing,
but since in many cases his functions aren't necessary, his place is frequently empty.

The right wing is formed by nine hunters stationed at some distance
from each other from *Sarelekua* to the peak of Mount Saiberry. Their
names are: *Traparia, Trapagibelekoa, Xokokua, Errekakoa, Arrigorrikoa, Arrixuri, Larrekoa, Debalde,* and *Saiberry.*

Traparia (his post is called *Trapa*) is the *Nausia* or leader of the
hunters. He is stationed in a basket at the top of an oak tree, a few
meters from the *Gainekoa* net. From his post, he overlooks the corridor
and part of the pass, directing the operation with shouts and whistles
(in Basque, *xistu*) and, by throwing his disks during the last stage of
the maneuver he forces the doves down into the nets at the end of the
corridor.

Trapagibelekoa (stationed behind *Trapa*) is also posted at the top
of a tree, a hundred meters east of *Traparia.* He awaits the arrival of
the doves from his spot, armed with disks to keep them from veering
back to the south over the mountain instead of continuing on the route
marked by the level ground that empties into *Sarelekua* or the bottleneck where the nets are placed.

Further to the east, in a canyon cut into the mountain, the *xatarlari*
or flag-bearers *Xokokua* (flag-bearer at the corner), *Errekakou* (the one
on the river) and *Arrigorrikoa* (the one on the red cliff) are posted. From
their stations, they overlook the ravine called Tombako-erreka (ravine
of the tomb). Their job is to shake flags and shout, thus keeping the
doves from crossing the peaks by flying through the depression formed
in the face of the mountain by a low hill in that spot.

Arrixurikoa (flag-bearer on the white cliff) is the name of the *xatar-lari* posted in a hut or shelter on Arrixuri peak, which is located on the western side of Mount Larria.

Larrekoa is a *butatzaile* or disk thrower who occupies the tower on Mount Larria, to the east of the *xatarlari* or flag-bearers mentioned above. The tower is a crude stone structure, like a column with a square base. On top of it is the observation post of the *butatzaile*. To climb to the top he uses a tall ladder.

Finally, on Debalde and Saiberry (Saiberri) peaks, there are two *butatzaile* or disk throwers stationed in small huts on the ground.

The *xatarlari* on the left wing are the ones best situated to see the *uso-multzu* (flock of doves) approaching the pass. By yelling *uuu, uuu, uuu* and snapping their *xatarr* or flags to make loud whiplash sounds, they keep any doves from breaking off from the flock and flying west. Additionally, they signal to the *butatzaile* on Saiberry (Saiberri), Debalde, and Larria as follows: when a flock of doves heads toward Mount Saiberry (Saiberri), they give three blasts on their trumpets; four blasts means the flock is heading for Mount Debalde; two means Mount Larria. When the flock heads straight down the middle of the refuge, they signal with one blast. This warns the *Trapagibeleko* to keep the doves from crossing the southern edge of the refuge and flying over the mountain to the left of the nets.

If the flock flies toward Larria, the *butatzaile* stationed there throws several paddles, or *karrota* (this is the Basque word for the wooden disks painted white on both sides, with a handle for throwing). These disks give the doves the impression that a hawk is plummeting toward them. This causes the flock to descend abruptly to a few scant meters above the ground in order to protect their bellies from attack by the predator.[8]

When the flock approaches Debalde or Saiberry, *Larrekoa* signals to the *butatzaile* stationed there by shouting for them to begin throwing their disks to keep the doves from flying up again and escaping over those mountains. The flag bearer on Arrixuri gives the same signal when a flock heads toward his post, shouting: *jo xatarra* (shake the flag), to force the doves to veer toward *Sarelekua*.

If the doves try to escape from the pass by flying over Tombako-erreka, the flag-bearers *Arrixurikoa, Arrigorrikoa, Errekakoa,* and *Xokokua* force them to change course by snapping their flags and shouting *uuu, uuu*.

These maneuvers keep the flock of doves zigzagging between the opposite flanks of the pass until they reach the final stage of their trajectory, that is, into the channel that opens into the mouth of the nets. If the flock makes any further attempt to veer toward the left, *Trapagibeleko* throws his disks, forcing the flock downward into the ravine. Then the *xatarlari* on the left wing go into action, snapping their flags. The doves fly up again and over the level ground of Legagorri toward *Sarelekua.* Now they are under the direct control of *Nausia* or *Traparia.*

If the flock is heading straight toward the mouth where the nets are placed, *Traparia* makes long, slow whistle sounds. He gives short, rapid whistles if the flock veers toward the upper region of Tombako-erreka: this alerts flag-bearer *Errekakoa,* who has to snap his flag to keep the doves from escaping from the dove pass on that side.

If the doves veer toward the other side and approach *Fardiko-harria,* *Trapari* alerts the *xatarlari* on Harrikoa peak, shouting: *Harrikoa, joizak* (*Harrikoa,* shake it). *Harrikoa* snaps his flag. If the doves head toward the side where *Aitzekoa* is stationed, the chief shouts: *Aitzekoa!* The latter snaps his flag. When it is necessary for *Orrazekoa* to wave his flag, *Traparia* shouts *koa, koa, koa.* Then, if the flock heads in the right direction, *Nausia* or *Traparia* makes a short blast on his whistle so everyone will stay quiet. When the flock heads straight toward the nets, *Nausia* makes a series of whistles, slow at first and then rapid, so the *sarezainak* will get ready with their hands on the triggers. As the flock nears the *Trapa* post, the chief stationed there throws several of his disks toward it. Then the doves descend almost to ground level. But this is their doom, because once they are on the same level as the nets, they will inevitably crash into the mesh. At that moment the *sarezain* quickly activate the moorings of the nets, which fall suddenly, trapping the doves between their meshes and the ground.

The five *sarezain* and the *karrotabiltzaile* rush toward the nets, remove the doves from the meshing, and put them in the cotton sacks that each one carries hanging from his waist. Afterward they meet in front of a hut called *Uso-etxola* (dove hut), located near the nets, they use scissors to cut one wing off each dove, and throw the doves through a window into the hut.

Any doves sold right on the site of the hunt are killed in front of *Uso-etxola,* since they don't need to be kept inside. There is a flat stone on the ground there, which they call *Usoak-hiltzeko-harria* (the stone for killing doves). The dove condemned to die on this sacrificial stone is thrown down on it with great force by a hunter, breaking its back. Thus it dies instantly.

After depositing the doves in *Uso-etxola,* the *sarezain* raise the nets and everyone takes up their posts to wait for another hunt.

The hunters work from dawn to dusk every day. Each man eats at his post. At nightfall, *Nausia* shouts *etxerat!* (Let's go home!), and immediately the *xatarlari* blow long trumpet blasts that are heard by all the hunters. This announces the end of the day. All the hunters gather in front of the *Uso-etxola*. There the division of the catch will take place.

From time immemorial, twelve houses of the community of Sara have shared by agreement the profits from this method of hunting in the dove passes of Nabarlatz and of Jauzmendia. Those houses are: Zugarria (which is a hospital today), Botikarioa (the storekeeper), Mielkoxepenea (today, the post office), Etxauzea, Barnetxea, Argainea, Bexienea, Moxoinea, Xerorainea, Etxazenea, Etxegaraya, and Hauziartzea.

The association pays the municipality of Sara 3,000 francs annually for the rights to the monopoly it enjoys to conduct the hunt in both dove passes. They hold a direct lease on the Nabarlatz pass, but sublease the one in Jauzmendia, paying residents of the town of Echalar (Etxalar) 2,800 francs annually, since the bottleneck of the hunt lies on land belonging to them. Until only a few years ago these rights cost only 1,200 francs, and before the year 1905 only 150 francs.

In the past, the privilege of belonging to the dove hunting association as a member was considered to be inherent to the houses cited above, and not to the families. For this reason, the owner of Bexienea was excluded from the association because he did not reside in that house.

Today, in addition to the owners who participate in the hunt through their farm workers or *mutilak*, eight other individuals called *ihiztariak* (hunters) are chosen by the association to take part. One of these is the *nausi*, or chief.

When a vacancy occurs in the group of *ihiztariak* because of death, illness, old age, or some other reason, his place is filled by one of the *mutilak* who has been in service to the association the longest.

The doves caught each day in the dove hunt are divided at the end of the day among the partners and the hunters. This division is carried out according to the terms approved by the association in the meeting held on January 15, 1905, which read as follows: "Beginning in 1905 the division of the cost of the bird-decoys, which up until this day was split equally between the hunters and the partners in the association, will be pro-rated among the total number of hunters and partners as follows: the hunters will deduct 8/20 of the total profit coming from the sales and 12/20 will be charged to the partners."

The twenty hunters gather in front of the *Uso-etxola* (dove hut). Two of them enter and begin handing the birds out in lots of three to the *nausi*, who stands in front of the door. He shouts *Fraile* and hands the first three doves to the *ihiztari* so named. He goes on calling out names and handing three doves to each of the other *ihiztariak*, that is, to *Xilardi, Iduzki* (from *Iduzkiagerreko-borda*), *Jean-Pierre, François, Larrekoa, Traparia,* and *Traparigibelekoa.* The lot for *Traparia* (the name designating the leader or *nausi*) is four doves. The leader continues naming and handing lots of three to each of the *mutilak*, or representatives of the owners, in the following order: Zugarria, Botikario, Mielkoxepe, Erretora, Mendiburu, Argain, Bexien, Moxoinekoa, Xerorainekoa, Etxaz, Lehenburu, and Hauziartz. The lot for *Erretora* (the name designating the Etxauzea farm's share) is four doves, one of which is for the priest of Sara who, on Sundays during hunting season, celebrates mass for the hunters at three-thirty in the morning.

The procedure is repeated as many times as necessary with the remaining doves, in the same order as indicated above, each time handing a lot of three doves to each participant, except for *Traparia* and *Erretora*, who are given four doves each as mentioned above. When there are fewer than sixty-two doves to be distributed, that is, when there aren't enough to hand out twenty lots, each participant is given one dove, in the order indicated. In the distribution the following day, the first order of business is to complete the lots that were incomplete the day before.

The *mutilak* deliver to their employers—the houses where they are employed—the doves to which they are entitled. The doves of the *ihiztariak* are taken to the Ustekabea house, which is the one responsible for selling them. The hunter Xilardi, the secretary of the group of *ihiztariak*, keeps the accounts for his companions.

The quantity of doves caught varies greatly from one year to the next.

The Abbot Dominique Lahetjuzan was the Vicar of Sara at the end of the eighteenth century and the beginning of the nineteenth. He produced a manuscript entitled "Recherches sur le moeurs, l'origine el l'idiome des basques" (Investigation into the Customs, Origins and Language of the Basques) that is kept in the Argainea house where he was born in the town of the same name. In that work he devotes several paragraphs to the hunting of doves that was practiced in that region during his time. In his words:

> On the day following our arrival in the community,[9] we went to see the lovely dove hunt they practice there. An identical hunt takes place in four other places on the slopes of the Pyrenees. The weather was beautiful and there were almost no birds in the air, yet we watched them trap some twenty *bixets* and an equal number of doves, which was enough to give us an idea of the total number caught. In earlier times, on some days the owners

of the nets received a profit of as many as sixty dozen live birds; twenty years later they barely caught that many during the entire hunting season. It is no longer profitable. A Society consisting of the principal inhabitants engage in it only for their own pleasure and that of visitors. It is rare for the catch to cover the cost of the investment. That's because in recent years the migration of doves and other birds has diminished, according to calculations by the hunters, by more than two-thirds, and it came to a halt during the latest war with the Spaniards.

This dove pass is located a league and a half from the town toward the mountain range separating France from Spain. It is split from top to bottom. This one is on the outcrop of Mount Navarlatz (which means rugged plain), which is easy to climb. A hunter lying on a basket constructed at the top of a beech tree of the right height directs the entire hunt. He is situated so that if his eyesight were keen enough he would have a view of all the birds migrating from that section of lowlands into the lower Pyrenees.

On the petition of a hunter, the Society will decide whether to prohibit the release of decoys. This can be overridden by unanimous agreement to allow their use by all petitioners because the goal of the hunt was the general pleasure and amusement of the different individuals who hunted with shotguns.

The chief hunter has under his command a group of boys each carrying a flag for scaring the doves. He places them at regular intervals on a line of peaks along the right side of the mountain, and when a flock approaches one of them, the boy scares them by shouting and waving the flag. The doves then veer toward another row of boys parallel to the first, who wave their flags like the first when the flock approaches them, causing it to veer from post to post and to enter a small channel at the end of which is the hunters' trap. He has an assistant who, like him, is perched atop a tree. He throws a fake sparrow-hawk over the flock, causing it to dip down; the chief hunter does the same, driving the ring-doves into one or two of the nets.

Each of these nets is ninety feet long with blinds made of evergreens placed at equal intervals along it where the trappers hide along with the onlookers; they release the ropes holding the nets when the dove is fifteen feet from it—if they release it too late, the dove will be killed or seriously injured on crashing into it at ordinary speed—even if it is stretched slackly sometimes the head falls on one side and the body on the other. As the nets are released, the feathers of one wing are pulled off so they can't fly unless they are lured by decoys. They are kept in a hole dug in the ground until they can be distributed.

* * *

Echalar (Etxalar) dove pass (*Etxelar'ko-usategieta*) is located to the southwest of the Sara pass, in the basin of the River Hiruetako-erreka. Its mouth is on a slope of Mount Yauzmendi, half a kilometer to the east of Leizarrieta Hill. All of the terrain through which the doves are herded is located in the jurisdiction of Sara; only the nets are on property belonging to Echalar. Therefore, the hunters from Echalar pay those from Sara the annual tribute mentioned above.

This dove pass has been exploited since time immemorial by two households of Echalar (Etxalar): Gaztelu and Arribiaga or Arribillaga.

Sixteen men classified in two categories participate in the hunt: seven *gizonak* or veteran hunters, and nine *motikuak* or assistants.

Three *gizonak* and three *motikuak* are responsible for the nets and their operation, so they are called by the generic name *sarezaleak*.

The remaining four *gizonak* are: *Trapa* (the leader) and *Trapabiela*, each located on a tower on the right side of the channel that empties into the nets; *Aritza* and *Bieltrapa*, stationed in a tree and on a makeshift platform, respectively, on the left side of the same channel. The four of them throw disks (which here are called *makila*).

The rest of the *motikuak* are stationed on peaks on both sides of the dove pass, following the *gizonak*. Those on the right side are called *Arrikua*, *Domikua*, and *Abatarri*, counting from the closest to the farthest from the nets. Those on the left side are: *Belata*, *Idoikua*, and *Larrekua*. All these men wave flags (in Basque, *xatarra*), except *Idoikua* who, in addition to the flag, also throws disks or *makilak*.

Abbot Dominique Lahetjuzan, in the manuscript cited above, has this to say about the dove pass of Echalar (Etxalar):

All the birds that escape the lower hunting ground fly to the upper section which is nearly half an hour along the road toward the border. This is not as costly and using it makes up for part of the expenses of the lower section. The Society exploits it jointly with the Spaniards. There are four nets, two belonging to the Spaniards, the other two belonging to the Society. They are stretched across the Spanish section since the rest of the hunt takes place on the French side.

From ancient times, the inhabitants of Echalar (Etxalar) have ceded the right to hunt doves to two property owners of the Commune only in the narrow channel where it takes place. Subsequently, they sought to take back this permission, but to no avail. One of the owners is a rich gentleman and the other a charcoal vendor. They have tried to force the latter to sell his hunting rights for a large sum of money ten times its value and which would have allowed him to live comfortably. He stubbornly resists this temptation of wealth or threats.

I asked a member of the Society, "Where do the doves go?" One flock, he told me, goes to the Canaries and to the southern mountains of Morocco, the rest stay in Spain. The latter are divided into two groups: two or three large flocks stop in the large forests of the Pyrenees several leagues from here, and four or five flocks settle more than a hundred leagues from here between the mountains of the Asturias all the way to those of Portugal.

I am indebted to the kindness of Monsieur Pierre Dop for giving me access to his archives in Argainea (Sara) and letting me transcribe the copy of the extract of a lawsuit relative to the dove pass of Echalar (Etxalar), which was presented before the ecclesiastical court of Pamplona in the year 1665. The litigants were: on one side, Juan de Goyechea, owner of the Gastelu [sic] estate in Echalar, and Domingo Iturria, a resident of the town of Sara; on the other, Don Juan Jauregui, Rector of Echalar. The former sought to prevent the latter from stretching his dove-hunting nets in the place called Nomparabos, 14.5 meters (24 cubits, according to one of the witnesses) from the site called Yauzmendi, where the former placed their nets, following ancient custom and hereditary right recognized by agreement of the kings of Spain and France. In the trial, among other documents, the following articles appeared, which in the archive of Argainea are written in French:

1) That my clients [these are the words of the attorney of the litigants], their relatives, grandparents and other ancestors, owners of the houses they now possess, called Anduecea and Petrisencenea in said village of Echalar (Etxalar) and that of Sara in the valley of Labort in the Kingdom of France, have held and continue to hold in tranquil and peaceful possession, since time immemorial, the right to hunt the doves that migrate through that site and channel called Yauzmendi which is within the confines of this Kingdom and that of France . . .

5) That in order to cause greater injury and prejudice, said Rector has cut down many trees and branches, opening a channel through said site (Nomparabos) thus altering the course of the doves away from

the site of Yauzmendi where my clients have their nets and continue to profit from the enclosures (fences), beaters and other devices belonging to them, causing them, as has been communicated in a variety of ways, a very serious loss as witnesses will testify."

The first witness, Juan de Luzu, a priest and interested party, fifty-one years of age, declared, among other things:

That his father came to the Yauzmendi site sixteen or twenty years ago to hunt doves, that on numerous occasions he placed a net at the site called Nomparabos with the permission and consent and license of the parties who held the rights to the site and channel of Yauzmendi without causing damage to said channel, and that the doves which he caught at the site of Nomparabos, with the consent and license of the interested parties, he shared in a proportion of one to four with the chief hunter (*trapario [sic]*), who is the person stationed on the tallest tree to throw the fake sparrow hawk (the disk) to force the doves back down into the channel; but that the Nomparabos site was heavily covered with trees, making it very hard for the doves to pass through there, whereas the Yauzmendi site had all the necessary qualities and conditions, until approximately two years ago when Don Juan de Jauregui, Rector of said village of Echalar (Etxalar), without the consent or knowledge of the parties, removed and cut down several trees and tree branches from the center of the Nomparabos channel, causing the doves that should have headed directly toward the site and channel of Yauzmendi to pass through the clearing cut in the Nomparabos site, especially if a tree accidentally fell blocking the proper channel of Yauzmendi. In that case, the aforementioned channel and hunt rightfully belonging to the aforementioned parties since time immemorial would be necessarily lost.[10]

The case having been resolved against the claimants, they appealed to the court in Calahorra. Although the disposition of the appeal is not known, the fact that the Rector of Echalar (Etxalar) did not continue stretching his nets in Nomparabos suggests that it did not favor the clergyman hunter.

Notes

1. *Ikuska* 1 (1947): 183.

2. J. M. Hiribarren, *Eskualdunac*, 119.

3. A. Arçuby, "Usages mortuaries à Sare," *Bulletin du Musée Basque* (Bayonne), nos. 3–4 (1927): 21–22.

4. Ibid., 21.

5. Ibid., 23.

6. *Karrota* is a disk made of alder wood measuring from one to two decimeters in diameter. The disk has a handle. These are used by the hunters posted near the nets, i.e., the *Traparia* and *Trapagibelekoa*.

7. From the French *trappe* (trap).

8. The *karrota* used by the *butatzaile* on Mount Larria, like those used on Saiberri and Debalde, are small, i.e., one decimeter in diameter. Those used by *Traparia* and *Trapagibelekoa* are larger (two decimeters in diameter) so as to produce their effect instantaneously because the doves are so close, and to prevent them from altering their course in any way to escape from the channel. Being larger, they fall to the ground more quickly.

9. He refers to the Plaza neighborhood in Sara.

10. The wind of hurricane force that blew on the night of the 15th to 16th of February of 1941 knocked down several of the thickest oaks and beeches flanking the mouth of the dove-hunting ground, producing wide gaps in their rows, which allowed the doves to change direction and, slipping through these openings, to cross the hill without falling into the nets.

Bibliography

Alcobé Noguer, Santiago. "Antropología de la población actual de las comarcas pirenaicas," *Pirineos* 1 (1945): 97–116.

Aranzadi, Telesforo de, and Florencio de Ansoleaga. *Exploración de catorce dólmenes del Aralar*. Pamplona: Imp. Provincial, 1918.

———. *Exploración de cinco dólmenes del Aralar*. Pamplona: Imp. Provincial, 1915.

Aranzadi, Telesforo de, and José Miguel de Barandiarán. "Exploración de la cueva de Urtiaga (en Itziar, Guipúzcoa), II." *Eusko-Jakintza* 2 (1948): 307–30.

———. *Exploración de ocho dólmenes de la sierra de Aralar*. San Sebastián: Imp. de la Diputación, 1924.

Aranzadi, Telesforo de, José Miguel de Barandiarán, and Enrique de Eguren. *Exploración de nueve dólmenes del Aralar guipuzcoano*. San Sebastián: Martín y Mena, 1919.

———. *Exploración de seis dólmenes de la sierra de Aizkorri*. San Sebastián: Martín, Mena y Cia., 1919.

———. *Exploración de seis dólmenes de la sierra de Urbasa (Navarra)*. San Sebastián: Imp. de la Diputación, 1923.

———. *Exploraciones de la cueva de Santimamiñe, 2º memoir: Los niveles con cerámica y el conchero*. Bilbao: Impr. de la Diputación, 1931.

———. *Grutas artificiales de Alava*. San Sebastián: [Eusko Ikaskuntza], 1923.

Arçuby, A. "Usages mortuaries à Sare." *Bulletin du Musée Basque* (Bayonne), nos. 3–4 (1927): 17–25.

Azkue, Resurrección María de. "Gernika'ko batzar baten." *Euskalerria-ren yakintza* (Madrid) 1 (1935): 299–301, 363.

Barandiarán, José Miguel de. "El arte rupestre en Alava." *Boletín de la Sociedad Aragonesa de Ciencias Naturales* (Zaragoza) 19 (March–April 1920): 65–98.

———. "Axular'en itzala." Lecture given at the Sorbonne on September 28, 1956; later published in *Gure Herria* 29, no. 2 (1957): 97–110.

————. "Contribución al estudio de la mitología vasca." In *Homenaje a Fritz Krüger*, vol. 1, 101–136. Mendoza, 1952.

————. "Creencias y ritos funerarios" [a series of articles on various towns in the Basque region]. *Anuario de la Sociedad de Eusko-folklore* (Vitoria) 3, 1923.

————. "De la vida tradicional vasca: Valores de algunos símbolos." In *Homenaje a don Luis de Hoyos*, vol. 2, 36–44. Madrid, 1950.

————. "Die prähistorischen Höhlen in der baskischen Mythologie." In *Paideuma* 2, notebooks 1–2 (1941): 66–83.

————. "Ele-zaar: Herensuge." *Eusko-jakintza* 4 (1950): 259–78.

————. "Ele-zaar, IV. Mendiko urrea." *Eusko-jakintza* 2 (1948): 345–46.

————. "Exploración de la cueva de Urtiaga (en Itziar-Guipúzcoa), I." *Eusko-jakintza* 1, nos. 5–6 (1947): 679–96.

————. *Fragmentos folklóricos. Paletnografía vasca.* San Sebastián: Imprenta de Martín, Mena y Ca., 1921. (Also published in *Euskalerriaren alde* 10, nos. 197–198, 202–204 (1920): pages 182–90, 224–32, 396–402, 431–43, 452–70.)

————. "Mari, o el genio de las montañas." In *Homenaje a D. Carmelo de Echegaray*, 245–68. San Sebastián: Imprenta de la Diputación de Guipúzcoa, 1928.

————. "Materiales para un estudio del pueblo vasco: en Liguinaga (Laguinge)." *Ikuska* 1, nos. 4–5 (1947): 126–31 and 177–84; 2 (1948): 9–24 and 78–84.

————. "Matériaux pour une étude du peuple basque: à Uhart-Mixe." *Ikuska* (Sare), nos. 4–5, (1947): 107–25; nos. 6–7 (1947): 167–75; nos. 8–9 (1948): 2–8; nos. 10–13 (1948): 84–93.

————. "Las montañas y los bosques." *Eusko-folklore* (Vitoria), no. 13 (1922): 1–2.

————. "La religion des anciens Basques." In *Compte rendu analytique de la IIIe session de la Semaine d'Ethnologie Religieuse* [held in Tilburg, Netherlands], 156–68. Enghien, 1923.

————. "La tierra." *Eusko-folklore* (Vitoria), no. 1 (1921): 1–2.

Barbier, Jean. *Légendes du Pays Basque d'aprés la tradition.* Paris: Delagrave, 1931.

Barcellos, Don Pedro de. *Livro dos Linhagens.* Portugal, [fourteenth century].

Barriola, Ignacio María. "La medicina popular en el País Vasco." *Real*

Sociedad Vascongada de los Amigos del País (San Sebastián), 1952: 82–83.

Caro Baroja, Julio. *Algunos mitos españoles y otros ensayos.* Madrid: Editora Nacional, 1944.

————. "Notas de folklore vasco." *Revista de dialectología y tradiciones populares* 2, 3rd Notebook (1946): 373–79.

————. "Sobre la religión antigua y el calendario del Pueblo Vasco." In *Trabajos del Instituto Bernardino de Sahagun*, vol. 6, 9–24. Madrid, 1948. (Reprinted in *Vasconiana* 2. Madrid: Minotauro, 1957.)

Cavaillès, Henri. *La transhumance pyrénéenne et la circulation des troupeaux dans les plaines de Gascogne.* París: Colin, 1931.

Cerquand, Jean François. *Légendes et récits populaires du Pays Basque* [part 1]. In *Bulletin de la Société des Sciences, Lettres et Arts de Pau* 8 (2e serie, vol. 4) (1874–75): 233–85.

Chaho, Joseph Agustín. *Biarritz, entre les Pyrénées et l'océan: itineraire pittoresque.* 2 vols. Bayonne: A. Andreossey, [1855].

Chalbaud, Luis. "La familia como forma típica y transcendental de la constitución social vasca." *I Congreso de Estudios Vascos* [1918], 41–64. N.p., 1919.

Delmas, Juan E. *Guía histórica descriptiva del viajero en el Señorío de Vizcaya.* Bilbao, 1864.

Echegaray, Bonifacio de. "Significación de algunos ritos funerarios del país vasco." *Revista internacional de los estudios vascos* 16 (1925): 94–118, 184–222.

————. "La vida civil y mercantil de los vascos a través de sus instituciones jurídicas." *Revista internacional de los estudios vascos* 13 (1922): 582–613, and 14 (1923): 27–60.

Echegaray, Carmelo de. "Provincia de Vizcaya." In *Geografía general del País Vasco-Navarro*, vol. 5, 672–990. Barcelona: Alberto Martín, 1917.

Fougères, Alain. *Les droits de famille et les successions au Pays Basque et en Béarn d'après les anciens texts.* Bergerac: Imp. Générale du Sud-Ouest, 1938.

García de Salazar, Lope. *Crónica de siete casas de Vizcaya y Castilla.* N.p., 1454. (reprint Madrid, 1914).

Hiribarren, Jean Martin. *Eskualdunac. Iberia, Cantabria, Eskal-Herriac, Eskal-herri bakhotcha eta harri darraicona.* Bayonne, 1853.

Lancre, Pierre de. *Tableau de l'inconstance des mauves anges et démons, ou il est amplement traité des sorciers et de la sorcellerie.* Paris, 1612. (English translation: On the Inconstancy of Witches: Pierre de Lancre's *Tableau de l'inconstance des mauves anges et démons* (1612), ed. Gerhild Scholz Williams (ASMAR vol. 16). Co-published by Arizona Center for Medieval and Renaissance Studies, Arizona State University (Tempe) and Brepols Publishers, Belgium, 2006).

Nussy Saint-Saëns, Marcel. *Contribution à un essai sur la coutume de Soule.* Bayonne: Le Livre, 1942.

Romeu Figueras, J. "Mitos tradicionales pirenaicos." *Pireneos* 6, nos. 15–16 (1950): 137–83.

Sacaze, Gaston. *Inscriptions antiques des Pyrénées.* Toulouse, 1892.

Seligmann, Siegfried. *Die magischen Heil-und-Schutzmittel aus der unbelebten Natur.* Stuttgart, 1927.

Staffe, Adolf. "Beiträge zur Monographie des Baskenrindes." *Revista internacional de los estudios vascos* 17 (1926): 34–93.

Vicario y de la Peña, Nicolás. *Derecho consuetudinario de Vizcaya.* Madrid: Asilo de Huérfanos del Sagrado Corazón de Jesús, 1901.

Vinson, Julien. "An Essay on the Basque Language." In *Basque Legends,* by Wentworth Webster, 219–33. London: Griffith & Farran, 1877.

———. *Le folk-lore du Pays Basque.* Paris: Maisonneuve et Cie., 1883.

von Schroeder, Leopold. *Arische Religion* (2 vols.). Leipzig: H. Haessel, 1923.

Webster, Wentworth. *Basque Legends.* London: Griffith & Farran, 1877.

Index